Sustainable & Responsible Investing 360°

Sustainable & Responsible Investing 360°

Lessons Learned from World Class Investors

R. Scott Arnell

ROWMAN & LITTLEFIELD
Lanham • Boulder • New York • London

Published by Rowman & Littlefield
An imprint of The Rowman & Littlefield Publishing Group, Inc.
4501 Forbes Boulevard, Suite 200, Lanham, Maryland 20706
www.rowman.com

86-90 Paul Street, London EC2A 4NE

British Library Cataloguing in Publication Information Available

Library of Congress Cataloging-in-Publication Data

Names: Arnell, R. Scott, 1957- author.
Title: Sustainable & responsible investing 360° : lessons learned from world class investors / R. Scott Arnell.
Other titles: Sustainable and responsible investing 360°
Description: Lanham : Rowman & Littlefield, [2022] | Includes bibliographical references and index. | Summary: "A must-read for anyone struggling to understand Impact Investing, ESG, SRI, and the myriad terms used to describe investing for positive impact. Hear from 27 experts managing trillions in funds about why sustainable and responsible investing matters, how they perform, and what the future of this investment strategy is"—Provided by publisher.
Identifiers: LCCN 2022010199 (print) | LCCN 2022010200 (ebook) | ISBN 9781538149041 (cloth ; alk. paper) | ISBN 9781538149058 (epub)
Subjects: LCSH: Investments. | Investments—Moral and ethical aspects.
Classification: LCC HG4521 .A7295 2022 (print) | LCC HG4521 (ebook) | DDC 332.6—dc23/eng/20220310
LC record available at https://lccn.loc.gov/2022010199
LC ebook record available at https://lccn.loc.gov/2022010200

∞™ The paper used in this publication meets the minimum requirements of American National Standard for Information Sciences—Permanence of Paper for Printed Library Materials, ANSI/NISO Z39.48-1992.

Contents

Acknowledgments

First, I must thank all of the investors whose professional experience, advice, and lessons form the essence of this book. You were all very gracious with your valuable time and so generous with your honest and candid insights. May everything you have shared in these pages inspire other investors to stand on your shoulders and build a more sustainable world for us all—and for the generations that follow.

To the Geneva Capital team, Jay, Vicky, Marcus, and Stephen, many thanks for your research, for combing through endless hours of recordings, and for your detail-checking and support. Jay, your insights, and meticulous nature kept this project from going off the rails numerous times. Vicky, you cleaned our transcripts and put on the finishing touches, and for this I thank you.

To Tom Kerr, you are a warrior king with the red pen. When I couldn't see the forest for the trees, your suggested edits distilled these often-rambling conversations into something readable and understandable. You were always there for me. Thank you, thank you, thank you.

To Raoul Davis, who relentlessly pursued me until I did this book project, are we good now?

The American author F. Scott Fitzgerald wrote, "There are no second acts in American lives." But I experienced a second act on a journey with my wife, Cathryn Arnell, as we dreamed and grew together. It has been everything I could have imagined and much, much more. You are an exceptional wife, my best friend and soul mate, a visionary leader, and a shepherd soul. Thank you for walking through this life with me.

How Did We Get Here?

It's been known by many names over the years—socially responsible, socially conscious, green, ethical—sustainable, responsible, and impact investing isn't new. There are a multiplicity of terms used within the industry for different categories and they are not all used universally. For simplification purposes in order to avoid clumsy usage of language, we'll use the acronym "SRI" to refer to all of the various forms of responsible investing that incorporate non-financial criteria in the process of making financial investment decisions.

SRI is getting increased attention as worries over social justice and other issues such as affordable housing shortages, business and judicial ethics, and climate change increase, prompting people to become more responsive to societal ills through their investments. It's a strategy that seeks to marry financial return with bringing about positive social and/or environmental change. Financial institutions, asset managers, family offices, and investment advisors all over the world are—or give the appearance they are—actively involved in making financial investments that both benefit society and the investor's bottom line.

The buzz around responsible investing began trending after the events of the world-wide recession of 2008—followed by the knock-on effects of the Euro's instability and subsequent geopolitical uncertainty—led to a global morality crisis. In the aftermath, people searched for an explanation on how our interconnected and interdependent economic and financial systems and associated social institutions had failed us so spectacularly.

People instinctively felt that there must be another way. It was easy to lash out at financial services and blame the industry for only playing a destructive role in our modern economic landscape. But when picking through the pieces in the wake of the Great Recession, it became apparent that there were ethical failures across a wide range of industries and with time, a new narrative emerged.

Traditionally we were taught to first maximize our wealth and then donate some of it toward social and environmental concerns. It was an unwritten paradigm universally understood, which compartmentalized and bifurcated two mindsets: 1) the ruthless, smart business brain that applies all of its acumen to market domination and returns on investment and 2) the charitable, careless brain that philanthropically gives back to society. But it was usually done using fewer critical facilities and without the control and accountability for results applied in the normal business environment.

Today people are increasingly shedding that paradigm in favor of blending those two mindsets. As a result, SRI has entered the mainstream. People no longer see investing and solving social problems as mutually exclusive. They want to invest their money where it actively benefits social and environmental concerns while also achieving competitive market rate returns—a kind of social capitalism.

We are living in an era of an unprecedented generational accumulation of wealth and will soon witness the largest transfer of wealth in history from baby boomers to millennials. It is estimated that the millennial generation accounts for 76 million people in North America and 148 million in Europe. Globally, they are expected to account for 75 percent of the workforce by 2025. They are the most highly educated and culturally diverse group of all generations and generally see their goal as making money by doing something good rather than by doing whatever. These young multi-millionaires, billionaires, and heirs will leave investment firms that cannot offer socially and environmentally beneficial investments in their portfolios and go to those that can.

Even though sustainable, responsible, and impact investing all strive to generate positive social and environmental benefits while achieving positive and competitive financial returns, there is little agreement on practical application. This book presents the stories—and tactics—of those financial pioneers who are leading the way to use investing as a force for good to improve the world and the lives of people in it.

R. Scott Arnell

Introduction

> It is not the critic who counts; not the man who points out how the strong man stumbles, or where the doer of deeds could have done them better. The credit belongs to the man who is actually in the arena, whose face is marred by dust and sweat and blood; who strives valiantly; who errs, who comes short again and again, because there is no effort without error and shortcoming; but who does actually strive to do the deeds; who knows great enthusiasms, the great devotions; who spends himself in a worthy cause; who at the best knows in the end the triumph of high achievement, and who at the worst, if he fails, at least fails while daring greatly, so that his place shall never be with those cold and timid souls who neither know victory nor defeat.
>
> —Theodore Roosevelt

It was nearly 2:00 a.m., somewhere in the sprawl of Mumbai, and I was bumping along in the back seat of a Kaali Peeli Fiat taxi on my way from one airport to another. I was traveling from Hong Kong to Switzerland, but my assistant had explained that the only way I could arrive in time for my Geneva meeting the next day was to change airports in Mumbai and catch a connecting flight. Anomalies like that were part of the international business life in the 1990s.

Still hot and sultry at that hour, all the windows were open in the cab because back then air conditioning wasn't an option. As the car slowed to a stop at a traffic signal, a mob of beggars suddenly descended from the shadows and their outstretched arms reached through the windows, straining toward me.

Still in a fog from interrupted airplane sleep, I felt like I was in some kind of a Kafka-esque movie scene. I looked up at a woman clutching a baby. She stared straight into my eyes; I was possibly her only hope that night. But hers was just one gaze from a dense press of desperate faces.

Can I give money to one and not the others? It wasn't possible to give money to all of them. I reflexively slid to the center of the car seat to position myself equidistantly from the pleading hands. The light changed and the taxi sped away, leaving those poor souls behind. But for the rest of the night, I contemplated their desperate circumstances while trying to reconcile the excesses of my own.

I've worked a lot in India over the years, so that wasn't my first experience with its poverty. But the juxtaposition of that unsettling street scene, coming just hours after leaving the marble and mirrored glass skyscraper's conference room in Hong Kong, all at once seemed surreal.

Some hours later, having flown through the night, I was back in Geneva. But the despairing eyes I had looked into earlier continued to haunt me. My world of corporate objectives seemed so distant, so disconnected from the harsh reality that most of the world lives. In retrospect, I can now see how that night in Mumbai planted a seed of unease that gnawed at me. But a busy life has a way of drowning out introspective moments, and back then I didn't understand those feelings well enough to articulate the questions I now ask.

What am I doing to positively impact my culture? How is my life's work affecting the world?

Fast forward a decade or more. After a varied career at multiple Fortune 500 companies, as well as some start-ups in several industries, I founded a financial advisory company in Geneva.

In the early days we were, like many firms, occupied with advising family offices, institutional investors, and high net-worth individuals on alternative investments. Coincidentally, a few years in, I started to hear that same voice in my head:

What am I doing to positively impact my culture? How is my life's work affecting the world?

At first it came occasionally, but later on it was louder and gained an intensity I had never before experienced.

A long career in building businesses all over the world allowed me to see that financial investments have direct consequences on people's lives. There are many factors that contribute to the great differences between the developed and the developing economies, but the availability of capital for investment is certainly a powerful one. Yet, spending most of my time in the gilded world of European money managers, it was hard to look at my life's work as contributing anything more than helping wealthy people become richer. I was generating alpha, and that wasn't what I wanted to do.

Then came the financial crisis of 2008, which cast a harsh light on the inherent conflicts of interest and the end-justifies-the-means financial investment system. A lot of savvy investors and investment professionals I knew on the Rue du Rhone in Geneva became uncomfortably aware that they had invested with people who wore no moral or ethical bathing suits when the tide unexpectedly went out.

As markets ground to a halt and mandates dried up, those long-fermenting questions were now bubbling to the surface. Like many others in my profession, I was at a pivot point and felt compelled to use the opportunity to hit my pause button and rethink, reevaluate, and refocus Geneva Capital's mission. I wanted to develop a business model for my company that was more holistic and more aligned with my values.

After a lot of soul-searching, I became determined that we would be led by a vision to mobilize capital into investments that would help create a better world for our children and future generations. But I qualified our mission by specifying that we'd strive to become the leading investment advisory firm enabling competitive, high-performance financial returns through sustainable, socially responsive, impactful investing.

In hindsight, articulating that vision turned out to be the easy part. While socially responsible investing was once again starting to trend, this time around it came with a twist: that for the sake of doing good, investors should be willing to accept lower financial returns. There was the usual overhyping, followed by skepticism and backlash. Nevertheless, over time, responsible investing successfully entered the mainstream. Today people are increasingly rejecting the idea that their business and financial investments are mutually exclusive from charitable and social justice goals.

That's why I refocused Geneva Capital as a solution to these problems. We only offer advice and assistance on companies, impact projects, and investment funds that have some kind of positive social or environmental impact—plus competitive or superior market rates of returns.

Assets under management invested in responsible investments have exploded. Nevertheless, there continues to be a great deal of confusion about how responsible investing is practically executed. There's little agreement on how to measure the social impact of these products, and investors also have trouble finding scalable investment deal flow. I've spoken with many people in different stages of implementing a sustainable investing platform who struggle to articulate and execute such a strategy.

When I was first approached to write this book, my initial thought was, "Does the world really need another book on investing? Is there anything really new to say?" As it turns out, because of the evolutionary state of sustainable investing and the relative naissance of that market, there is plenty to be said that's new. But I'm not the person to say it. I'll leave that to the qualified experts and brilliant innovators who are out there every day charting new waters and blazing new trails.

My goal with this book is to create a set of virtual advisors for anyone attempting this journey. To the extent that's it's possible, I also want to shed light upon and democratize responsible investing. I want to share tactics and solutions that were previously only used by professional investors with extensive experience and great resources at their disposal. Inevitably, the journey to sustainable investing is different for each investor. But I hope you will find principles here that will help you more clearly define your road map to execution. Ultimately, my objective is to empower individual as well as professional investors to deploy capital in a more sustainably life-giving way.

I am not writing this book as any kind of thought leader or self-anointed expert. If I have learned anything that has allowed me to have any success in my career, it's how much there is that I don't know. I don't have the answers, but I do have plenty of questions, and I took the opportunity to ask them of professionals with years of experience in this arena. They've pushed themselves, experimented, tried, failed, grown, and ultimately succeeded. Not all of their insights will be applicable to your particular situation. But perhaps some principles or nuggets of wisdom from their journey will help you along the path of yours.

These days there is much fanfare and bluster around sustainable investing. But in the end, it's the people who are mobilizing capital into worthy investments that are changing the world for the better. Clarifying your values and finding your true purpose in life is a worthy achievement. If you can then align those with your financial investments it will allow you to not just embrace those ideals, but live them on a daily basis—while positively impacting the rest of the world, for generations to come.

My intention was to create this book in easy-to-navigate stand-alone sections. You can consume it from beginning to end or turn to a specific topic of interest. The first part of the book offers a basic overview of Socially Responsible and Sustainable Investing. There you'll find selected definitions used throughout the book, and a high-level summary of the advantages and challenges of different investment approaches.

The remainder of the book is devoted to interviews with different professional investors, and those are presented in sections organized by various types of investment focus and investor class. Each interview is intended to be a conversation with someone who has proven their know-how, has plowed new ground, and can explain the *why* behind their investment approach.

By sharing their knowledge and experiences through accessible and thought-provoking dialogue, these investors and company leaders can benefit both new investors and seasoned professionals looking to expand their investment horizons. Together they offer a collective vision for building sustainable profits, while creating better communities throughout the world.

Complementary SRI Self-Assessment Guide

SRI360°: Lessons Learned from World Class Investors was written for a range of professional investors. It's for those already actively pursuing sustainable and responsible investing activities, those interested in more closely aligning their investments with their values, and those just beginning the process of trying to figure out where to start. But for many individuals and companies, incorporating nonfinancial criteria and performance indicators into the investment decision-making process is unfamiliar territory and can be confusing.

In my experience, two key points must be clearly understood before you can begin to build a solid and successful SRI initiative in your organization:

1. Who inside and/or outside your company is driving this shift toward SRI?
2. Why are they interested in SRI and what are their motivations?

Establishing the answers to these two questions will help you create a clear understanding why an SRI initiative will be of value to your company and your clients. However, to form clear answers to these two questions, you must first ask other questions because a lack of motivational clarity leads to a culture within a firm that renders SRI confusing, unfocused, and reduces the effectiveness of sales efforts. Answering these key questions before building out an SRI program provides the foundation upon which to build the corporate culture necessary to succeed.

The good news is that we have created an SRI self-assessment resource guide, built around a step-by-step questionnaire designed to help you accelerate the process and avoid costly mistakes down the road. The questionnaire is divided into two parts: 1) an internal questionnaire for use within your organization and 2) an external questionnaire for use with your clients.

The questionnaire for the company is designed to find SRI supporters within your organization and their motivations by asking individuals for their views using a combination of open-ended questions and multiple-choice tables. From these responses, you can develop a clear, concise mission statement for the initiative, which will build internal awareness and align the motivations with a concrete strategy.

The client questionnaire includes only questions relevant to them. It seeks to assess demand by focusing not only on traditional investment issues such as risk and return, but also on family values, philanthropy, legacy, natural resources, and future generations.

This questionnaire is the absolute first step in establishing an SRI initiative. Even if you are already part-way down the road, going through this process will help clarify and focus your program. It is based on the same questionnaire we have used when assisting clients in establishing their SRI activities.

To download a complementary copy of the self-assessment guide, go to SRI360.com/self-assessment-guide or visit our companion website at SRI360.com and request it there.

Visit SRI360.com for additional articles, full-length recorded interviews and more SRI lessons learned from world-class investors who are driving positive change with market returns that go beyond the niceties of SRI. You will find out what they're doing, and how they're doing it.

Chapter One

Why Sustainable and Responsible Investing?

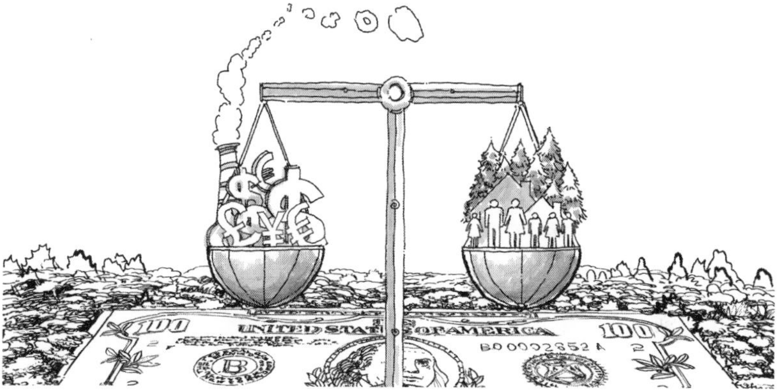

Much of our world is in chaos. For many, multigenerational war is a way of life. Natural disasters are no longer the exception, they are commonplace. They shred our landscape, while simultaneously destroying and demanding more of our limited and valuable resources. Societal unrest tears at the seams of civilization. Hope that the worldwide web would bring people together now casts a shadow of cynicism, as social media accentuates and inflames tribal differences.

Financial markets prefer peace and quiet, because don't we all? In the absence of calm, those markets react the way we do, becoming imbalanced, distorted, and volatile. Sometimes panic ensues, triggered by a fight or flight reaction. Bubbles expand and burst, portfolios go bust, and people and their communities are subjected to painful economic step functions. Naturally, painful outcomes circle around to exacerbate and perpetuate the cycle.

But humans are incredibly adaptable. Soon we are no longer shocked or dismayed by screaming headlines and dire news broadcasts. The mind can't abide constant turbulence, so we acclimate with desensitization that moves the dial another degree toward numbness. Click the mouse, change the channel, swipe to the next story, and search for relief, for answers, for a positive reckoning.

Otherwise, it's all a bit overwhelming and can send you into a funk. But the world around us reflects our own choices, our own decisions, and ultimately the actions we take day after day. We owe ourselves some thoughtful reflection of our own.

I am not a social scientist nor an economist, just someone who's paid some dues as he dragged his suitcase around the world to make a living in an international business career. Along the way, I accumulated a healthy amount of observations, traveling in a lot of different countries, on a regular basis over several decades. Some things have become vividly apparent: Despite amazing advances in technology, developing markets, increased access to information and improved productivity, we are witnessing huge, unintended consequences. They are clearly the result of large and complex global interdependencies that were not anticipated—and are still not well understood.

I'm no Einstein, but anyone paying attention sees glimpses of what our future may look like should we continue down the same path without any course correction. As the real Einstein observed, "We cannot solve our problems with the same thinking we used when we created them."

Socially, we are at a crossroads. If you get off track in the woods and go one way, you may be hopelessly lost by nightfall. Head in the right direction and you'll be home in time to tuck your children into bed. I've read that when making your final ascent to the top of Mount Everest, if you don't reach certain mileposts by a certain time of day, you won't make it back down before the temperatures plunge and you die of hypothermia. Despite knowing that, many climbers experience muddled thinking due to a dangerous mix of ambition and lack of oxygen. They proceed, convinced they'll make it and survive. But no one ever has.

Climate scientists plead with us to heed their warnings, which are supported by mountains of evidence. Meanwhile, the clock keeps ticking, we're on a slippery slope, and time is of the essence.

Understanding and overcoming social and environmental challenges is moving to the forefront, as the most pressing matter of our current generation. Our planet's sustainability and survival may depend on what we do, and how soon we do it. I believe we now need large-scale investment that offers competitive financial and economic returns fueled by mission-driven social and environmental solutions. A lot of people much smarter than me happen to agree.

ENTER SUSTAINABLE AND RESPONSIBLE INVESTING

In the early days of what was dubbed "socially conscious investing," it was basically a strategy for eliminating the bad apples. Investors conducted negative screening, which meant "avoiding investments in," to weed out specific companies and industries that did not align with positive social and environmental outlooks and outcomes. Those strategies ultimately led investors to sacrifice returns for values-oriented investment decisions.

In recent years, however, these investors have begun to screen investments to include those that actively drive constructive change forward. With an estimated global population increase of two billion people by 2050, the demands for food, energy, and water will inspire and propel innovative technology enhancements and additional investments in infrastructure to overcome those challenges.[1] There are important trends already in motion that provide investors a heightened awareness of the impact of their financial investments. There is accelerated momentum toward the creation of proactive investment strategies that hold public companies and governments accountable for measurably improved social and environmental outcomes.

MIGRATING INTO THE MAINSTREAM

While this type of "married to values" investment approach has been around for some time, within the last several years it has gone mainstream. Sustainable ROI is not measured only monetarily but in ways that include the value of clean water, sanitation, energy generation and distribution, increased biodiversity, improved health care, more efficient transportation, and other similarly positive outcomes.[2]

These investment opportunities are arising both in the developed and developing world, and the need for sustainable development is increasingly obvious. The private sector will continue to play an important role in redefining business as usual, and the financial industry is in a unique position to mobilize capital into investments that generate not just social and environmental benefits but competitive financial returns.

Despite the significant increase in these investments within recent years, there is still much work to be done. Fortunately, the opportunities for sustainable and responsible investing are vast. Many of the world's largest investment companies are already making significant strides to deploy capital for social and environmental outcomes. It is only a matter of time before sustainable and responsible investing becomes not only the industry standard, but a key ingredient in the recipe for socio-economic success.

SUSTAINABLE AND RESPONSIBLE INVESTING ACRONYMS AND "SRI"

A term thrown around quite a bit is "Responsible Investing."[3] This tends to be used as a broad umbrella term for all strategies that seek to include some dimension of social or environmental impact within the investment analysis and evaluation of investments within a portfolio. Depending on the strategy, the goal may be to better manage risk, but increasingly it is to generate long-term, sustainable returns.

Meanwhile, "Environmental, Social, and Governance" (ESG) investing is a strategy that relies on a set of standards for a company's operations, by which investors can assess their investment adherence to what is, again variably, considered as best practice.[4] Each of the three facets of ESG investing are carefully scrutinized to understand the overall impact of a company's operational footprint. "Impact Investing," on the other hand, actively seeks to generate positive social and environmental outcomes.[5] Then there is "Climate and Sustainable Finance," which generally refers to the subset of investing that specifically looks at mitigation and adaptation to environmental challenges.[6]

SRI (sometimes also referred to as "Ethical Investing"), includes ethical preferences when it comes to particular investments.[7] For example, SRI may exclude certain industries or particular companies based on investor ethics (e.g., those who make and sell arms, tobacco, or fossil fuels).

Over the years, I have spoken with hundreds of professional investors on this subject, and there's no clear consensus regarding the terminology we use to talk about a responsible investment approach. There is no shortage of terminologies and acronyms from which to choose, and there are no one-size-fits-all definitions to qualify and quantify a sustainable and responsible investment. There is, however, general consensus among those I've spoken with that I should just keep it simple for the purpose of this book. To that end, I will use SRI to refer to a whole slew of different methods and strategies, all of which consider the social and environmental footprint that investments create and leave in their wake.

I understand the potential for confusion as some professionals will quickly protest and say, "Hey, that only refers to negative screening of public equities!" But it doesn't in the specific context of this book. I've decided to appropriate the term SRI because it is widely recognized as one of the oldest and most referenced acronyms in the responsible investment industry, by both professional investors and the public at large.

So to be clear, when I use the acronym "SRI" in this book, I'm using it as an abbreviated way to refer to the Sustainable and Responsible Investment category as a whole.

"I DON'T HAVE TO TELL YOU THINGS ARE BAD . . ."

"I don't have to tell you things are bad. Everybody knows things are bad. We know the air is unfit to breathe and our food is unfit to eat, and we sit watching our TVs while some local newscaster tells us that today we had fifteen homicides and sixty-three violent crimes—as if that's the way it's supposed to be."[8]

That's an excerpt from the on-air rant of fictional, low-ratings national TV news anchor Howard Beale. He's wonderfully portrayed by actor Peter Finch in the 1976 movie *Network.*

Ignoring the teleprompter, Beale blurts out all of his frustrations about the world he lives in, before shouting, "*I'm as mad as hell and I'm not going to take this anymore!*" He then urges all viewers to open their windows and do the same. Although his lines were scripted nearly half a century ago, they still ring true and seem more relevant today than ever before.

Maybe that's because what's now percolating to the surface has been simmering for a long, long time. The challenges we face didn't arrive overnight. But often the problem in mounting meaningful change comes from the lack of shared experience. It is difficult to get people from different backgrounds and circumstances, who come from different cultures and parts of the world, to agree on how to prioritize our problems.

Whether the issues are human rights and social justice, or energy generation, climate change, and the environment, people are not all impacted by them in the same way. Many may feel that their daily lives are not at all affected by some of these issues.

Then the COVID-19 pandemic came along, dealing a global punch with a universally adverse impact felt around the world in a matter of months. Not everyone's life was impacted by the pandemic in the same way, but everyone has been touched by it in ways that were immediate and personal. There is no single occurrence in recent history more relevant than the COVID-19 pandemic in terms of bringing home the fact that all of us, everywhere, are truly interdependent and interconnected. Regardless of color, creed, or country, nobody on the planet was exempt. COVID-19 made it clear that even seemingly distant problems from geographically far away parts of the world can have a very real and profound local impact.

The arrival of COVID-19 reminded us of serious issues many would much rather not have to think about. Who could have imagined something of this magnitude, requiring social distancing, uncomfortable and annoying face masks, constant disinfecting, and a sense that we were confined—against our will—to house arrest.

At no other point in history have we been more poignantly reminded of the inequities which still exist between countries, races, and social classes. Many white-collar workers could make a good living while safely at home, in a relatively spacious environment supported by latest communication technologies. In fact, they may have saved significant amounts of money, thanks to fewer transportation expenses. They may have had more time to spend with loved ones like spouses and children, since they no longer had to commute to and from work.

In contrast, most blue-collar positions were deemed non-essential, and they were either laid off or their place of business was forced to close, either temporarily or permanently. Those lower-income workers often lived in more congested urban areas where access to healthy amenities is limited, but the risk of contracting the virus was higher. Those who did remain employed may have been much more likely to catch COVID-19, and even die, as a result of increased exposure to others within the workplace.[9]

The pandemic also brought into glaring focus the reality that what many people take for granted is unavailable to others. That can include the availability of everything from nearby grocery stores, pharmacies, outdoor spaces, and broadband connectivity. The disparities can be very real obstacles to success that is dependent upon such fundamentals as education, health care, and food security. Once the pandemic becomes a thing of the past, these inequalities can have a negative impact for life—on one's earning power as well as their mental and physical well-being.

Race was another trigger topic during the pandemic. A disproportionate number of higher-risk essential worker roles are held by people of color. Communities of color already suffered higher mortality rates due to being under-resourced and subjected to other hardships.[10] Abuse of police authority and excessive force was highlighted by media coverage and public protests.

COVID-19 created or amplified adverse economic and public health consequences, as those outcomes were felt throughout the world. Due to the world's interconnectivity, the aggressive virus spread with unfettered ease. That can be attributed to interactions between human populations and interactions of humans with nature, as natural habitats are encroached upon by a growing human population and appetite for natural resources. But there is a delicate balance within the planet's ecosystem. One result is zoonotic diseases emerging and spreading at a rate previously unimaginable. With increasing frequency, deadly viruses cross over from the animal kingdom to humankind.[11]

Unless and until we pay proper attention to these situations and take collective steps to stymie these growing threats to public health, we can expect continued widespread socio-economic impact. If we continue to ignore these realities, we will reap the tragic, catastrophic consequences.

COVID-19 PULLED BACK THE CURTAIN

Before the COVID-19 world, there was a tendency to gauge the impact of human behavior mostly in terms of climate change. Even that is a topic of fierce debate, although there is no arguing about the existence of symptoms like rising ocean temperatures and sea levels, the increasing frequency of extreme weather events, and shortages of vital resources like fresh water and clean air. The crew of the Titanic would have only been able to see the tip of the iceberg, while the real scale of the threat loomed massively large beneath the surface. Similarly, we are only beginning to comprehend the full magnitude of the consequences we will incur if we proceed full steam ahead, without regard for environmental stewardship.

One silver lining noted during the pandemic was that due to unfortunate lockdowns that curtailed much human activity, the earth responded with surprising resiliency. Positive changes in such things as greenhouse gas emissions and depletion of the ozone were recorded.[12] Damage that many climate scientists and computer models estimated would take decades to reverse was apparently healed within a matter of months.[13] Nature just needed the opportunity, and our social changes under COVID-19 restrictions provided that. The healing isn't permanent, nor is it significant in the grand scheme of things. But it does provide evidence that humankind has the power to reclaim much of what has been lost. Now climate scientists are more confident that if there's a will, there's a way.

The maintenance of healthy forests may be one option, versus unrelenting, systematic deforestation. Carbon dioxide emissions are reportedly at the highest levels in 650,000 years.[14] The global temperature is 2.1 degrees higher than it was a little more than 100 years ago.[15] Arctic ice, which we rely on for nearly 70 percent of drinking water, is literally evaporating into thin air.[16] The ice sheets are losing an incredible 427 billion metric tons each year, while the sea level is rising 3.3 meters per year.[17]

The list of threats and causes is long and getting longer. But the time to act is short and getting shorter. If you wake up and realize your home is on fire, you may not have the luxury of going to investigate who or what is to blame. You first have to deal with the fire before it kills you, using whatever resources and strategies you have at your immediate disposal.

It seems that our first priority should be to do what we can to ensure that future generations don't face an existential threat. Then we can take our time to retrospectively figure out who or what was to blame for today's climate crisis.

"I HAVE NOT YET BEGUN TO FIGHT"

I'm old enough to remember being instructed in grade school that the world was going to run out of oil in just a few years. Varying estimates of the timeline were given, none of which were immediate. But all predicted the demise of the fossil fuel industry within my lifetime, if not sooner, and that's a lot to lay on an innocent kid in middle school. I vividly remember being more than a little freaked-out and thinking to myself, "My future is screwed." I imagined living in some kind of dystopian, Mad Max world, wringing my hands from worry and for warmth, while huddling over a barrel fire in some grim, barren landscape I used to call home, sweet home.

Of course, none of that happened. Humans adapted and developed previously unknown technologies to extract oil. New oil fields were discovered, shale oil extraction completely turned the industry around, and a myriad of alternative energy technologies have been developed, including many promising ones that are still in their infancy. As enormous as some of the challenges we face may appear, the human race has demonstrated that we have no desire to sit on the sidelines as spectators to our own extinction.

The encouraging news is that, for the most part, a lot of the solutions we so desperately need right now already exist. Technological advances, powered by the best and the brightest, will continue to reveal even more innovative remedies. I have observed, however, that even the geniuses among us do tend to be motivated by tangible compensation. Their innovations and inventions can also cost a pretty penny to develop and, perhaps more importantly, deploy. We now have COVID-19 vaccines and therapies, but inevitably there are debates about how much money is being spent to get them into people's arms.

When it comes to solving the world's problems, there are countless things I do not know. But one thing I know for sure is that the solutions we want are going to demand a massive investment of capital. On the other hand, just look at how fast several COVID-19 vaccinations were developed and deployed for a previously unknown disease in less than a year. That's a great example of what we are capable of, when the world's best minds and significant investment capital are mobilized to remedy a global problem.

BEEN THERE, DONE THAT

In 2015, the United Nations set 17 interlinked global goals to be achieved by 2030; designed as a "blueprint to achieve a better and more sustainable future for all."[18] This plan, called "Agenda 2030," is estimated to cost $2.5–3 trillion per year for developing countries alone.[19] Financing at this level can't come from governments alone. That's especially true since the largest investment gaps will likely incur in countries that are the most at risk of being left behind. Fortunately, the private markets that have the capacity to fill the funding gaps are showing an increased appetite for SRI. Their appetite confirms my hunch, that the ultimate cost of doing nothing would be exponentially higher.

The SRI industry has evolved over time. Some commentators—typically and predictably those investment firms that only recently entered the sector—claim that the idea of investing for impact is new. New to them, perhaps, but scholars tell us that placing "social righteousness" above "business interest" was advocated by Confucius, circa 500 B.C. Similar welfare goals were a component of the investment philosophy of seventeenth-century Quakers. With the recent acceleration in investment in social housing, it's worth remembering that the world's first-known social housing complex was established by a wealthy merchant in Augsburg, Germany, in 1516.[20]

In the 1970s, SRI began to be adopted more widely, often by faith-based organizations keen to screen out those companies considered at odds to their core values (e.g., tobacco, weapons, alcohol, and pornography). Progressive foundations including the Ford Foundation developed "Program-Related Investments."[21] These were philanthropic investments that provided capital to initiatives deemed worthwhile, but with an expectation of recovering the principal and, when possible, additional returns.

By 1989, pioneering public market investors like Jupiter Asset Management had launched some of the earliest mainstream responsible investment funds. Impax Asset Management with support from the International Finance Corporation was founded in 1998 to invest in companies whose work might reduce resource scarcity. Less than ten years later, the Rockefeller Foundation debuted "Impact Investing," the most recent and fastest-growing SRI strategy to arrive on the scene.

Much of the early shift toward SRI in the private markets was thanks to the creative imagination of the nonprofit sector. While most foundations had long since removed any cognitive dissonance within their public equity and fixed income portfolios (e.g., a healthcare charity screening out cancer-causing tobacco stocks) they also began to realize their efforts were merely a drop in the bucket compared to the deep ocean of the institutional investment market. In 2019, for instance, U.S. charitable giving was estimated at $449 billion,[22] versus $160 trillion transacted in equity and debt markets.[23]

Forward-thinking donors recognized that the scale of challenges required far more capital than they had available. But, they thought, what if solutions to poverty and climate change like micro-drip irrigation in Africa, low-cost maternal healthcare in India, and micro solar grids in Cambodia could deliver sufficient return for investors to lure institutional investment? In that case, the $11.5 trillion that the United Nations estimates is needed to deliver all 17 of the Sustainable Development Goals suddenly seems perfectly manageable. Despite gloom and doom predictions, solutions are achievable—as long as we have the vision and resolve to invest in them.

I'm reminded of the story from the American Revolution, about naval commander John Paul Jones. When asked by his British counterpart, who had severely damaged Jones' ship, if he was ready to surrender, Jones famously responded "We have not yet begun to fight!" Soon

Jones emerged victorious. There's cause for optimism, even if the odds may not appear to be in our favor.

THE TIMES THEY ARE A-CHANGIN'

While SRI has been around for a longer time than is often acknowledged, it only became a mainstream phenomenon within the past few years. While many veterans continue to invest as they have done for years (and we profile a number of them in this book), what has been most striking is that major financial services groups, many of which are household names, have recently launched their own SRI impact-oriented offerings.

In 2015, Goldman Sachs acquired Imprint Capital.[24] Since 2016, huge private equity firms like TPG (The Rise Fund), Bain (Double Impact), Partners Group (LIFE), and Blackstone have launched investment funds with discrete impact investment strategies. The Rise Fund alone raised $2 billion for its first fund, and another $2 billion, as of 2020, for its second.[25]

In 2019, Schroders—the UK's largest asset manager—acquired the emerging market impact specialist Blue Orchard (who we speak with in chapter 7).[26] A year later, it listed the Schroder BSC Social Impact Trust (alongside Big Society Capital), specifically targeting homelessness, learning disabilities, and housing for survivors of domestic abuse. According to U.S. SIF Foundation's 2020 *Report on US Sustainable and Impact Investing Trends*, responsible and sustainable investing now represents a total of $17.1 trillion AUM, or 33 percent of all U.S. assets under management.[27]

In the words of Bob Dylan, "The times they are a-changin.'"

TAMING THE 400-POUND GORILLA IN THE ROOM

One of the largest catalysts for this change has likely been the entrance of long-dated asset investors, such as insurance companies and pension funds. These investors are capable of taking very long-term perspectives because of the liability-matching nature of their portfolios (e.g., pension funds are investing pension contributions now to fund payouts when pensioners retire). But they are also acutely aware that they are ultimately beholden to their beneficiaries—the retirement savers themselves. Those beneficiaries have been increasingly activist, demanding say-so regarding where their funds are invested and with whom.

This has caused a transformation among pension fund managers who have changed their investment approach from a fanatical adherence to fiduciary duty (a Friedman-like profit maximization philosophy, forsaking all else) to a far more holistic stewardship. After all, what is the point of providing for a retirement fifty years from now, if there is no livable planet left by then?

There is, of course, another hard-numbers dimension to their concern. Climate change has impossibly complex negative implications, from rising sea levels and crop failure to mass migration and war. These forecasted calamities represent catastrophically systemic risk to their portfolio's investment returns, and no amount of strategic asset allocation can diversify away from such exposure. Rather than building a portfolio to avoid climate change exposure, these huge institutional investors have recognized that they need to address the potential crisis head-on. As much as possible, they need to preemptively mitigate climate change itself. Having acknowledged the 400-pound gorilla in the room, they want to bring it under control before it wreaks more havoc.

GAINING TRACTION AND ALTITUDE

These recognized risks, of course, do not only potentially impact the future. The present value of any company or asset depends upon its projected future cashflow. Futuristic climate scenarios already affect current valuations and investment returns. For example, by the year 2100, rising sea levels are expected to cause up to $1 trillion in losses in U.S. real estate alone.[28] A report published by First Street Foundation estimated that $16 billion was already lost in just 17 states between 2005 and 2017.[29]

Those calculations can fundamentally change an investment thesis in the stock market. The 2011 Carbon Tracker's report on "stranded assets" in the oil and gas industry pointed out that if temperature rise is limited, through a combination of regulation and change in practices, reduced fossil fuel demand will substantially decrease the amount of these reserves that will never be able to be monetized.[30] Previously, major oil companies had been valued, in part, based on the amount of oil reserves they owned but had not yet recovered. While the Carbon Tracker report was ridiculed by oil execs at the time, their core premise has now been validated by massive asset write-downs across the industry. In 2020, BP's new CEO went to great pains to explain that it is no longer an oil company, but rather an energy company with net zero carbon ambitions by 2050.[31]

WIDE ROAD AHEAD

While there has been great momentum over the last few years, much work remains. Also, while statistics on SRI can be reassuring, the devil, as they say, is often in the details.

For instance, most impact assets under management remain in public equities. That may appear to affect the weighted average cost of capital for listed corporates, making it cheaper for positive companies to raise capital and grow—while making it more difficult and expensive for negative companies to do the same. But it is hard to verify that investors trading shares are driving meaningful outcomes. BP's recent change in strategy, for example, is less likely due to downward pressure on its share price caused by ESG investors divesting oil shares. A more plausible explanation is that this move was the result of BP recognizing that their core business is within a sunset industry, and that to survive they need to reinvent themselves.

On the other hand, the picture is different within the realm of fixed income, with growth of green bond issuance over the last couple of years, especially during the pandemic. When green bonds are issued, new funding is raised with very strict parameters. Those stipulate how the funds can and can't be used, such as investment in green infrastructure by an energy company, or energy efficiency investments for a hospitality business. These expenditures are subsequently verified by objective third parties, so that the lenders are assured that the use of funds is consistent with the premise upon which the funding was raised.

But significant gaps across asset classes remain. While companies like Mirova were an early mover in the space (by acquiring Althelia Ecosphere in 2017), none of the world's largest asset managers follow dedicated investment policies related to biodiversity. That's despite current extinction rates that are estimated to be as much as 1,000 times higher than they should be.[32] Meanwhile, in venture capital, only 2.8 percent of funding goes to founders who are women.[33]

Data will be a key part of the solution; you can't manage what you can't measure! But data is already proving to be no silver bullet. Current frameworks often score companies based on inputs rather than outputs. That skews the results toward disclosure and transparency and disproportionality rewards those large companies that can afford dedicated reporting staff, relative to their smaller but possibly more sustainable competitors. Furthermore, investors are already noticing significant discrepancies between ESG ratings of the same company. For example, in terms of ESG, MSCI ranks Tesla as one of the best global car manufacturers, while FTSE ranks it as last.[34] This is due to differences in the underlying methodologies, which need to be reconciled if investors are ever going to be able to compare asset managers in a meaningful way, in terms of their ESG performance.

Developments in regulation may help. The Financial Stability Board's Taskforce of Climate-related Financial Disclosures (TCFD) has been an important enabler over the last couple of years and has demonstrated the power of disclosure even when it is voluntary. As usual, governments are followers rather than leaders. But once they enshrine policies through regulation, the stick can be far more persuasive than the carrot.

In 2020, the Canadian government announced that any company seeking COVID-19 relief must disclose its environmental impact, in line with TCFD recommendations.[35] Later that year, the UK became the first country in the world to make TCFD disclosures mandatory by 2025.[36] Post-Brexit, they will also adopt a UK taxonomy—based on the new EU taxonomy—that specifically establishes what can and cannot be defined as "sustainable."[37] This is in reaction to claims of greenwashing in the investment industry (marketing investments as sustainable when they are not) and should further bolster investor confidence as new impact-oriented strategies are introduced.

We will look at all these matters throughout this book and hear opinions on each from different investors who are actually in the trenches. They are those whose "faces are marred by blood and sweat and dust," in the words of Theodore Roosevelt. I hope that this approach will give you a far broader sense of the prevailing, and ever-evolving, debate(s).

Occasionally, we will touch on frontier strategies, those that are still experimental and are not yet deployed on a meaningfully significant scale. Since green bonds have enjoyed recent success, will we soon see the rise of blue bonds to protect our marine ecosystems? Where we have seen tradeable carbon emissions, will we soon see a range of other tradeable ecosystem services, from soil and water credits to Net Biodiversity Gains?

Only time will tell. My grandparents, who immigrated from Sweden to America in the early twentieth century, used to tell me in their heavily accented English, "the afternoon knows what morning may only wish for, or suspect."

"Start where you are. Don't get too wrapped up in the language and the terms and the labels. Anything can be viewed through an impact lens and can be managed on that basis. So, if you're in a firm doing whatever type of investing, all you have to do is start asking uncomfortable questions. About the practice, about the process . . . and you become an impact investor."

THE EVOLUTION OF IMPACT
JED EMERSON
TIEDEMANN ADVISORS
TIEDEMANNADVISORS.COM
LI: https://www.linkedin.com/in/jedemerson
TW: @BlendedValue

Jed Emerson is an internationally recognized thought leader in impact investing, social entrepreneurship and strategic philanthropy and the Managing Director and Global Lead Impact Investing with Tiedemann Advisors. He has extensive experience leading, staffing, and advising funds, firms, social ventures, and foundations in pursuance of financial performance alongside social/environmental impact. Emerson has authored numerous articles and papers on the subject, including the first book on impact investing (*Impact Investing: Transforming How We Make Money While Making a Difference*), which won the 2012 Nautilus Gold Book Award. In 2018 he released his eighth book, *The Purpose of Capital: Elements of Impact, Financial Flows and Natural Being.*[38]

Originator of the *Blended Value* concept, Emerson is a Senior Fellow with the Center for Social Investment at Heidelberg University and has held faculty appointments at Oxford, Harvard, Stanford, and Kellogg business schools.

Take us back to your early career—what was the catalyst for your transition from Larkin Street Youth Services to the founding team at REDF?[39]

When I was in my teens, all I wanted to do was run a nonprofit and change the world. I did that with Larkin Street when we got that program off the ground, despite a lot of political issues with other groups that thought they should be running it. We launched and then, about three or four months after that, the program facility burned to the ground and one of my staff was killed, so I had to re-launch it. This was also in the middle of the AIDS epidemic, so it was a very intense period.

After about three or four years, I began taking stock and thinking about where I was. I realized all the things I'd loved about social work turned out to be wrong. I think at that time, a lot of people moved to San Francisco to just be radical. I learned how to play really good social service politics as a result and human service politics can be really nasty. Part of the thing I realized was that capital in the nonprofit sector—especially at that time—moved on the basis of politics, perception, and persuasion—but not performance.

I reached a point where I realized my job as executive director was basically either to play politics to get the funding we needed or to give talks and make people cry about street kids so they would write me cheques. Or it was to schmooze foundation program officers and get them to think that we were the next best thing and fund us. I realized I didn't want to spend the rest of my life being assessed based on those kinds of metrics, if you will, which had nothing to do with transforming lives or creating actual change.

I was pretty burnt out after that experience, so I decided I needed to get into something else. At the time, I didn't know what that was. This was before social entrepreneurship or venture philanthropy or impact investing. You really had to choose to either go into the nonprofit or the for-profit sector. There wasn't any kind of middle ground. I knew I didn't want to do foundation work or government work or nonprofits.

About that time, a gentleman who ran a number of foundations for different families in the Bay Area reached out and said he had a donor who was interested in free enterprise and market-based approaches to social issues. I told him that I didn't think it was a great idea, because if you believed in free enterprise approaches to homelessness, you'd have all these homeless entrepreneurs. And since I didn't see any, maybe the market wasn't doing so good in our communities!

He called me later to say the client wanted to hire me to do the research because if I didn't think it was a good idea, he trusted me not just to sell them a bill of goods. "You're going to be critical," he told me and asked if I would consider just doing the research part.

Who was this gentleman who wanted your help?

So, it turned out it was George R. Roberts (one of the three founding partners of Kohlberg Kravis Roberts & Co., KKR). He had come to a very similar place to where I had come, but obviously from a very different journey. His challenge to me was whether we could create a way to approach philanthropic and charitable giving that was informed by investment and business acumen and practices.

Was that your initial premise or framework?

That was the starting place: how do you use finance to create community level change, as opposed to how do you do grantmaking? And so, that was the kind of initial frame that I then explored and came back to him with a strategy that we executed together for the next eleven years.

One of the things that we did at that time, in the mid-1990s, was to convene what I'm pretty sure was the first working group to create a formal methodology to calculate Social Return on Investment (SROI).

At the time it was very chic to say, "Oh, we're investing for social returns!" I would ask for-profit, mission-driven investors, "How do you calculate the return on that part of your portfolio?" And they would literally laugh at me and say, "Oh, no, it's a metaphor. We don't actually *invest* for social returns. We're just investing for financial returns that have social value somewhere in the mix." I would say "Well, let me share our Excel templates with you. We actually monetize specifically the economic value of social impact. We do a discounted cash flow analysis to time zero, based on the time zero valuation of the enterprise. We look then at the performance of our capital over time relative to that economic value we created." It was very rudimentary, but it was something nobody had really sat down and actually done at that point.

The generation of business people at that time was Patagonia, Body Shop, Ben and Jerry's. It was that kind of period of business development—businesses that were being started to really create an advanced social and environmental value as well as financial return for investors. That's how I kind of found myself in the middle of all those different conversations that, to my mind, were all the same.

But, because each of these folks entered from their own silo, they all thought they were very unique. To my mind, all they were doing—either on a nonprofit or for-profit or a charitable or a market rate basis in terms of capital—they were all grappling with the limitations of a bifurcated value proposition that asks you to either do well or do good. You either make a grant or you make an investment.

What I realized by the end of the 1990s was I had kind of naturally gone to this place where I was agnostic about the investment vehicles. I didn't care if it was a grant, high-risk loan, recoverable grant, or if it was market rate, venture, seed, whatever. And in terms of organizational form, I didn't care if it was a nonprofit or a for-profit or a hybrid or co-operative. That's because to me, it's all just types of capital and types of organizational form. The real question is, what are you trying to do? Or more specifically, how do you understand the nature of the value you're trying to create in a market, in a community, or in an ecosystem?

When you have clarity on *that*, then you can start talking about what the best kind of organizational forms are. What's the right structure of capital to really drive the value you're trying to capture? And that's how I came up with the concept of Blended Value and what that all became.[40]

And where did that eventually lead?

I came to this place where I accidentally fell into family office work. Because families don't think in terms of instruments and structures. They think in terms of what they're trying to do as a family, like, "What are our values? What do we believe in? Can we create a foundation? Should we do that? Should we start a company that has our family values?" I mean, they don't start with the solution; they start with the questions.

I had an opportunity to begin working with a woman out of Hong Kong named Annie Chen, of RS Group Asia. I've worked with Annie and her team for over ten years now on this idea of how you take a holistic approach to wealth management and have that be the operating assumption, versus we're a for-profit, we're a nonprofit, or what have you. I've called that Total Portfolio Management—how you manage philanthropic, near market, and market rate capital in order to optimize the value you seek to create in the world.

I then ended up being the senior strategic adviser to Liesel Pritzker and her initiative, which is the Blue Haven Initiative out of Boston. I was with them for six years or so. I worked with another family out of Hawaii, another out of Colorado, but all with this idea of "How do you utilize all of your assets for impact?"

In the midst of all this, of course, in terms of my own journey, the whole field was blowing up all around us. In 2008–2009 when we had the financial crisis, it was really striking because at the time there was this infusion of very traditional finance people who felt completely betrayed by finance. People don't really acknowledge this, but capitalism is premised on a faith in capitalism. It's like a religious kind of thing, where you have the Wall Street priests and you have the doctrines and rituals and practices; it's very religiously oriented. And they felt betrayed by God, their God of Manna, if you will. And so, they came into this space looking for meaning, purpose, and value.

That's when I think the talent base within impact investing really took off because you had all these folks who were very serious financial people. I mean, we were serious financial people, too, but I'd never run a $500 million investment portfolio on Wall Street. That wasn't what I did. But there were now people in our field who had and, broadly speaking, I think the adoption and translation of this to the mainstream really accelerated around that period.

Can you explain what you mean by Total Portfolio Management?

There are a couple of different aspects. The first is a recognition that all capital has impact and all companies have impact. The issue isn't whether you're an impact investor or not. You are an impact investor when you deploy capital in the world that does things in the world. That's what it's all about.

That's what Total Portfolio Management is about, and why I call it *management* and not activation. Your portfolio is already activated and it's doing things all over the place and most of it is probably bad. But management means you have intentionality, you have strategy, you have metrics. You're approaching the understanding of the impact your capital has in the world in a more intentional way. That's the framing of TPM, which I think is important.

Related to that is, to my mind, that we have to understand the value we're trying to create is itself whole and integrated and non-divisible. There is no such thing as doing well and then doing good. There's no such thing as externalities. In traditional finance and economics, you basically say here's the stuff we can measure and assess inside this little square. Things that are intangible, but at the same time we understand are priceless, we're going to put outside of our calculus because we don't have the right way to think about that. You have then, whatever it is, 350 years of people basically pretending the off-balance sheet stuff doesn't matter.

I think what has happened in the progression of this work and conversation is that initially it did begin as a values conversation around "I don't want to invest in tobacco, alcohol, firearms." Then it became, well, if you can screen out bad companies, can you screen-in good companies?

And so that's what evolved in the 1980s—best in class investing. You had a lot of strategies looking for good companies in bad sectors, or just good companies. Then folks started doing the ESG piece and saying, okay, environmental, social, and governance factors are material to your ability to make money—they represent off balance sheet risk to managers and investors. And if you're not thinking about that off balance sheet risk, then it will jeopardize your ability to optimize financial return. So, if all you care about is making money, you *still* have to think about this stuff. It has nothing to do with morality. It has nothing to do with anything other than the materiality question—how are these elements material to your ability to make money? Which, of course, laid the foundation for the expansion of ESG Integration.

And then [in 2008–2009] people started saying, well, guess what? The wheels have just come off. I think this is part of what happened with the financial crisis. It's part of what happened during the pandemic, combined with the events of George Floyd's murder and the light that was shown on racial and economic injustice. And then the pandemic's effect of kind of pulling back the curtain and showing in stark terms the real effect of social and economic inequity, and the fact that all these so-called essential workers were being paid minimum wage and were basically viewed as though you could sacrifice them. And that people like you and I, it was okay for us to go to our second homes and just get Amazon to deliver. So, it raised a whole set of issues regarding business, ethics, investing and the type of world we wanted to be investing in. This is why I think some of this has just taken such a sharp edge now, is that people are really saying, okay, all capital has impact. All companies have impact. Can you manage that impact for positive social and environmental intentionality and with direction? Can you manage for positive net impact?

Smartphones and social media have played a large role in bringing the awareness of business practices and their impact on our world into mainstream consciousness. What role do you see technology playing in responsible investing going forward?

I think technology has enabled a whole host of issues to surface that we traditionally have not adequately paid attention to. I guess the one tweak to that I would add would be to say that the trick is that the technology hasn't done anything new—its simply showed a reality we have ignored. So, it's a tool and we need to be careful not to confuse a tool with a task.

I would argue what that tool shows you is the truth of the notion of the illusion of separation because, in the absence of that tool, you could pretend what happened to a company in India didn't matter to an investor in the United States. Like you could pretend the world was separate and that your own wealth and money was distinct from somebody else's poverty. I think what technology has enabled us to do is very literally, take a picture of those connections and make us realize there really is no separation between self and other. And that this is the reality.

You've previously flagged pandemics as being a significant corporate risk before we ever knew about COVID-19, and the UN has estimated that 50 percent of GDP is dependent on nature. How can or should investors address these types of risks in the market?

We first need to acknowledge that ecosystems provide services to local communities, to cities, to all of us. And that for the most part, we have done a very, very poor job of accurately pricing those ecosystem services. We have created an economic order that allows many companies to offload their environmental costs to the Commons and not actually carry that cost as part of their price of doing business. I—and many others, have argued—many of the companies that today are thought to be very profitable would not be profitable if they had to actually carry that ecosystem rent, if you will, that they're paying at very marginal, artificially low levels. We really need to step back and think very differently about how we price nature services, how we think about carbon taxes, how we think about cap and trade, how we think about all these issues.

With more large investors entering the responsible investment market, how can investors diagnose who's credible and who's not? And who's greenwashing or impact-washing?

I think you've got to wash off some of the grime in order to see the green. That's part of what this opportunity is. Basically, anybody who's involved in finance as it currently is made up in the United States and the Western cultural frame is involved in extractive economic practices. I mean, that is the whole premise of traditional investing. You invest to get something back. We need to recognize—there's a phrase I heard last year—"you have to own your ugly."

We can modify it, we can change, we can redirect. When it comes to separating out the wheat from chaff, we need to look at who the actors are, their own track records. Like, are they Johnny-come-lately to the conversation? Or have they actually advanced net positive impact over time? Do they speak with a level of honesty about the challenges?

I think one of the biggest challenges certainly in the investment advisory and fund manager's space is that the whole conversation is premised on best ideas, best solutions. And so there's no opportunity to fail, right? You basically have to say, "We have the best idea, we have the best team. This is the best investment strategy." You can't say "Well, we're still working out that off balance sheet risk thing . . ," or "There are still parts of this that are in development. . . ."

I think it really entails a level of confidence. Walter Brueggemann talks about the importance of what he calls *humbition* which is his idea that while we have to have serious ambition for what we hope to achieve in the world,[41] we have to approach the pursuit of that ambition with deep humility. And that's really the power of evolving what in Buddhist tradition is often referred to as "beginners mind." You have to have confidence in what you're trying to do. You have to be okay with who you are in that process. And you have to operate from a place of humility in the course of pursuing the ideas you believe in.

When I look at advisors, I'm looking for who speaks with a level of authenticity, who has a level of performance relative to these ideas and practices, who is asking better questions around what this is and where it could go—as opposed to constantly selling solutions.

If you had to name the single most important challenge in the sustainable and responsible investment space at this time, what would it be?

I would say it is this question of how to scale with authenticity and how to keep the integrity of the practice as we go about the task of changing the face of systemic capitalism.

What do you know now about ESG, responsible and impact investing, that you wish you knew back in 2000 when you started Blended Value?

I wish I had understood the degree to which this is all just one big parade. We may have different marching bands but at the end of the day, it's all the same parade. And I watch the amount of energy other people put into defending this practice against that practice, or this mindset or this label. It makes no sense to me because it's all one thing. It's all about how we seek to create integrated, holistic value in the world—whether you call it Blended Value or Integrated Value or Shared Value. So, I wish I myself and the field had become aware of that earlier, because I think that it would have saved a lot of hassle.

Describe an investment that you were convinced ticked all the boxes, but in the end did not have the impact you expected—and what you learned from that.

When I think back on the different investments that we've made over time, it's less that the investments have turned out differently than we might've thought as it is that the overall strategies have had to evolve and change and become something other than where we started. So, in almost every case, certainly with the families that I've worked with, it's been a process of evolution and development and refinement of the strategy that we've been executing, as opposed to having one strategy and saying, "Okay, this is it. We're going to ride this horse into the ground."

I think the bigger lesson for me is the need to have conviction and to be focused on and disciplined with the execution of your strategy, and also to recognize that it's simply one strategy. And strategies, circumstances, and contexts all shift. We have to have a dynamic approach to managing wealth in this regard, as opposed to locking-in and saying, "Here's how we think about portfolio structure. Here's how we think about the definition of performance." (Which, of course, is always financial!) Even, "Here's how we think about this definition of an asset class."

So, I think it's the idea that we have to, on the one hand, have the courage of our convictions, but, on the other hand, allow our confidence to evolve and shift and grow.

If someone wants to get into the sustainable, responsible investment space, how would you advise them to do so?

I would advise a couple of things. One is start where you are. I mean, don't get too wrapped up in the language and the terms and the labels. Anything can be viewed through an impact lens and can be managed on that basis. So, if you're in a firm that is doing whatever type of investing, all you have to do is start asking uncomfortable questions about the practice and the process and you can become an impact investor.

I think the other part is to read. I am genuinely shocked at the number of people who have come into this space in the last twenty years who lead with their ignorance. It's not that they're stupid, it's that they don't know what they don't know because they think this is a new idea. They think because they were successful in finance, all they've got to do is learn some of this terminology and they can be successful in impact.

It's just curious to watch. And then you talk to those same people five or 10 years later, and they're like, "Oh my God, the things I didn't know, I can't believe it." Well, maybe you could have been quiet for a little bit of the first part and just listened to the field. I don't mean listen to me. Just listen to the people who were actually doing the work. I think reading and just listening to the experience of the folks who've gone before can position you to make much better mistakes than they made. And that's what it's all about, it's taking risk and capturing opportunity.

Chapter Two

Why SRI Is a Future-Proof Trend

There are two major tsunami-like structural trends driving the inevitable growth of SRI. Both originate from one phenomenon: demographic change.

THE POP GOES BOOM

The first of these is relentless global population growth. It's worth reminding ourselves that while our species has walked the earth for more than 300,000 years, up until 500 years ago there were only 450 million people on the planet. Since then, our population has ballooned to at least 7.8 billion. Needless to say, this relentless growth will require extraordinary investment if our societies and planet are expected to equitably support an estimated 10.9 billion population by 2100.[1]

On the environmental side, humans consume huge amounts of resources. But we have destroyed more than a third of those in just the last 30 years, according to the World Wildlife Fund.[2] Nevertheless, we keep consuming, at an ever-more voracious rate. Our world consumes an estimated equivalent of 1.75 planets worth of resources.[3] While the average American consumes the equivalent of five planets, the average person in India consumes a relatively scant 0.7 planets.[4] If we are to support what certainly looks like an unsustainable human population, then huge investments need to fuel innovations that increase resource efficiency and/or shift consumption from non-renewable to renewable resources (e.g., from coal to solar).

It will also require significant behavioral change. For example, our global food system is as damaging to biodiversity as our energy system is to climate change. But an Oxford University study found that if everyone eliminated meat and dairy from their diets, it would lead to a 49 percent reduction in greenhouse gases, and a 76 percent reduction in land used for food production (agriculture being one of the leading causes of deforestation).[5]

While universal veganism may prove unrealistic, a "flexitarian" diet (characterized by significantly reduced meat consumption) would have a significant positive impact. Companies like those developing lab-grown meat or plant-based alternatives are already receiving substantial venture capital and significant private equity. The company Beyond Meat—having IPO'd in May 2019 at a valuation of $3.8 billion[6]—had a market cap of $7.27 billion in September 2021.[7] That was following the announcement of its strategic partnership with PepsiCo, one of the largest food and beverage companies in the world.[8]

We also need significant social investment to reduce existing inequalities and simultaneously curb population growth. Like many think tanks, the Brookings Institute has emphasized the direct relationship between girls' education and population growth.[9] This is because the vast majority of population growth is expected to be in developing countries where, thanks to improvements in healthcare, mortality rates have declined more rapidly than fertility rates.[10] Data from the World Bank shows a clear trend: low educational attainment for girls is associated with higher population growth and is especially costly in part because of the relationships between educational attainment, child marriage, and early childbearing, and the risks that they entail for young mothers and their children.[11]

These are complex and perhaps wicked problems because they intersect with everything from poverty alleviation and gender discrimination to cultural and religious expectations. There are, however, clear and necessary investment opportunities across the board, from educational and broadband infrastructure to telemedicine. Recently, the UN's 17 interlinked Sustainable Development Goals, outlines as a "blueprint to achieve a better and more sustainable future for all," were adopted by the investment community to help identify key themes, ranging from Goal 2 (Zero Hunger) to Goal 6 (Clean Water and Sanitation).[12] While investors can consider their own priorities and frameworks, these goals have proven to be a useful guide.

MILLENNIALS BANK THE GREAT WEALTH TRANSFER

The second and perhaps less obvious demographic wave driving responsible investment is the extraordinary intergenerational wealth transfer. Dubbed "The Great Wealth Transfer," it moves massive wealth from the Baby Boomer generation to Millennials over the coming decades. While estimates run the gamut, from $30 trillion to more than double that amount, the sums are historically enormous.[13]

The game-changing importance of this transfer is due to the decidedly different social, environmental, and financial investment perspective of Millennials compared to Boomers. Millennials were born roughly between 1981 and 1996 and entered adulthood during the 2007–2008 Global Financial Crisis. That jarring experience significantly undermined their trust in long-standing institutions. A recent ShareBuilder survey found that 60 percent of Millennials are skeptical of financial markets.[14] Neither do they trust government, the justice system, or corporations to always do the right thing. As the first generation to have grown up with digital technology, however, they are keenly aware that a universe of information is at their fingertips. They are also conscious of the voice and power that social media gives them, to influence corporate and governmental change.

Today Millennials are the largest segment of the world population, and they also comprise the biggest workforce. They are unafraid to advocate and agitate for issues they feel strongly about. Facebook, for example, faced a "virtual walkout" in 2020 by its young workforce over Donald J. Trump's posts.[15] A year before, Google employees protested the company's participation in efforts to enforce U.S. immigration policies they disagreed with, and hate speech broadcast on Google's YouTube platform.[16] Their passionately held values are equally manifested in their consumer habits and preferences.

A PURPOSE-DRIVEN GENERATION

Millennials are, above all, a purpose-driven generation.

In a survey conducted by American Express, 68 percent said they wanted to make a positive difference in the world, while 81 percent said a successful business needs to have a genuine purpose.[17] Millennial spending power as a percentage of overall spending will increase over the next few decades and Boomer spending will decline. The generational handover of financial power will subsequently determine which companies and industries thrive, and which ones fade toward irrelevance and obsolescence.

The Great Wealth Transfer, and the different values of the Millennial generation, represent double-barrel challenges for the private wealth investment industry, as well as the global asset management groups that serve them.

The first challenge is that (according to a Brooks Macdonald report forecast) 53 percent of Millennial inheritors will change or leave their financial advisors upon inheritance.[18] That potential churn represents an existential crisis for the investment industry in terms of Assets Under Management (AUM). The second related issue is that for those asset managers to succeed and nurture strong relationships to retain AUM, they must recalibrate toward the purpose-driven demands of their new clients. They will need to offer investment products and services that attract the interest, and align with the values, of Millennials.

For Millennials, investment beliefs and personal values are no longer in separate, dichotomous silos. They are not willing to invest in ways that create a personal conflict of values. They won't agree to get rich by investing in Big Oil, in order to engage philanthropically to promote climate change. Their portfolios must be inherently consistent with their values, otherwise they'll reject those portfolios as being at cross-purposes. Or, to put it bluntly as younger generations often do, they'll consider them downright hypocritical.

The myth that social and environmental outcomes come at the expense of financial returns will have to be dispelled in a demonstrable and easily understood way. Disingenuous practices like "greenwashing" will have to be exposed, called out, and rejected. Wealth managers will need to communicate to clients their own values, much more transparently, and provide a broader range of sustainable investment practices and products.

A 2017 Morgan Stanley report found that 86 percent of Millennials are interested in investing in companies or funds aimed at generating market-rate financial returns coupled with the intentional pursuit of positive social and/or environmental outcomes. The report also noted that 90 percent say they want sustainable investing as an option within their 401(k) retirement plans. Eighty-four percent believe that their investments have the power to help lift people out of poverty.[19] A more recent deVere Group survey reported that 77 percent of Millennial investors consider ESG issues a top priority for them, when assessing investments.[20]

Given this seismic shift, the entire private wealth management and asset manager industry will need to transform itself, a move that is already underway. The bottom line is, investment firms that offer responsible and sustainable fund strategies will be positioned to succeed two-fold. Not only will the underlying companies that they invest in be more likely to outperform, but those funds will be best positioned to gather assets and grow AUM. The Millennials, who now hold the purse strings, are demanding those kinds of SRI products and strategies.

In the chapters that follow, we will hear from some of the leaders in the field—recognized experts already positioned to capitalize on these mega trends.

"One of our super trends is millennial values. As millennials are getting into their peak earnings years, how is their earning power going to drive change, what products and services do they want to buy, and how are they going to use financial services? When you wrap a sustainability lens around millennial values, it leads you to interesting thematics."

SUSTAINABLE INVESTING
MARISA DREW
CREDIT SUISSE
CREDIT-SUISSE.COM
LI: https://www.linkedin.com/in/marisa-drew-9532088/

Marisa Drew is the Chief Sustainability Officer and Global Head of Sustainability Strategy, Advisory, and Finance at Credit Suisse in London. She is responsible for setting the strategy and directing, coordinating, and facilitating activities across the bank that lead to sustainable investing on behalf of the bank's private wealth, institutional, and corporate clients.

Drew established the Impact Advisory and Finance department following her role as Global Co-Head of the Global Markets Solutions Group encompassing Equity Capital Markets, Debt Capital Markets, Leveraged Finance and Equity and Debt Structured Derivatives Products.

She has been in the investment banking business for over thirty years, joining Credit Suisse to establish the Leveraged Finance Origination Group after working at Merrill Lynch's European Leveraged Finance Group, a private equity firm and the investment bank, Kidder Peabody.

She sits on the Harvard Women's Leadership Board, on the advisory boards of Room-to-Read and the Lessons for Life Foundation, is a Trustee of the Credit Suisse Foundation, and is active in her industry's recruitment, diversity, and philanthropic initiatives.

Drew received a BA in Finance and Marketing from the University of Virginia's McIntire School of Commerce and an MBA with distinction from the Wharton School.

Describe the evolution of your role from creating the Impact Advisory and Finance department to becoming the Chief Sustainability Officer.

The Impact Advisory and Finance role was very much designed to be a client facing, client service effort. It ranged from helping to create and facilitate investment products that drove environmental or social outcomes to providing advice.

I set about building an expert team who were facile with this topic, and who had been involved in the sustainability arena for many years and were in a position to deliver their expertise. Then I identified where raising capital was needed to fund people's sustainability journeys. That's a natural home for me because that's classic investment banking and capital markets services. Whether it was taking a sustainability disruptor public or providing dedicated debt capital for them to realize their transition ambitions, it was very familiar territory—just with a sustainability lens. It was a global remit, so it spanned across our private banking, institutional and corporate client base.

That was the early generation of our effort. The impact finance market, however, is just a small subset of the overall sustainable finance arena. As we've evolved and taken on a broader remit to include all of ESG investing, we've renamed the group Sustainability Strategy Advisory and Finance (SSAF), to reflect this wider universe of sustainability.

A year ago, I took on the additional role of Chief Sustainability Officer (CSO) for the bank, and that is all about Credit Suisse as an enterprise. The questions I tackle in this role are: What's the ambition of the bank? What is our sustainability strategy? How do we embed it into the organization? What are the initiatives around sustainability as an organization that we're going to pursue? As an example, we've made a commitment to achieve net zero emissions by 2050, using science-based targets. All of those sorts of things are encompassed within the CSO title. So, I've got these two hats which is great because my scope now covers front to back, from the client all the way through to our organization and operations.

Were you able to leverage your investment banking background into the sustainability area?

A hundred percent, because at its core I believe that one of my primary mandates is to help mobilize capital at scale to help solve some of the world's biggest environmental and social challenges. And if you are truly going to create scale in the private sector, you need to be able to speak the language of the institutional investment community.

Those who are coming up through sustainability who were previously working for an NGO or a development bank would have a harder time doing this within a complex highly regulated bank like ours, because it's not a world they are familiar with. Most of my career has been spent in the traditional capital markets, capital raising, dealing every day with institutional investors. So, what they need is intuitive to me, what structures work for them, which don't, and what their particular requirements are around liquidity or collateral coverage or return hurdles for a given asset class, etc. This is all a natural stomping ground for me. If I'm going to successfully deliver sustainable investment solutions, I need to be able to do it in a format that speaks to them.

Sustainability sectors that are underinvested are often the case because there have not been institutional grade investment opportunities available. In the oceans for instance, the feedback we got when we delved into this space was "Yes, I'd like to invest in the oceans, but there's nothing there for me. There might be some small venture stage stuff around, but nothing that we can put money to work in at scale in a structure that works for us." Having faced this at other points in my career albeit in a different context, it was so natural for me to rethink how we could present credible sustainable investments to these classes of investors and use structuring technology like credit enhancements or derivatives to find solutions.

Another area of common ground is in raising growth capital for early-stage companies. I was previously responsible for our ECM origination business—the IPO world—helping to take new and often disruptive companies public. Today, many of the disruptors are sustainability companies at heart run by mission-driven entrepreneurs trying to solve environmental or social problems with their business models—these are the new companies coming to the IPO markets. So, despite the fact that on the surface it doesn't seem like there's a big link between running capital markets businesses and sustainability, there are more similarities than one would think.

Another bit of familiar territory with what I see in the sustainability maturity curve was what I experienced in helping to build the leverage finance asset class in Europe. When I moved to Credit Suisse in 2003 to run our corporate LevFin (Leveraged Finance) franchise, the market in Europe was nascent. You didn't have a common language or set of standards. And despite its extraordinary growth at the time, there was a healthy dose of skepticism among many on the sidelines about the claims of certain structures and there were too few case studies to prove out the risk adjusted return thesis. The regulatory environment was also just catching up to the growth in the asset class.

We had to systematically build a market with common terminology and one with depth, liquidity and confidence, *and* we had to deliver on the market's risk/return promises in order to achieve true scale. In so many respects that's just what we're doing in sustainable finance. So many of the same principles apply. You see many, many analogues. In the realm of taxonomy, just google the words "responsible or sustainable investing." You'll find five different definitions. But when markets can rely on the same principles and adopted standards, capital flows. There's a lot there that I think has been very instructive from my prior life.

Describe an example of a product that you developed where you saw the opportunity to scale the offering to a ticket size that institutional investors are interested in.

I was seeing that all of our clients were increasingly using the UN Sustainable Development Goals as their language for how to express the categories of themes that they might want to invest in. And with that becoming the language, it allowed us to use that as a framework for how we create investment opportunities.

If we look at the case of SDG 14, which is "Life Below Water" (i.e., the oceans), I can illustrate our approach. I had said to the team let's map the SDGs, on the one hand to find out where there has been a fair bit of capital flowing and it's working very well, but where we just need more of it and we can play a role to help scale, scale, scale. On the other hand, let's also challenge ourselves in the places where there's a dearth of capital, to ask why. Is it because it's fundamentally an uninvestible SDG (recognizing the SDGs were never designed to be an investment framework)? Or is it just because no one has rolled up their sleeves and tried to figure it out?

That work led us to oceans. Knowing how critical this resource is to planetary health and being personally passionate about the oceans, we commissioned an institutional poll. We went to the largest asset managers in the world and asked them a series of questions about whether they were interested in investing in the oceans. If not, why not? Most of the responses came back saying that the desire was there but the investment opportunities were not.

So, we said let's get to work to change the equation. The investors were asking for a direct link between their capital and ocean-friendly outcomes. They wanted to be sure that the capital was going to make a tangible impact. That ultimately led us to create a fund focused on using the power of shareholder engagement to drive corporate change, so that we can really deliver that conservation impact while generating attractive returns. We did it in partnership with another asset manager [in the spirit of SDG 17, "Partnerships"] because of their focus and track record on shareholder engagement, plus their affiliation with an ocean NGO, a charitable foundation that had been working in the oceans for decades.

We felt that was a powerful combination to bring together. We launched last October, and we're well north of $600 million of capital invested in that fund less than a year later. That's a pretty seminal thing because five years ago, if you had asked anybody "Could you mobilize $600 million of private investors' capital for ocean conservation?" they would have thought you were crazy.

Is that all in public equities?

Correct. So, it's liquid. That was key. The investors in this instance wanted a fund they could trade in and out of—the liquidity was important to them, and they were keen to be in the public equity risk asset class. Beyond this, they wanted that direct link to the ocean outcomes which we were able to deliver for them. When you have the right theme, the right structure and mission-alignment, the capital really can scale. This fund is just one example of many we are creating and very excited to be a part of.

Introduce Credit Suisse's dedicated sustainable and impact offerings and activities.

I genuinely believe that we've shown real leadership in the impact space in particular, and that's the tougher end of the spectrum because it's very deliberate with investor additionality, outcomes achievement, and measurement. We approach impact in an extremely serious and dedicated way. Impact investments are just one sleeve of our overall sustainability offering, however and our ambition over time will be to have a full suite of SDG thematic opportunities across our product shelf as well as across the risk spectrum and across asset classes. What we would hope at some point—and that's the Holy Grail—is that if a client says, I really care about any SDG, whether it be oceans or healthcare or education, but I really want it to be in an equity or a PE strategy, we can deliver it.

With another lens, we look at what we call the Supertrend themes which are developed by our CIO's research team. The Supertrends are the big, big themes of the future, that will drive markets and economies over the next decade or so. And we have now wrapped a sustainability view around Supertrends within my team to identify the sustainable solutions and companies that are poised to capitalize on these trends.

As a specific example, one of our Supertrends is "Millennial Values." This trend speaks to the changing nature of the millennial demographic and how powerful that force is, as the millennials are entering their peak earnings years—we know the millennials think differently as consumers and investors than prior generations and they are advocates and activists when it comes to social and environmental topics. We explore how that's going to drive societal change, how they behave differently, what products and services they want to buy, and how they are going to use financial services. When you wrap a sustainability lens around millennial values, it leads you to interesting thematics, and we've created a millennial values fund that invests in those themes and companies that resonate with and serve this population.

The last published report of our sustainable AUM was when we issued our inaugural sustainability report in April 2021, which reported over CHF 100 billion of sustainable AUM.

Was this increased focus toward sustainable investing driven by the private wealth business?

When we began the journey, the early investors in many of those impact funds were progressive experimental private clients who were probably very active philanthropically but liked the idea of being able to allocate some pocket of investment money for return, to do positive things. We also had institutional investors, but they were smaller in nature. You weren't talking about the big mainstream Fidelity's or PIMCOs in the space at that time.

What you've had in the intervening period in the sustainable finance market is incredible enabling conditions. You've had this maturation of millennials who do think differently about investing. Then you marry that with the acute reality of climate change and this sense of urgency.

You have the government investment dollars behind mitigation. You have the corporates that are having to migrate their business models and the media attention to it, the everything attention to it—and when it becomes real for you, when it's your property underwater or burning from wildfires or whatever the issue is that's affecting you, it's a call to action.

While we are experiencing a wall of institutional money flowing into sustainable investing now, I think people as individuals are driving this at its heart, because now they feel the necessity to do everything they can to contribute to the change they want to see, both as private and professional investors. This whole wave of big walls of capital who want to follow ESG principles has become the baseline. The enabling conditions and drivers supporting the explosive interest in sustainability is really coming from everywhere.

What is Credit Suisse's Young Investors Organization?

The YIO (Young Investors Organization) is an organization supported by Credit Suisse that we helped found, but they're self-governed, so it's an independent group—their own organization. It is for the nextgen (under 35s) of our top wealth clients and, for lack of a better description, it's almost like a club. There are some 2,000-plus members and it is an incredibly phenomenal group. I have a lot of interaction with the group, and I am inspired by them.

They are entrepreneurs in their own right or, in many cases, they might be inheriting family businesses and they're grappling with the weight of that. They're grappling in the sustainability context often about very, very serious issues that speak to this millennial values question. Some of them don't like the businesses they're inheriting because they might be in high carbon emitting industries contributing to climate change, and that bothers them. In other cases, they're seizing that moment to say, "When I have the reins of my family company, I am going to transform it into a more environmentally friendly or socially friendly business model." What I see is an incredible passion and determination to try to create a better world for themselves than the one that they're inheriting. And they can do it as entrepreneurs, they can do it as corporate leaders, they can do it with their money.

We also see in them a big behavior change, and I think that is a little bit of what Viola Steinhoff Werner (Founder of the Young Investors Organization and a Managing Director at Credit Suisse) is alluding to as it relates to financial services and the [pending] great wealth transfer [to the millennial generation], because they do think differently. What they want from any bank is very different than what our generation wants, and what they ask of a bank is very different.

They ask questions like, "What is your green footprint as a bank?" or "How many IPOs have you done for sustainable companies?" So, to be able to serve them properly, we need to be part of that dialogue. We also have to help them on the journey because they are looking for advice, particularly in the sustainability arena, about how to translate that passion or emotion into their business lives or investing habits.

What are some of the conversations your private bankers are having with younger millennials, and what types of products are they demanding?

The conversations are very much around the notion of how they incorporate sustainability into their lives, broadly defined. It could be as a business owner or a soon-to-be business owner if you're in that family corporation. It could be as an entrepreneur. How do I tell my sustainability story with my start-up because I believe that I should lead with that?

Many of the businesses that the YIO cohorts are starting as entrepreneurs lead with the mission. Their ethos is, "I want to solve an environmental problem. I'm creating a business around it." That's very different than entrepreneurs of the prior generation, which were, "I've got a great idea and I hope to go raise money for it." The conversation with them is how to do it in an authentic and robust way. Also how do they express their sustainability narrative and present their investment thesis in a way that will resonate with the investment community? Or it's, "I am now in a position where I can start investing, so how can I make sure that my money is having impact?"

I also sometimes have a conversation, which again, I don't think we would've ever had 10 or 20 years ago, which is, "My parents don't understand how serious I am about this. Can Credit Suisse tell them that impact investing is a serious thing, and that you can generate serious financial returns? Because they're not listening to me. If you, Credit Suisse, say it's real, then my parents might listen to you."

Being in the middle of these conversations, helping to bridge these generational gaps and ideologies about what financial investing should or should not be or can or cannot achieve was a surprising place to find myself. I have in some cases become a kind of guidance counselor or family broker between the older and younger generation.

You can't over-generalize because, as always, this is an individual discussion with an individual person, and everybody has a different view and approach. But I find the receptivity of the younger generation to the concept of impact investing, the concept of sustainable finance, as being just natural to them. Not all of them care about that, but the vast majority do.

You believe in the power of a partnership approach, rather than trying to do it all in-house, don't you?

You are absolutely 100 percent right about that. It's very much in the ethos ever since I began building IAF. I felt very strongly that when we're talking about some of the world's biggest challenges, there is no one person or organization that has a lock on good ideas. And I do believe—and I say this often—that the power of 1 + 1 in the sustainability arena is way more than 2. The reason is because different partners bring unique attributes to the table. They can provide a different type of expertise, or a different lens. There might be an approach that we hadn't thought of because this is a relatively new field. With our partnerships there's a lot of experimentation and innovation happening.

My view is, if we can collaborate with partners and break the silos of historical banking—which was in the past very provincial with the idea that 'if you're my competitor, I can't possibly do something together with you'—you come to better outcomes. For example, the Ocean Engagement Fund with Rockefeller Asset Management has been a beautiful marriage and they brought to the table a 30-year track record of engagement history with demonstrable results. They also brought this affiliation with the Ocean Foundation. At Credit Suisse we are not climate scientists, nor are we an NGO. But their foundation was very deeply engaged with what can actually matter to the oceans.

If you think about these two aspects of what Rockefeller brought, plus Credit Suisse's structuring and distribution power, it's just a complete win-win. We felt similarly when collaborating with BlackRock, one of the largest asset managers in the world to create a new sustainable fund partnership. We are the combination of two mission-driven, very aligned organizations motivated to use our platforms trying to drive change from an ethos point of view. They, as a large asset manager, and us as a huge private bank—a powerful combination. Our recently announced fund partnership with JP Morgan is the same thing.

In virtually every one of our impact investments or sustainable investments that we're creating in-house, we're doing it with a collaboration partner. Sometimes it can be a financial services organization. But oftentimes it's an NGO, because they're experts on the ground, working day to day, in the weeds. And their knowledge, expertise and insight can help ensure that the dollars end up doing the good that we aspire to.

What does a credible path to Net Zero look like for a bulge bracket investment bank?

The biggest challenge in getting to true Net Zero for a bank ahead are the decisions we will make on who we bank (and not bank), what businesses that we take on and who we lend to. All these decisions need to be aligned with our emissions reduction commitment. That piece is definitely a work in process. The way we're approaching it is by comprehensively mapping the universe of our clients and activities. The 'biggest bang for the buck' will be identifying and ensuring that the highest carbon emitting industries that we bank are on a Paris-aligned transition pathway alongside us. If they are committed to Net Zero, then it becomes easy for us to support them in that transition.

The way we approach this challenge is that we're systematically going through each of the highest carbon emitting industries that we have exposure to as a bank. We're placing them on a spectrum of grid ranging from the most progressive to transition down to those who are not indicating that they intend to address their emissions. If they don't want to transition, there must come a time when we'll have to part ways, because it won't be in alignment with our sustainability commitment. But the word 'transition' is very operative. We can't do this overnight, and our clients can't change their entire business models overnight, but we need to be actively using all our available resources to accelerate the drive toward those outcomes.

In terms of modelling emissions trajectories, it is complicated, and we are looking at questions such as, "What's the right measurement? Is it carbon intensity? Is it aggregate carbon emissions, different things for different industries?" We're getting input from third-party sources to help inform us because, in some cases, there isn't a truly green pathway yet for certain industries or we do not have the data to accurately measure carbon footprints.

Aviation is a good example because there is no green aviation fuel today. If a zero carbon option does not exist today, we want to help our clients adopt the most impactful ways to reduce their footprint in the interim. And at some point, I am hopeful that there will be an answer for all industries to be truly Paris-aligned in their operations.

Finally, we have to consider how we treat the stub, if you will, which is today the part of any business which you can't abate. There we have to purchase carbon offsets or work toward offsetting in some way, by accessing nature-based solutions like planting trees or using mechanisms for carbon capture and storage. Our belief is that offsetting should only be for the tail that you can't abate. You don't want to use offsets as an excuse to keep doing business the same old way. You have to do the hard work operationally to be part of the overall transition to true Net Zero.

Do you face internal struggles with the profitability of traditional non-sustainable products and getting open discussions about this, about hydrocarbons, for example?

So, without question, anytime you're in transition there are tension points. But, at the same time, I think the broad understanding, the mandate that we've committed to—which is to achieve Net Zero across our Scope 1, [Scope] 2, [and Scope] 3, emissions including our business activities that we do with clients—we've made that decision. We've crossed that threshold.

Therefore, the organization now has to figure out the most sensible way to do that. We're a profit-making organization. It does not involve firing all our clients in any high carbon emitting industry and jettisoning them. That's not logical, and frankly, if we did that, we wouldn't have an ability to engage with them anyway. There's power in our ability to provide capital to them, both to help the transition, and to use that as leverage, to have them engage. And it represents a tremendous business opportunity for the bank if we get this right.

These are the tools that are at our disposal, and we think that we've got a big role to play in that participation. But there's no doubt that you need to work through these things because those bankers who cover traditional industries, they also have to transition. So, as always, when you're asking anybody to change their behavior or what they've done for 20 or 30 years, it requires a re-education and a process.

But I have to say, the necessity of climate change is such a call to action that it's not, as maybe in years past, "Who are these ideological people in this fringe area of sustainability getting in the way of my business?" That was the perception, right, that people in sustainability weren't serious businesspeople or weren't guided by the need to make profits. Those debates are gone. People now know the world has got to change and I think that provides a groundswell to get the full organization behind what we're trying to accomplish.

How would you advise someone who wants to get into the sustainable investment space?

I would say for someone early in their career, don't necessarily sweat the sustainability bit. If you really want to be in the investment world, first get a good solid grounding in either investment structuring, product creation, capital markets or sales—or any other area that's broadly in and around that investment space—being a relationship manager, etc.

The sustainability piece, because this is such a high, high, organic growth area that now touches all aspects of finance and it will be so for decades to come, almost by definition, you'll get exposure to sustainability as an overlay because you can't be a good relationship manager if you can't talk to your clients about sustainability. You can't be a good product creator these days, creating investment products, if you don't understand the ESG overlay. That's almost a necessity that'll come as part of getting that good, grounded finance foundation. If you want to specialize later in sustainability there will be plenty of opportunities that will be available as sustainable finance truly does become the "new norm."

Chapter Three

Aligning Investment Portfolios with SRI Values

Every investment we make impacts the world.

We don't often think of it in that way. Even when managing our personal finances, the investment process can be detached and impersonal:

We log in; we transfer. We analyze and allocate. We sell. We buy. We log out.

Even in private equity, where the investing process is very hands-on with due diligence, it is easy to lose sight of the correlation between our choices and actions and the greater cause and effect. Nevertheless, every investment we make, no matter what asset class, has some kind of impact in our world and on our quality of life—either positive or negative. Every euro invested is another proverbial chaos theory butterfly wing fluttering with potential somewhere on the planet. Every investment makes some contribution to the multiplier effect and our shared collective outcome. That's as true for investments that expressly target the achievement of worthy environmental, social, or governance goals as it is for those that are completely indifferent to any implications or results beyond increased wealth.

The truth is, whenever we make an investment, we are allocating capital to make specific activities become a reality in our world. Like it or not, ours is a shared reality and planet, and after we invest, the world—in some way or another—becomes a different place than it was before we acted.

The genesis of this book was to stimulate conversations that would inspire more investors to weigh the broader impact that their portfolio returns have on others—including future generations. Portfolios yield financial returns that investors ponder and scrutinize with intentional deliberation. But restricting that consideration to issues that are solely financial grossly underestimates the power of our investments. After all, they also offer profound opportunities to generate environmental or social value, based on our particular interests and concerns. To leave those out of the equation is to leave sustainable, scalable, quantifiable value on the table.

Until now, when investors tried to incorporate impact criteria into their portfolios they often felt that they were limited to only one, or a handful, of investment strategies. Their only options seemed to be within a single or just a select few asset classes capable of achieving their SRI objectives. For instance, they may have implemented negative screening only within their public equity portfolio. Or maybe they included a number of cleantech investments in their venture capital allocation.

At the same time, they often still held traditional investments that either had negligible impact or, in some cases, were actually completely at odds with their personal or institutional values. Needless to say, from a total allocation perspective, this also meant that they were only applying SRI principles to a rather insignificant percentage of their entire investment portfolio. Likewise, at a macro-level, it meant that only a very small fraction of the world's capital was being channeled toward financing a better future for us all.

Over time, institutional investors became interested in applying a more holistic approach and began looking for opportunities to apply SRI principles across more asset classes. Most SRI attention recently has been focused on private equity, but in terms of scale and total impact, the largest opportunity has always been with public equities. They typically have a larger allocation within traditional investment portfolios, specifically institutional portfolios and also within personally managed retirement portfolios.

ALIGNING YOUR PORTFOLIO WITH YOUR MISSION

Most people working in the professional world are familiar with mission statements. If you're old enough to have lived through the 1990s, you may remember Dilbert's Mission Statement Generator created by Scott Adams, the author of the American comic strip, *Dilbert*, known for its satirical office humor about white-collar, micromanaged office life.[1] The Mission Statement Generator was an online webpage where you selected your nouns, verbs, adjectives, and adverbs, and then clicked a button. The website would generate a customized mission statement that would read something similar to this:

"Our challenge is to enthusiastically administrate world-class deliverables so that we may endeavor to assertively fashion mission-critical methods of empowerment."

The humor was derived from the all-too-painful truth that oftentimes corporate mission statements were either meaningless or obliviously disconnected from observable day-to-day corporate culture. Mission statements are often joked about because many times they are in conflict with the more nuanced and complex reality of daily life experiences. Or, worse still, they are frequently crafted (sometimes intentionally) as "word salad," a verbose jumble of business-speak that uses lots and lots of words and, in the end, basically says nothing at all—or at least nothing that can be measured.

A mission statement only means and stands for something if it changes how we act and, ultimately, the outcomes we achieve. Steven Covey famously explained in his book, *Seven Habits of Successful People*, that in order to get in touch with your meaningful mission, you should begin with the end in mind. You determine what the result is that you want to achieve and then work backward to identify what steps you must take to get there. In my introductory comments to this book, I described how I had wanted to get from Hong Kong to Geneva by a certain time, not to Mumbai. But to do that in the most expedient way, my assistant reverse-engineered my airline reservations, realizing that landing in India was the right next step to take.

Applying this in the investment world, there are opportunities to leverage all aspects of an investment portfolio. But we just might need to frame our approach differently in order to align our portfolio with our stated mission.

Accordingly, I've loosely structured the interviews in this book around the concept of "Total Portfolio Activation," which was first introduced as an investment framework in 2012 by the Tellus Institute.[2] While still not widely referenced by investors, the concepts are being more and more broadly implemented. The framework prescribes an approach that encompasses and considers the alignment of your entire portfolio—not just particular elements of it. The point is to maximize social and environmental impact, alongside your required financial returns. This concept proposes a ten-step process that any investor can deploy, to identify a portfolio's impact opportunity potential and then reallocate assets across the entire portfolio, as needed.

Today, the largest of asset owners—from Dutch pension funds to U.S. insurance companies—are considering how to best apply their SRI policies across every asset class. Those range from debt investment in green bonds to renewable energy infrastructure; from specific impact themes in public and private equity to microfinance; and from agroforestry to social housing.

The essential emphasis of this book's collection of interviews is that your entire investment portfolio, whatever your underlying asset class allocations may be, can be aligned to your SRI priorities—your personal or institutional "mission statement" (whether they be climate change or gender diversity or anything in between). We each have the power of personal agency that we can, and rightfully should, exercise when making investments. Once we frame things this way at an individual level, the financial markets will follow our lead.

ASSET CLASSES

"Asset classes" are different categories of investments, grouped according to similar characteristics. Instruments within the same asset class often behave similarly to each other but differently from others, exhibiting low correlations and, in some instances, negative correlations in terms of performance. Multiple asset classes are therefore often used by investors to diversify away risk and will frequently appear together in a balanced portfolio.

Investors who learn the social and environmental functions across different asset classes (and the potential strategies that can generate impact results within each one) can actively and strategically construct an entire investment portfolio to influence outcomes consistent with their objectives. Obviously, certain asset classes by their nature lend themselves to generating certain types of impact. That's why investors with specific areas of concern will need to increase allocations to the activities and investments that target them.

For the purposes of this book, I have concentrated on six asset classes that are most commonly found in a diversified professional investor's portfolio:

1. Public Equities
2. Fixed Income
3. Private Equity
4. Private Debt
5. Venture Capital
6. Real Assets

I've also chosen to organize the interviews in this book by these same asset classes, rather than alphabetically or by underlying impact theme. I did that for three key reasons, with the concept of a "values aligned portfolio" in mind:

First, I want to help investors (whether individual or institutional) understand the opportunities for SRI across all asset classes, and to specifically highlight examples in asset classes that they may not have previously considered. For example, some investors who are highly skilled in certain asset classes may be unaware of the opportunities available in others. By organizing them this way, these interviews may motivate readers to expand their thinking into other asset classes, with a view toward a more holistic portfolio approach.

Secondly, I hope to emphasize the variety of investment strategies and themes that coexist *within* each asset class. The industry has evolved far beyond the point where it was a stark and binary choice between either ESG screening your public equity portfolio or not. We are all unique, and today portfolios can reflect our individual values, personal priorities, and primary concerns.

Within your public equity portfolio alone, for instance, you might choose to champion female representation within corporate leadership teams. Or you may want to invest in only those companies aligned with a circular bioeconomy (e.g., by investing in Lombard Odier's LO Funds-Natural Capital, who we speak with in the next chapter). Maybe you'd prefer to finance impact outcomes (e.g., by buying shares in BlackRock's Global Impact fund also in the following chapter). There is no one size that is presumed to fit all values. SRI investors must seek out and invest in those strategies which resonate the most with their own values and financial objectives.

Last but not least, my goal was to make this book as useful as possible for each reader, according to their interests. If you know you're mainly open to venture capital opportunities, skip straight to that chapter. Perhaps you later become curious to learn what fixed income funds you could own in your pension pot. Dip back into chapter 5 to learn more about potential options and the differences between green bonds, transition bonds, and social bond strategies.

For those of you who already know what impact theme you're most passionate about, just look it up in the Index. There I'll show you exactly which interviews discuss your topic of interest. Although I've only been able to include a select number of practitioner interviews in this book, I've attempted to curate something for everyone.

Chapter Four

Public Equities

The primary core asset class in most investment portfolios is likely a selection of shares of stock which are freely traded on a publicly regulated platform such as the New York or London stock exchanges. This chapter focuses on SRI strategies and insights for buying and selling of those shares of publicly owned companies.

A share of stock represents fractional ownership in a company and entitles the holder of the share to participate in the company's potential financial success. Shares are collectively known as "stock," or "capital stock." The shares of public companies are available to purchase by the general public, in contrast to shares of private companies that can only be purchased by a closed group of investors.

Compared with many other asset classes, public equities are a relatively liquid asset, and those traded in large volume on the main stock exchanges can usually be bought and sold within seconds.

With public equities, there is no predictable investment return, because there is no obligation to pay any type of income to shareholders. The value of such investments rises, falls, or remains flat based on many factors, not the least of which is the company's financial performance. Some stocks also provide income in the form of a dividend, which is an additional payment made by the company to its shareholders, regardless of whether the stock has gained or lost value on the market.

While investing in public equities through the stock market is probably the most accessible way for even the most passive investor to invest, there is potential volatility. For example, the investor is exposed to the risk of financial loss due to factors that affect entire markets or asset classes, such as stock market crashes or economic recessions. Volatility may be triggered by unexpected events that rattle the markets—such as war, natural disaster, or pandemic.

DISCLOSURES AND TRANSPARENCY

One aspect of investing in public companies that can be particularly attractive and reassuring, compared to investing in private companies (see chapter 6) relates to disclosure requirements. Depending on the jurisdiction, public companies are usually legally bound and naturally motivated (to ensure their continued access to the capital markets), to publicly release all financially relevant information. This includes their current financial status, analysis of their strengths and weaknesses, and an assessment of the future of the company. Typically, such data must be released to both government regulators and shareholders, in a timely fashion.

Historically, these public disclosures were purely financial. But over the past few decades, and driven by early actors in the SRI field, it has become more commonplace for companies to voluntarily report on certain social and environmental metrics, as well.

Therefore, these disclosures are no longer just evaluated by investment analysts and prospective investors. They are also scrutinized by the media and by nonprofit groups such as Greenpeace that are positioned to hold companies accountable for their activities.

SRI MOVES FROM A NEGATIVE TO A POSITIVE APPROACH

SRI started largely in the public equity markets through SRI mutual funds commonly using "screening and exclusion" to avoid investments in companies that were determined to have negative social or environmental exposures. As negative screening gave way to investors searching for a framework to consider risks to sustainability, investors developed criteria to evaluate a company's environmental, social, and governance risks and practices in order to determine the worth of a company.

Over the last decade, investors began to recognize the materiality of risks that lie beyond what a purely financial statement analysis might reveal. The use of ESG metrics within investment strategies gained more momentum and attention, eventually becoming a mainstream investment approach.

Originally, there was a strong suspicion that these strategies would come at the expense of financial performance, because they were necessarily limiting exposure to the broad investment universe. But today there is a growing body of compelling evidence that they can help investors select better companies, provide a competitive advantage, and, ultimately, generate superior market returns. Subsequently, the negative consequences are growing and accruing for companies that fail to adapt to this new investment paradigm.

DISCLOSURE 2.0: MAN BITES DOG

Social and environmental disclosures evolved from early CSR (corporate social responsibility) reports where there was no uniformity of metrics, disclosures were qualitative rather than quantitative, and there was no third-party verification. These days, however, they are ever more fully integrated into annual reports and aligned with recognized industry standards (e.g., the GHG Protocol for carbon emission accounting), so investors can now compare company impact on a like-for-like, apples-to-apples basis.

This shift has, to a large extent, been driven by large asset owners putting pressure on companies to report on negative externalities and invisible natural resource dependencies. But governments are also increasingly recognizing the urgency of any number of social and environmental challenges, and their critical obligations to address and solve them. They are also increasingly bound by legal obligations to global treaties.

One example of this disclosure momentum in action is the Taskforce for Climate-related Financial Disclosure (TCFD). It was established in December 2015 with the goal of developing a set of voluntary climate-related disclosures to help inform public equity investors of the financial risks posed by climate change. The TCFD released its first recommendations in June 2017 and originally compliance was intended to be voluntary. However, in September 2020, New Zealand became the first country to make them mandatory. Three months later, the UK became the first G-20 country to follow suit.

A Taskforce for Nature-related Financial Disclosure (TNFD),—covering the global risk of biodiversity collapse, was established in June 2021. Within its first two or three years, it is no doubt expected to achieve the same level of impact and influence that the TCFD has demonstrated.

THE CARROT AND THE STICK

These disclosures allow sustainable investors to closely monitor the social and environmental risks, policies, and progress of each public company. They can then proactively advocate that company management improve policies (and capital expenditures) where necessary (e.g., gender diversity, worker pay, energy efficiency). Sustainable and responsible investors, as we will see in the following interviews, can wield significant power around these issues, through their right to vote proportionately to the number of shares they own.

The power of this kind of voting is most influential when used by major investment management institutions on behalf of their own underlying investors. Often, in coalition with other sustainable investors who care about driving the same positive policy change, they are able to submit shareholder resolutions themselves and force significant corporate behavior change.

When public equity investors leverage their power as active owners, that can translate into very significant influence and impact. After all, the total market capitalization of all stocks worldwide is approximately $70 trillion.

SECOND-WAVE SRI IS ON THE HORIZON

The next decade will likely bring a new wave of shareholder-driven accountability. Europe, for example, has traditionally been a leader when it comes to SRI, and a new wave of European regulations will accelerate how investment managers account for SRI factors. Meanwhile, things are also rapidly changing in this regard in the United States.

Of course, SRI investing comes down to the incorporation of nonfinancial criteria into the investment decision-making process. But when it is time to execute, SRI terms and definitions are wide-ranging and their inherently subjective nature can make these factors hard to quantify.

But not to worry. The professional investors profiled in this chapter have developed their own insightful philosophies and keen approaches to affect positive change through their commercial investment activities in the public equity markets.

"ESG is about how companies operate—treating society, the environment, and thinking about their governance in constructive ways. It's about the *how*. We care about ESG. But the critical difference is that impact investing is about *what* the company is making. These are companies solving the world's great social and environmental problems."

FUNDAMENTAL EQUITY IMPACT INVESTING
ERIC RICE
BLACKROCK
BLACKROCK.COM
LI: https://www.linkedin.com/in/eric-m-rice-9472b3/

Eric Rice is Head of Impact Investing at BlackRock and the portfolio manager and the architect of the world's first diversified public markets impact investing strategy, Global Impact. Global Impact is an alpha-oriented strategy that invests in companies whose goods and services help address the world's great problems, as defined by the UN Sustainable Development Goals. He also collaborates with other investors at BlackRock to help germinate additional impact and sustainable investing strategies.

Rice, who lives in San Francisco, joined BlackRock from Wellington Management in 2019, where he had been for more than 20 years. Previously, he worked as a World Bank country economist and a diplomat in Rwanda with the U.S. Department of State. He earned a PhD in economics from Harvard University and an AB degree in economics from the University of California at Berkeley.

How did you come to impact investing from traditional investing?

For more than a decade I was a conventional investor at Wellington. All was going well, but I always kept a file of clippings of interesting job openings in economic development. The file helped me to think about what I might do next someday. In those days there wasn't anything like impact investing. So that was the file I kept.

Then, with the advent of impact investing and social entrepreneurship that friends of mine were doing in the private markets—the Bay Area started to become a hotbed of such activity 12 or 13 years ago—that became interesting to me. So that was the end of my clipping file because I thought this is the thing that really brings together the two halves of my career: finance and economic development.

How did you come to join BlackRock?

At Wellington, I was the portfolio manager of the impact strategy that I created. At the time, when I proposed to do an impact investing strategy, Wellington had no strategies in sustainability or impact. There was no head of sustainable investing, there was no sense of sustainable investing at that time, or almost any place. So, I had to explain to my managers and colleagues what sustainable investing was, and that's completely understandable because those were early days—eight, nine years ago.

I had to sell the idea and when I got approval to start working on it, the message was, "remember, this is not your day job; this is a nights and weekends project for you." So, I assembled some friends who wanted to work on something like that. We were a shoestring band of investors inventing this thing as we went along, and no one ever imagined it was going to accumulate a billion dollars of assets. But it did, quite quickly, even though at Wellington we'd never really been well resourced. We were just this little band of people doing our thing.

After a few years, BlackRock recruited my team and, when they came to us, their message was, "We're all-in on sustainability. Everything that you've read and what Larry Fink has said and written is true, and here you'll meet all our people who are also believers." I wasn't interested to go to a place where one person, even if it's the head person, had this vision but that vision wasn't integrated throughout. We got clear messages that this was everything that BlackRock was going to move toward.

BlackRock's message to us was, if we're moving toward sustainability, then impact investing has to be the flagship of that effort. How can we be a sustainable investment firm if we don't have an impact strategy, or if we don't have a proliferation of impact strategies? And it was very encouraging that across the whole firm, people were saying, "We have a few things to get right and integrate into our firm, and one of those is sustainability."

Describe the BlackRock Global Impact fund.

It sits on the fundamental equities platform and is informed by the early strategies of people I knew who were doing impact investing in private markets—which is the only impact investing that existed at that point. I worked with some of them to think through how we could do an authentic public-equities impact strategy. What would it take to bring the best characteristics of impact investing in the private markets, adapt them to public markets, and then enjoy the scale and diversification that you have in public markets?

Most of it's pretty straightforward, but it takes some work. I mean, we set a high bar for companies to be included in our investible universe, which then makes them eligible to be in our portfolio. We have deep due diligence, the kind you would expect with venture and PE funds. We also have a long holding period of five years minimum when we go into a new position. Again, that's comparable to what's done in VC and PE, and it enables us to have quite an engaged relationship with our managements. We use that long, engaged relationship to become a trusted partner with C-suite management of our portfolio companies. We understand what they're trying to accomplish, and they understand that we want them to make good long-term decisions. We also engage with them on how they can be more impactful, on introductions we might make for them, on projects we can help them to undertake that they might not have quite the bandwidth to take on. We've had some great success with that.

I guess the last thing I'd say is there's a funny misconception about public markets. We often hear, "Well, private markets—that's where companies need funding. Once they go public, they're done." But it's not one and done. We have companies that have run into trouble because they're negative free cash flow, need to raise money, and sometimes the market's not open to that. But if they have long-term investors who know what they're doing, we can fund their sometimes-unloved secondary issuance, which we've done.

The moment of leaving the private markets to go into the public markets is, from an impact point of view, a perilous moment. The CEOs and CFOs we talk with want to be sure the new roster of investors when they go public isn't just hedge funds or other short-term investors who will flip their holdings. They want investors who will hold their shares for years, and so that's an important role for us, too. And then when they need to raise money again in secondaries for projects or whatever, they want to know that they have partners who are there and who will be likely to participate.

There are various ways in which we can engage. The engagement may not be, say, to find a new CEO for a tiny company—as you might see in venture investing—but there are analogous forms of engagement that are also quite powerful.

What is your role as Head of Impact Investing at BlackRock?

My day job is to run the Global Impact fund, which we have a couple different versions. But my remit more broadly is to look for other investors and other potential strategies that could work. It's to find other investors who always wanted to find more meaning in their jobs and are looking for how to do an impact investing strategy. They will typically know how to invest, but they might not know what's involved in managing and reporting impact. Then sometimes the role is to think about new strategies that "BlackRock should certainly be creating," and to find the interested and willing team that might launch it.

So, it's intended that I will be the person running some fundamental strategies, but also the person helping foster others, and in fact not just in public equities. We have people in credit and in private markets who are working on developing strategies. We have an amazing strategy that's focused on opportunities for minorities in the United States, a very new thing—investing in minority entrepreneurs and in projects that are oriented to minority populations. These days, there is a whole set of interesting impactful areas where we are launching.

Are there themes that you're focused on or limited from investing in?

Our themes are based on initial research we did years ago, around what companies can do to solve the great problems in the world. One thing to recognize is that we launched Global Impact before there were UN SDGs. So, when the UN SDGs came along we could see that they're a useful organizing principle, but they don't correspond neatly to what companies do. Companies don't end inequality or world hunger.

Companies have a lot of areas they do work on. A particular example that's interesting is gender equality. There is no company whose key function is to solve gender inequality, but there are companies that educate girls, there are companies that solve women's health problems, and there are companies that do microlending only to women.

There are a lot of levers that we have, but an SDG is not really the right way to structure that. We structure around "people" and "planet" themes. People themes are the kind of things that you would expect: affordable housing, public health, access to education, digital inclusion, financial inclusion. Then on the environmental side, which we also do, it's about renewables, about electrification and efficiency, about remediating and reducing pollution.

So, it's fairly broad based across themes. We wanted a mainstream global fund that could better meet the needs of someone who currently has their money invested in an unsustainable non-impact global fund.

What do you benchmark against?

MSCI All Country World. We wanted a very standard benchmark, because that's the opportunity cost of our clients moving money into BlackRock Global Impact.

How does impact investing in public equities at BlackRock differ from your ESG investing in public equities?

It's a very straightforward distinction. ESG is about how companies operate. ESG can be about a company making furniture or steel or whatever, and it looks for those companies that are doing it in a good way. Those that are treating society, treating the environment, and thinking about their governance in constructive ways. So, it's about the *how*. In contrast, impact investing is about *what* the company is making, and the critical difference is that these are companies working to solve the world's great social and environmental problems with their goods and services.

Yes, we care about ESG for those companies too; we don't want badly behaved renewables companies. But even if you have famous companies making ice cream—and I do love ice cream—and they are great to their employees and about the environment—they're not solving great world problems.

Why are materiality, additionality, and measurability the important qualifiers and differentiators for your fund versus an ESG fund?

Of course, I wouldn't take credit for those criteria because they come directly from impact investing in the private markets. But I call them out as what makes Global Impact an impact strategy rather than a thematic strategy.

Materiality is simply the idea that the majority of what each company does must be impact. I mean, you could have a strategy that doesn't require materiality, that looks at a company that has one line of business that is highly impactful. There are conglomerates that have divisions that are highly impactful. But what our clients want, I think, is more pure expressions of impact. They want access to companies that they don't find in any of their other portfolios.

And it turns out that our strict 50 percent materiality hurdle is enough to ensure that the portfolio ends up being close to 100 percent impact.

The second qualifier, additionality, is even more critical. For instance, we have a theme around sustainable food, agriculture, and water, right? There are thematic funds that would invest in those companies that bring water to European cities and U.S. cities just as they have for decades and that represent no theory of change, they're just doing what they do. But additionality means that we invest only in those water companies that are bringing new technologies, new business models, or that are serving a clientele that hadn't been served before. If these companies didn't exist, then big problems wouldn't be getting solved. That's a critical difference between an impact strategy and a thematic strategy.

Ultimately, we subject each of our 1,000 eligible universe companies to a basic plausibility thesis: if you ask me about any company in that universe, it should be straightforward to explain why it is an impact company at its core.

And finally, measurability is the basic idea that one can't know if one's investments are achieving impact unless that impact can be measured and reported. Throughout the year, we track and quantify the social and environmental impact of each company we invest in, using the best industry standards of measurement, and then report them annually to our clients.

Explain how buying and selling public equities on the secondary market drives impact.

We buy, but we don't do a lot of selling, and no more than a VC firm that buys and then sells shares onto PE, or PE fund that takes something public. I would say that our long-term holding period is something that's critically important in understanding what we do. And half of the portfolio consists of the same holdings as we had eight years ago when we launched. So, it's not like we're buying and selling the way one would normally expect in public markets.

A lot of what's in the portfolio now is shares of companies where we were early investors in their IPO, and where it was very important that we be part of what the literature calls a "responsible exit." The responsible exit from being private enables a company to have new shareholders that understand that the company is investing for a long-term future that's impactful. We have that high bar for what constitutes an impact company, but it's also important for us to be there to support them financially as needed and to try to bolster their impact.

One thing we do that I think no one else does in public markets is impact engagement. What I mean by that is we work closely with our companies—and this will remind you more of VC than PE. For instance, we have a company that we're invested in that is a job board for Asia, for the Australasia region. They don't offer a lot of training of job seekers, so there's no mechanism to prepare jobseekers to get better jobs than they might otherwise get. We also invest in online training and education companies that happen to be in the United States, and what they don't have is an Asian or international presence. So, we've introduced them and encouraged them to move in the direction of sharing their complementary services.

We've also done that with financial literacy. We've started a program to take some existing online financial literacy programs in companies, whether we invest in them or not, and bring those programs into financial institutions that are doing microlending or virtual wallets, or whatever it may be. And we're finding ways for them to upgrade the financial literacy of those clients and prospective clients.

So, there are a lot of things that one can do. We can help match-make our companies with developing country markets where they're not operating, to make inroads there. There may be reasons why they don't have the bandwidth or don't have the infrastructure to do it, but we can help them to find that.

This is a core part of your impact engagement and not a one-off?

It's not one-off, but rather one-by-one in the way that venture capital has its impact one-by-one. We have someone who spends much of her time identifying these opportunities, working with the companies, and then bringing our analysts into the process. We call this impact engagement 2.0. It's something that, now that we're at BlackRock, we have the capacity to do, and it is what transforms what we're doing to be more like VC and PE impact investment than anything before.

We found that there are lots of avenues for our impact engagement 2.0. You know, a company is focused on its survival, is focused on growing, is focused on doing what its core competency is. And there may be other things that they just haven't gotten to. If we can help that along, it's great.

Explain your screening process.

Whatever you may think of ESG screens, and they're certainly a mixed bag, there's nothing that exists like screens for impact. Identification of impact companies happens company by company through fundamental research. And we have a whole process for assuring that any company that is proposed for the universe goes through this process.

Consider, for example an education company in a developing country. It's educating people—what could be bad about that? But in some developing countries, private education serves only elites and therefore is a vehicle of inequality. The UN SDG on education doesn't just target education, but it also calls for greater equality and access. So, we would reject those companies that are for elite education because we're looking for companies that are providing more mass education. Our themes are about access. And you vet that by looking through everything that's written by and on the company, about whom they're educating, how they do it, and what the innovations are. There's no shortcut.

Do you have a checklist that demonstrates what you are looking for in your screening process?

Happily, it's publicly available and it's not ours. What we rely on is industry standards, industry best practices. So, we subscribe to the IFC operating principles as a high-level approach. But then we use the Impact Management Project (IMP) "dimensions of impact" as our standard, and there's a clear set of criteria around what the impact is, who's impacted, what the risks are, and so on.

How credible is the investment industry's pathway to net zero and is it realistic for an asset manager to map its entire portfolio footprint?

I think that Scope 3[1] is critical for understanding investment management, because it's one thing for BlackRock to run its operations in a clean way. But that's not really what Net Zero is about. Net Zero involves assessing every holding in our trillions of dollars of AUM. BlackRock and the industry are building capacity to track that carefully, to set out a path for a more sustainable redeployment of assets and to know where the pain points are. Naturally, fossil fuels are among the most important industries where our investors have begun tilting away from such holdings. BlackRock already has fossil-fuel free strategies. We also have engagements, as we did very publicly with ExxonMobil, saying, we can't accept your demonstrated failure to engage or show leadership toward Net Zero.

When we think of the world economy moving to a 1.5- or 2-degree world, it's like the way an enormous ship changes direction. Importantly, the world is moving now—but still it's gradual. Well, BlackRock represents a significant percentage of that world economy and, thanks to the leadership of our CEO and others, we are now pushing for and sometimes even leading that redirection. But the economy is not going to stop using oil tomorrow. So, while BlackRock will still be invested in every sector, we offer a range of opportunities for clients to purge their portfolios of the activities they find objectionable or destructive, for example through our many sustainable and impact funds. And we need to keep pushing increasingly on every lever that we have. On the companies. On governments. On our joint trade associations. To find ways collectively. And what I see in 2021 is that our path toward 2030 is encouraging.

What is the single most important challenge in the public equity impact investing space at this time?

It's clear: impact washing. Why? Because fund managers see a big fat opportunity to relabel their strategies as impact or to tilt their strategies toward something that resembles impact. But you have to do impact investing right, and there's a lot of bad product out there. A lack of authenticity in impact investing could easily undermine this nascent industry.

"If you aren't including ESG factors in your investment process and are just simply buying broad benchmark products, you're losing value and you're also firmly separating any concept of having responsibility for the impact of money."

GLOBAL PUBLIC EQUITIES
MATT PATSKY
TRILLIUM ASSET MANAGEMENT
TRILLIUMINVEST.COM
LI: https://www.linkedin.com/in/mattpatsky/
TW: @MattPatsky

Matt Patsky is CEO and Lead Portfolio Manager of the Trillium ESG Global Equity strategy and Portfolio Manager of the Trillium Sustainable Opportunities strategy. Matt has over three decades of experience in investment research and socially and environmentally responsible investment management. He began his career at Lehman Brothers in 1984 and in 1994 became the first sell-side analyst in the United States to publish on the topic of socially responsible investing.

Patsky currently serves on the board of TONIIC and has previously served on the boards of Environmental League of Massachusetts, Shared Interest, Pro Mujer, US SIF, and Root Capital. He is also a member of the Social Venture Circle (SVC) and the CFA Society Boston and is a CFA® charterholder.

How does Trillium Asset Management incorporate ESG factors in the investment process?

I start from a fundamental belief that these factors are material. And if you start with a fundamental belief that they're material, you start at the absolute opposite 180-degree end of the way in which most professional institutional investors historically have interpreted this entire field. I have a fiduciary obligation to include environmental, social, and governance in the investment process and not to do so is a violation of my fiduciary responsibilities. So, when you start there, then you're just realizing that most of the world doesn't think that way. How do we change the way the world thinks? How do we convince the world that these factors really do matter? And that a simple factor of how you treat your employees—just to pick one out—how does that matter in the building of a sustainable business and value creation?

And you can go through and do this with almost all these issues. No, it's not necessarily easily boiled down to a financial metric, but it matters. And we can demonstrate why and how it ends up playing into the building of a sustainable business model and creation of shareholder value.

So, that's pulling it back and saying let's do it from not necessarily a values perspective, even though it's perfectly fine to include your values in the investment process, and we certainly do that. But rather, this is just simply saying, I don't care what firm you work for. I don't care what your style is. If you aren't including environmental, social, and governance factors in your investment process, I am firmly of the belief that you are in violation of your fiduciary duty. And I am also firmly of the belief that if you are just simply buying broad benchmark products you're losing value and you're also firmly separating any concept of having responsibility for the impact of money. You've thrown that out the window.

What's most disturbing to me was the evolution of what we were seeing and why we did the Total Portfolio Activation framework. We were seeing people say, "no, impact investing is about investing in some direct deals, and some direct loan funds, and then you buy broad market index ETFs or index products, and this is your impact portfolio."

And that's BS. You can't ignore the impact of the largest portion of your investments, because there is the ability to have meaningful impact on companies and to change behavior of companies.

But there's this belief system that all I'm really doing in the secondary market is trading shares, right? And it's true, I'm not having a great deal of influence on the capital flows into a business when I'm trading shares in the secondary markets.

But there are influences and we can talk about what happened in tobacco, what's happening in fossil fuels, or what's happened in industries where there's been a recognition of underlying liabilities that need to be recognized and addressed, or negative societal or environmental impacts that need to be addressed. How that plays out in terms of the cost to these companies' capital is the bigger picture macro.

If I can drive enough people to recognize that just going back 30 years there was liability sitting on the books of the tobacco companies that was unrecognized, you start to influence a company's cost of capital. And we did. And the divestment campaign actually led to having some impact on the cost of capital for the tobacco companies.

Provide an overview of Trillium Asset Management.

Trillium Asset Management was founded by Joan Bavaria in 1982 with the mission to "Provide for the financial needs of our clients, while leveraging their capital for positive social and environmental impact in alignment with their values." Trillium right now has about $4.6 billion in assets under management with another $800 million in assets under advisement. So total assets under advisement are about $5.4 billion. When I came into the firm eleven years ago, we were around $700 million, so we've participated in the growth of Impact Investing.

What we now have are eight equity strategies, some of which are available in mutual fund form. That started because we had a meeting back in 2010 about how the minimums we were taking for separately managed accounts had grown from $250,000 to $2 million. And that we were excluding most people from being able to invest in alignment with their values with us. If we wanted to democratize impact investing, we needed to provide a vehicle that allowed more people to invest in our strategies. That led us to two major pushes. One, we went to the broker dealer channel and said, "we can be your partner with a true impact product offering." And we got on the platforms of Merrill, Morgan [Stanley], UBS, Raymond James, basically we got on the platforms of two dozen firms where we're approved and on the buy list for people looking for ESG or impact investing.

In addition, we decided we were going to launch mutual funds. As you look at us now, we have a global equity mutual fund that actually was merged-in because we acquired it. We have a SMID (small to mid-sized market capitalization) mutual fund and we were going to launch a domestic equity strategy, but when we filed with the SEC to launch our own large cap core mutual fund, John Hancock came knocking and said, "We want that strategy. We want to launch it, we want to market that." Recognizing that we had minimal marketing/sales capability, we partnered with John Hancock. It's certainly been a slower build than we would have expected, but it's now just hit over $200 million so it is doing well for us.

Our global equity is now almost $900 million and SMID has been a struggle, it's about $30 million. So, the majority of the asset pools are still in separately managed accounts for us in those eight strategies.

When you hear us talk about sustainable opportunities, we are speaking about a strategy—not a fund. We haven't put it in fund form yet, but we are in negotiations with a partner to launch it in fund form.

Describe how you invest in your global equity strategy and obtain impact by investing in equities on the secondary market.

The structure of it is we're looking for high quality companies that are leaders in environmental, social, and governance that also have strong potential for financial return. It's actually our most highly diversified strategy and it's right now over 127 names across the globe.

The way in which we have impact is mostly through coalition. And remember, we started in 1982, really taking from the playbook of the trade unions and the nuns. The nuns were active too, and that was "as an owner, I have certain rights." Now, most people who are owners don't exercise those rights. Companies are quite used to the shareholders being very passive, and particularly the big pools of money that come in from index products. If you look through the last 40 years, there's been usually no correspondence at all around asking for any change in behavior or asking questions at all about environmental, social, or governance characteristics. This is one of the reasons we witnessed explosive growth in CEO compensation over the past four decades as a growing number of investors moved to passive investing and the large players in the index space blindly voted with management on all proxy issues. That is just starting to change now, but it was unusual for an owner to actually pick up the phone, call company management, and start talking about these issues.

Explain the power of coalitions behind your shareholder engagement.

If you were to look at why [companies' management] cares about what Trillium is coming to them with, it's because they know that there are a whole bunch of other organizations through ICCR (Interfaith Center on Corporate Responsibility) that are going to be behind us. They're increasingly aware now that we are usually arm-in-arm with AFL-CIO (American Federation of Labor and Congress of Industrial Organizations), AFSME (American Federation of State and Municipal Employees), normally in partnership with the state of New York's pension plan, the city of New York's pension plan, California's pension plans, both CalPERS and CalSTRS. There are numerous others because we've forged alliances with all the New England states retirement plans, and the state retirement plans of Pennsylvania, Illinois, North Carolina, and others.

So, at this point, the coalition is strong enough that we will come in and say, "we'd like to see this change and if we don't see this change, we're going to file a shareholder resolution." If we file a shareholder resolution, it's actually highly probable that we will get the endorsement of both ISS (Institutional Shareholder Services) and Glass Lewis, and with those two, we could get a majority vote the first time this goes to ballot. And that's embarrassing for companies.

So, what you're seeing now is—and it is an amazing evolution of the impact of shareholders—is that increasingly companies are willing to resolve the issue without you having to file a shareholder proposal. We had over 600 engagements with companies last year. In only 36 did we have to file a shareholder resolution.

Increasingly what happens now when we go to the extent of filing a shareholder resolution is that once the board is aware of it, the media is aware of it, the institutional shareholders are aware of it, and the management has heightened pressure to address the issue. When company management goes to write the opposition statement, you have to just think about what's going on in their heads. They're sitting there and they're writing "We don't think it's necessary to address gender pay inequity as suggested in this proposal, because. . . ." What's the reason? And in half the cases they're coming back to us and saying, "We've decided we agree with your proposal. We'd like you to withdraw your resolution and we'd like to work on a satisfactory solution for you." So, it's been getting easier and more collaborative over time.

What are you benchmarking against?

We're benchmarking against traditional benchmarks because we've always wanted to prove that inclusion of ESG is beneficial, I don't want to show you that I did okay versus the WilderHill clean tech portfolio or an ESG index. I want to show you that I did okay against the MSCI World. I want to show you that I did okay against the S&P 500. Our objective is to demonstrate that we can compete and outperform against the broad market benchmarks.

I would say our approach looks very much like any traditional investment firm, with the caveat that we're including environmental, social, and governance as meaningful factors in the investment process. Generally speaking, all the names you see that make it into our portfolio are going to already be better than ESG stories.

Are you targeting companies based on untapped potential to engage?

There are plenty of times where we will go after an opportunity where see both a great investment opportunity and where we believe there will be a willingness for a company to engage on issues that we think will help improve the company's operations in regards to it's ESG profile. However, we're not an activist shareholder that's buying up ExxonMobil in a portfolio and saying, we're going to make this a clean energy giant by changing the behavior of ExxonMobil management and getting them to completely shift their business model. I salute those who've done it but it doesn't fit our profile. People sometimes look at our portfolio and say, "I don't understand, you own Microsoft, everyone owns Microsoft. Aren't you just like every other fund?" My response is that you need to look at what's not in the portfolio to really understand what's different about how we're selecting companies, because we're looking for the better ESG players. And yes, Microsoft has a good ESG profile.

I'll give you an example of a name you won't find: you will not find Amazon in any of our portfolios. It's not on our buy list. It can't make it onto our buy list because they still have huge societal issues and negative impacts that we can't accept, even though we know the trend is really strong for e-commerce. We've decided to play e-commerce through other names like Etsy, which have a much stronger ESG profile.

Is there a performance issue that you may have given up?

That's a big question, and I don't know whether ultimately some of the problems that Amazon has created catch up with them. I mean, when we go in and sit down and do attribution-versus-benchmark by not being in Amazon we have lost performance. That's just a fact. But we've delivered performance over benchmark without owning Amazon.

We don't own Facebook. Why don't we own Facebook? Well, because the governance structure is terrible. Mark Zuckerberg reports to Mark Zuckerberg. Anytime you see the CEO also being the chair of the board, you've got a governance problem and it should be addressed. And we asked that it be addressed because we were in Facebook and we decided that we were going to actively press for change in Facebook's governance. While we did get a positive vote of the non-Zuckerberg shareholders—63 percent in favor of our shareholder proposal asking for the separation of the roles of CEO and Board Chair, the Facebook Board refused to act. We failed to get the action we were asking for and ended up liquidating our position and taking it off of our buy list.

What represents "greenwashing" to you in the current ESG public equities landscape?

Here's an example of the worst of the worst that can happen. It's when people see the marketing opportunity, they run to it and forget about authenticity and the accuracy of the label. So our dear friends at State Street launch a fossil fuel free index product. In order to make sure that they were tracking the benchmark at the time they launched, they decided they were going to have 7 percent fossil fuel exposure in a product being launched called "fossil fuel free."

We were in the media calling them out on it and they finally changed the name to "fossil fuel reserves free." And they still have exposure to fossil fuels, but the consumer has no clue and thinks they're buying a fossil fuel free fund, even if it's called "fossil fuel reserves free."

State Street also did a gender-lens fund offering. You may have seen the guerrilla marketing they did. They put the statue of the fearless girl in front of the bull on Wall Street and that was part of their marketing campaign for their strategy, for which they got the ticker symbol SHE. *I wish State Street would put the same level of thought into the design of their product offerings as they do into their marketing efforts.* When you look at it, they did a screen of requiring two women on the board and one woman in the C-suite. With that, they put the resulting universe into the index. And that's the end of their screen. What did gender lens mean to them?

Did they look at whether or not there's pay equity in the firm? Did they look at whether or not women are being promoted in the firm? Did they look at whether or not they have forced arbitration for sexual assault? All these issues need to be thought of when you're talking about consideration of gender issues and yet they weren't. Is the product or service helpful for improving the lives of women and girls? Basic things that we ask all the time about companies.

I was alerted to this fund because I got a call from a salesperson from State Street trying to sell it to me saying, "we think this is really going to be good fit for your clients, given that you care about gender." And I'm thinking, "this is ridiculously bad and my clients would fire me if I put them in this." So, there's a lot of that going on.

When I look at BlackRock and all the efforts that they're making, that's real. They've put real resources into it. They've got 75 people focused on this and they really do care. They're actually calling companies and asking for change. That's not happening at State Street nor Vanguard or Fidelity. But when I throw stones, it's usually at a specific product that's mislabeled, rather than the asset management companies.

Explain your Community Impact Investing certificates of deposit and promissory notes.

This is really about credit analysis and it's the same as you would do for fixed income portfolios. But we're looking at community finance institutions that are designated in the U.S. and usually have additional support coming from banks. Banks in the United States are required to provide a certain amount of support for community. So, you'll see them using the part of their assets that are required by regulations to be reinvested in the local community.

CDFI's (Community Development Finance Institutions) are the primary place we go for what is really a part of the cash allocation for our clients. If our clients have a requirement that they want to keep 5 percent in cash, we're going to try to find places like community banks or short-term CDs in banking institutions that are local, including credit unions.

With CDFIs, it's maybe one year rolling notes. We're not usually going out more than three years. We're doing a very small portion of an allocation to it. It is historically low yield, but it's usually better than you can get from a money market fund, better than you can usually get from a bank deposit. Default rates for us have been very low. If you were to look over the history of almost 40 years of doing this, the default rates have been minuscule, well less than one percent, so it's not been a risky investment.

One of the newer areas that we've tried to work on is . . . if Community Development Finance Institutions want to raise money that is longer term, we have encouraged them to use instruments that include a CUSIP number. So, making it a registered instrument that allows us to consider it as part of our fixed income allocation. There we've had great success in getting people to do notes as long as seven years. In most cases, they're able to even get it rated and we're usually able to get a premium in yield versus an equivalent investment grade corporate. So, we've been able to invest part of our fixed income portfolio into these. Our total private portfolio invested mostly in CDFIs is around $40 million. Our total fixed income portfolio is $400 million, so if the CDFIs can tap into the fixed income market, there's a lot more ability to raise significant assets.

Are the risk-adjusted returns commercial or concessionary?

Considering default rates and everything else, it oddly looks to be non-concessionary. But I would still argue that there's a concessionary element to it when risk is considered because it's generally harder to assess the risk in a CDFI than it is for a typical corporate bond. We are therefore very careful about under what circumstances we use CDFIs in portfolios and generally use them in larger portfolios where we and the client feel concessionary returns are acceptable.

What's a concrete example of the impact that these certificate investments have?

Let's discuss the promissory notes to Root Capital because it's a name people often know and it's easy to identify what the work is they're doing there. They're predominantly doing loans to agricultural co-ops in the developing world and providing money well below what would be the market if these institutions were able to go to banks. For an environmentally fragile area, lets consider the Chiapas region of Mexico.

They actually go in with technical expertise, they go in with the loan capital, and they've helped them to organize and form the co-op. They're helping them with capital to buy equipment to further process agricultural products and in the case of Chiapas, one of the great success stories is a coffee co-operative they helped the farmers form. They helped them with washing stations and drying stations to further process specialty coffee, and then they connected them with Starbucks and Green Mountain Coffee Roasters for the end buyer to actually cut out all the middlemen.

In the process, the community's income went up five-fold. I actually went to visit the community and I was just shocked. They now have running water, they have electricity, they have a school. So we went representing the investors from Trillium several years ago and we were there dressed in shorts and t-shirts as it's hot. And this young man shows up dressed in a suit and tie and we're all wondering what would make someone think that made any sense? Generally speaking, the clothing of the cooperative workers is appropriate for the work they're doing and of course they were not dressed up. I didn't expect a guy in a suit and tie. It's hot and humid. He comes over and they just said, "He wanted to thank you himself. He's the first graduate from our new school. The first one in the community to get a high school diploma. That was made possible because of the quintupling of the income of the community, and he's been accepted to university in Mexico City. He wanted to personally thank you all."

That is the impact! You're changing lives and putting money in places where it normally wouldn't get to in the system by depositing at the local Bank of America or investing in an S&P Index Fund; which is not having that kind of positive impact in people's lives. And you're doing that over and over again because you're touching, first hundreds, then thousands, then millions. When you look at it in an aggregate of all of the effort from the Impact Investing field, it's incredible.

What is the single most important challenge in the ESG public equities investment space right now?

It is getting harmonization and standardization of what we're asking companies to report so that we have the ability to compare across industry and then across the entire system of how companies are doing. That's number one and number two is I need more of a timeline of data. I need 10 years of history so that I can analyze how people are progressing. We keep saying that specifically on DEI (Diversity, Equity, and Inclusion), unless people are releasing data, I don't have any way of judging their progress. You can make all the comments you want about caring about DEI. You can go ahead and donate to the NAACP like Morgan Stanley did and that's nice. I think it was $5 million to the NAACP as part of your response to what happened with George Floyd, but I don't know how you're doing, unless you release your EE0-1 (Equal Employment Opportunity Form 1) data and release it over a timeline so that I can start to see if you're actually doing anything. Are you making progress? So, we need the data, we need it standardized, and we need it for multiple years. Then we can really have the ability to make sense of it all.

How would you advise someone who wants to get experience in the SRI sustainable investment space?

You could get into Sustainable/Impact Investing now with almost every asset management firm and almost every asset owner because everybody's looking at getting into this field. It's kind of exploded to where really you could go into the state of New York's retirement plan and work on sustainable investing. You could go into almost every European pension plan. They've all got to be working on how to do more of this. It's an exciting time to be entering the field as it has now truly gone mainstream.

"Over half of the global GDP directly relies on natural capital . . . while we are not integrating natural capital challenges into investment decision-making, nor do we have suitable global policies to effectively address these, breaching the planetary boundaries."

NATURAL CAPITAL
ALINA DONETS
LOMBARD ODIER INVESTMENT MANAGERS
LI: linkedin.com/in/alina-donets
AM.LOMBARDODIER.COM

Alina Donets is a globally recognized specialist in water and sustainable investment, having developed several new strategies with proprietary impact, thematic, and ESG-centered processes. She is a portfolio manager of the LO Funds-Natural Capital at Lombard Odier Investment Managers and has been managing sustainability portfolios for more than eight years. Previously, she co-managed the Allianz Global Water strategy at Allianz Global Investors and was an investment manager on Pictet Water Fund at Pictet Asset Management.

How do you describe what you do?

I am the lead portfolio manager on our fund called LO Funds-Natural Capital at Lombard Odier, launched in November 2020. As we speak, the fund has about $900 million in assets under management.

As the lead portfolio manager, my day-to-day responsibilities are constructing the high conviction portfolio of 40 to 50 publicly listed companies. All of them either contribute to the preservation of natural capital or create solutions for harnessing the power of nature via the circular-bioeconomy. We are active shareholders, which means we also do a lot of engagement work [with portfolio companies].

But my contributions to the company extend beyond just simple stock selection. I also partake in the organization of our capabilities around the ESG integration and work on streamlining and developing our sustainability reporting. A lot of my work contributes to the overall improvement in our approach to sustainability and ensuring that it's positively aligned with the positioning and the capability of the Natural Capital fund itself.

What do you mean by "high conviction" portfolio?

We aim to be quite concentrated in our investments. Traditionally, broad and diversified global equity funds, or perhaps those that have a regional style and bias, consist of anywhere between 60 to 100 companies in a portfolio. Our fund aims to build a strong conviction, based on understanding a business from the bottom-up. We invest in companies which have a targeted substantial sustainability contribution, are financially sound, and offer an attractive investment opportunity. The portfolio construction process aims to minimize the factor risks and maximize the contribution of idiosyncratic risk to overall performance of the fund.

The consequence is a portfolio consisting of 40 to 50 companies that's quite concentrated, with a strong, detailed, and rigorous view on each of the holdings in the portfolio. Our turnover would be anywhere between 30 to 40 percent. This means that, on average, we hold a company for three, or maybe just under three years.

How do you define natural capital?

Natural capital is basically all the resources that we get from nature. Starting with the non-renewable resources, such as minerals that we extract from nature or other materials that we then transform and utilize in our economy and society. There are also renewable and regenerative resources that we utilize as direct inputs, such as water. And finally, ecosystem services which are crucial for many parts of human and economic activity, for example, bees that pollinate the agricultural fields that eventually produce food to feed the population. Natural capital is an aggregation of all the resources in nature. It is vital that we ensure that we fully utilize and harness the power of the regenerative aspects of natural capital and preserve those that have a finite resource.

Why should we invest in those resources?

I think there are two key parameters or factors to consider: First, it is estimated that over half of global GDP directly or indirectly relies on natural capital or natural resources, be it in the form of physical resources or ecosystem services. That means that as a population, we are hugely reliant on nature and natural resources. Secondly, we are not utilizing these resources efficiently and effectively. We are over-extracting or overusing these resources, which creates a negative impact on the planet. That can be from either utilizing or extracting the resources

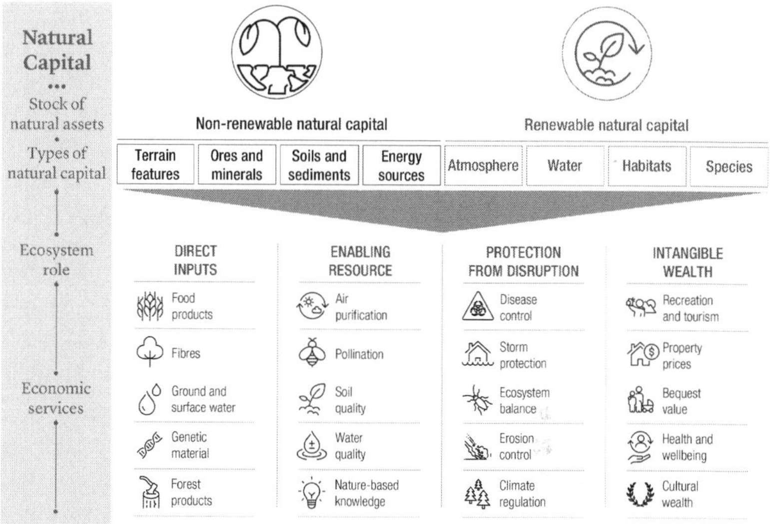

Lombard Odier Investment Managers, 2021. ***Source:*** **Used with permission of Lombard Odier Investment Managers**

quicker than they can replenish themselves, or from creating negative externalities such as pollution, that eventually harm nature, and reduce its efficiency and resourcefulness.

As a whole, the concepts and understanding of global sustainability are all still relatively underdeveloped and poorly integrated. We have already seen, over the last decade or two, an improved understanding of climate change, including the root causes and the long-term consequences. That has over time translated into a willingness to address climate change, with specific policies addressing both mitigation and adaptation. When it comes to natural capital, it's a much broader environmental challenge, but equally important and equally challenging. Unfortunately, there isn't yet a fully aligned consensus on how to measure and evaluate the different aspects of this challenge, what needs to be done to mitigate it, and how to do it.

At Lombard Odier, we recognize the need to actively incorporate the sustainability challenges, and opportunities, in the financial system and global investments. Our LO Climate Transition and LO Natural Capital funds are based on our Lombard Odier framework for sustainability, which we call CLIC™. The "CLIC"[2] methodology is a starting point on which we establish the key objectives of the investments that need to be undertaken to address crucial environmental and social challenges. CLIC™ stands for Circular, Lean, Inclusive and Clean—the key aspects of the future economic model we need to aim for. The Natural Capital fund aims at the "Circular" and "Lean" aspects, by investing in companies that develop solutions for the circular bio-economy and a lean industry.

We are also developing supportive measurement tools alongside our investment approach. One existing tool that we utilize across our portfolios is the temperature alignment measurement which we call ITR (Implied Temperature Rise). It assesses the temperature alignment of companies relative to the Paris Agreement goal of keeping climate change within 1.5°C of pre-industrial levels. Specifically for the Natural Capital fund, we are also currently developing similar tools to measure relevant metrics such as biodiversity and natural capital depletion.

One of the theories that we use is the framework of planetary boundaries. It serves as a foundation around which we're hoping to build measurement tools that will allow us to quantify the risks and the whole positive impact [of natural capital investing]. This approach will allow us to monitor and assess where we stand in terms of current and future utilization of and footprint on some of the key natural resources—relative to a sustainable manner of utilizing them. We aim to use it as a framework that helps to support, organize, and bring transparency into our investments in natural capital.

Planetary boundaries have been developed by the thought-leaders at the Stockholm Resilience Center and subsequently widely adopted as an effective framework for assessing the health of the planet. We use it as a foundation for developing a proprietary toolset at Lombard Odier aimed to translate this theory and the concept of sustainability in the way we manage and address resources, and operate as a human society, into an input in the investment process.

You use the term "Planetary Boundaries"; what does that mean?

Planetary boundaries is a theory developed around the natural boundaries within which the planet functions in equilibrium. These include, for example, levels of biodiversity, or certain key chemical elements in natural habitat. What we have already recognized, for example, is that nitrogen and phosphorus pollution stemming from agricultural activities have increased to levels where that has significant negative impact on biodiversity. We exceeded the limits of the planet to actually absorb and manage these, affecting the environmental balance. There are a number of relevant metrics that we are monitoring and assessing.

The problem is that at a global level, many of these metrics are not integrated into economic decision-making, with measures such as GDP or traditional financial assessment tools not taking account of, or valuing, nature. Therefore, we're still at the point where a lot of the natural capital issues are not effectively addressed, despite the urgent need to do so.

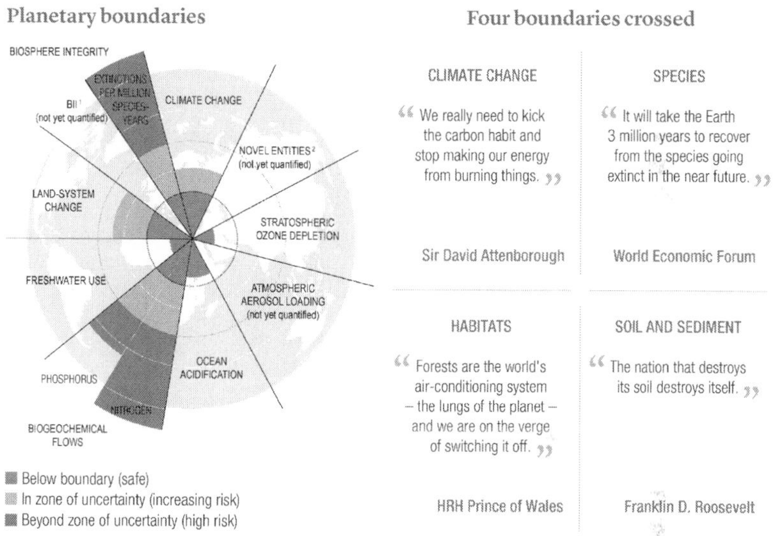

Lombard Odier Investment Managers, 2021. *Source:* Used with permission of Lombard Odier Investment Managers.

What's the difference between Lombard Odier's "WILD" and "CLIC" frameworks?

WILD (Wasteful, Idle, Lopsided, and Dirty) and CLIC™ (Circular, Lean, Inclusive and Clean) are two acronyms that we use to describe the old, and the sought-for economic model, respectively. The CLIC™ framework that we have developed is used as a basis for a range of investment solutions, including the Natural Capital fund.

The WILD acronym describes the traditional economic model. In such a model, linear business approach prevails—you take resources, make products, and then waste the resources disposed along that process. In order to protect the environment while meeting global demand, we need to create a sustainable circular economic model. The Natural Capital fund targets investments that unlock this transition to a Circular and Lean economic model.

There are other parts to the WILD and CLIC™ concept. For example, the transition from Dirty to Clean. One of the key challenges with pollution is carbon emissions, and the dire consequences in the form of climate change. The LO Funds-Climate Transition targets investment in companies that offer solutions for climate change and are set to thrive in a carbon-constrained world.

So, in summary, the WILD concept represents the traditional approach that we have lived with for centuries, and CLIC™ represents the number of targets that we, as a company, think are essential to achieve when it comes to sustainable investing. A number of our investment solutions are set to address these challenges by investing in companies that develop solutions for a Circular, Lean, Inclusive, and Clean economy.

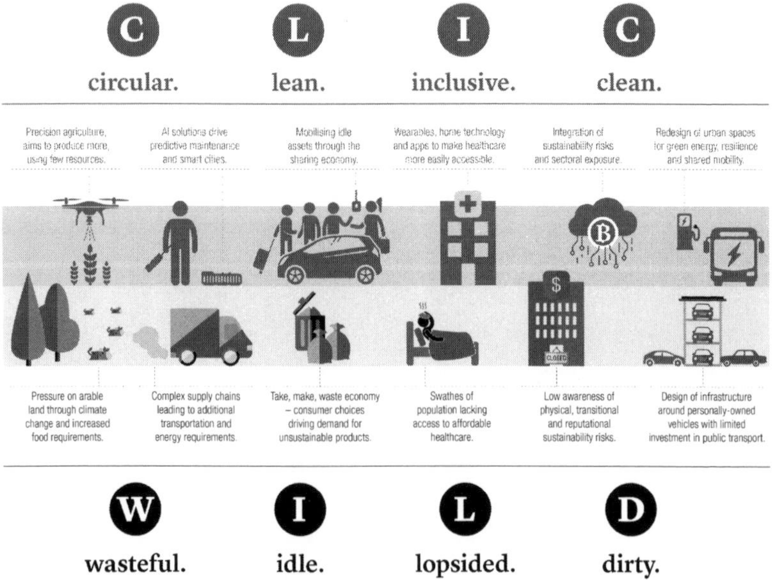

Lombard Odier Investment Managers, 2021. *Source:* Used with permission of Lombard Odier Investment Managers.

When in that decision-making process do you apply CLIC™?

The CLIC™ methodology and the focus on preserving natural capital and harnessing nature really comes at the first stages, when we define the investment opportunity. The identified universe currently stands at approximately 600 companies active in the businesses that create positive outcomes for nature. As the next stage, we start looking for the most attractive investment opportunities. An assessment of the technology that the companies produce and the environmental benefits of it are an important constituent to the analysis, but we equally assess a number of other factors along the financial performance and ESG characteristics.

How do you use this methodology to select companies to invest in?

It's important to realize that all of these objectives and benefits of natural capital that these different businesses and business activities have are very difficult to prioritize. I would almost call it ethically challenging to assess which of them needs to be addressed more, right? Because it depends on a number of different factors. It depends, among others, on the cost of the technology, or the necessity or pressure that you see with a certain particular environmental issue. It also depends on how well the specific company is able to scale that technology. There are really a lot of points that come into consideration when attempting to understand the importance of the positive environmental contributions. Therefore, CLIC™ serves as a tool for organizing our research into sustainability challenges and definition of the investment opportunity set.

So, how do you score this?

Instead of trying to score or create a prescriptive approach to assessments of the importance of the sustainability contributions or positive impact that we're creating, we have come to an assumption that all of these topics are equally important. So, the actual selection of the companies for the portfolio will be based on the conviction that we create around a specific company, instead of a result of scoring the environmental challenges. That means that the ability of the company to contribute to positive objectives they can achieve with a product or the service that they produce is integrated in the assessment of the business as one of components of a conviction formation. There are a number of other factors that we need to consider. For example, do the financials of this company reflect the opportunity, or are they strong enough to actually bring this opportunity forward? Is this company an attractive return on investment? Is this company well managed, when it comes to business quality and the ESG parameters?

Can you give an example?

One of the investments that has been there since we launched the fund is Advanced Drainage Systems, a company that creates solutions around stormwater management. The reason why this is important for nature is that global urbanization and development of cities significantly alters the water cycle. Creating urban areas prevents the absorption of water into the ground, which subsequently changes the water balance and distribution of water in the area, with negative impacts on ecosystems and biodiversity.

Equally important is that inefficient stormwater management can actually wash a lot of pollution from the city back into the natural habitats. Effective drainage systems are necessary to minimize the alteration of the underlying biodiversity and ecosystems.

Advanced Drainage Systems develops sophisticated systems and products that allow for an efficient and effective implementation of these stormwater solutions. On top of that, they are one of the companies that realized the value of sustainability, not only from the perspective of the end use of their product, but also from the design of the product. Over half of the raw materials they use are recycled plastics. Their product design helps to close the loop in the economy.

This is one of the perfect examples of a company that creates products that have a strong, positive contribution to resource management. They created that solution in the recognition of the sustainability benefits, which actually led to significant market share opportunity gains for them.

What's the difference between LO Funds-Climate Transition and LO Funds-Natural Capital ?

Both funds are investing in companies that develop technologies solving sustainability challenges, but we are addressing different challenges within the CLIC™ framework. The Climate Transition fund invests in solutions that help to solve the climate challenge, address carbon emission issues and help to build resilience to climate change—this helps address the clean part of CLIC™, although it is also indirectly tied to circularity, leanness, and inclusivity.

In the Natural Capital fund, we're focusing more on the issue of circularity and lean operations. I am not directly investing in climate-related transition, and do not specifically target reducing carbon emissions—even if many of the companies in the natural capital investment universe create solutions that help with this challenge and the assessment of the companies' temperature alignment is part of the investment process. The Natural Capital fund is investing in companies that help to create a leaner utilization of resources during the manufacturing and consumption processes, help combat the waste challenge, and create biologically based solutions that help replace some of the finite or damaging resources that we're currently utilizing in our economy.

What do you benchmark the Natural Capital fund against?

I would say we are benchmark agnostic. Our conviction is that investing in companies that create solutions for natural capital is in the long run more attractive financially, and not just in terms of sustainability objectives. Therefore, we would expect to outperform the market. The fund has a focus on smaller-to-medium market capitalization companies. Thus, the reference index is the MSCI All Country World Small-to-Medium Market Capitalization Index.

Do public equities allow for a targeted impact approach, since they are typically large companies with both positive and negative impacts under the same umbrella?

First of all, when it comes to the purity of the companies or their exposure to the activity that interests us, we would not invest in a company that has less than 30 percent of their business in activities that positively contribute to natural capital preservation or harnessing of nature. The average for the portfolio, however, is much higher than 30 percent. Over time, we are getting closer to 60 to 70 percent exposure when you look at the average fund value.

We also actively monitor the remaining business activities, as well as assess the business practices along environmental, social, and governance factors to ensure that the companies we invest in do not create any harm "on the other end." All these aspects are integrated in our investment process and take place before we make any investment.

At the same time, we're not passive investors. We don't just select companies for investment but aim for continued active stewardship of these investments. There is a very active and large engagement program for the Natural Capital fund. We aim to meet with the companies, not only to discuss any particular issues that we might see along the environmental, social, and governance aspects—but also to emphasize the reasons for our investment and support strategic focus and transparency on the key business activities that create positive impact.

It is important to communicate the sustainable investment objectives and link these to the technology that the investees have developed. We actually truly believe that capital allocation and effective communication can eventually translate into improved decision-making at the corporate level, as well. I have seen for years how companies eventually start appreciating the source or the foundation of the interest of their investors and start focusing and allocating more capital toward businesses that actually interest their key long-term investors. We think that capital allocation in active engagement eventually helps to increase exposure to the right business activities.

What do you consider the most important current challenge in the SRI public equity space?

Transparency, because better information allows for improved effectiveness of capital allocation. It allows for better communication. It supports better outcomes for the planet and the investors.

"We're really talking about a system change. But you can only change the system if you change every moving part . . . the way you measure, the way you incentivize, the way you report. And the complexity of integrating ESG properly into the system is something that I think we all underestimate."

QUANTITATIVE SUSTAINABLE INVESTING
DANIEL KLIER
THE ARABESQUE GROUP
ARABESQUE.COM
LI: https://www.linkedin.com/in/daniel-klier-463615/
TW: @DanielOKlier

Dr. Daniel Klier is CEO of Arabesque S-Ray and President of Arabesque Holding. Prior to joining Arabesque, Klier was Global Head of Sustainable Finance for HSBC, where he developed the global climate strategy for the bank and led the development of the sustainable finance business across the corporate bank, retail bank, and asset management business. He joined HSBC in 2013 as Group Head of Strategy in London, following nine years as a Partner at McKinsey & Company.

Klier, who is a member of the Board of Sustainable Energy for All, has also chaired the Bank of England Climate Risk Working Group and the Sustainable Finance Working Group at the Institute of International Finance.

As you are both President of Arabesque and CEO of Arabesque S-Ray, what are your responsibilities within each role?

Arabesque was originally founded as an asset manager, but then fairly quickly realized that if you want to be a leading sustainability asset manager, you need to have two things. First, you need better ESG data. That's when this business, Arabesque S-Ray was created, focused on ESG data. Second, you need a technology platform to manage this data because the human brain can no longer handle the amount of financial and nonfinancial information that you can find in the world. That's when the AI platform was created.

So, one role that I have is to lead the data business, because obviously it will be a huge component of any sustainability transformation. But then secondly, the president of the group has to really help pull together the bigger narrative of how we are, as a group, helping reshape the financial system in a positive way.

Can you give me an overview of Arabesque and your mission as a company?

Our mission is to mainstream sustainable finance. We have three businesses: we have an investment management, asset management business where we create funds and manage funds—anything from ESG funds to very specific climate pathway funds. The second is we have Arabesque S-Ray which is our ESG data business. We provide ESG data and analytics. So, if you are an investor and you want to know your climate alignment, we provide that. If you are a big pension fund, if you want to understand your exposure to human rights risks, we provide that information. The third business is an AI platform, which is a platform that allows you to customize investment strategies. So, if you say, "I want to invest in global equities, but I want to exclude certain things and I want to overemphasize companies that are one and a half degree aligned," the AI platform not only calculates a strategy for you, but also actively manages it—it brings together active management with customization at the cost of passive strategies. Those are the three platforms that we provide.

What is quantitative investing and how does this investment philosophy differ from other investment strategies?

Well, the main thing is that we don't have a human bias in our sustainability decisions, so everything that we do is purely data driven. We collect 150 million ESG data points and we combine that with all the financial information that we get. We have the AI platform that the team has built which forecasts 30,000 equity prices every day, based on all of this information coming together, so we don't have human judgment in the process. Every score that we build, and every investment decision is purely data driven.

If you are a large company and you want to understand your ESG score, you can double click and double click and double click, and you arrive at the raw [underlying] data. If you are an investor and you want to understand what drives your investment choices, there's an algorithm behind that which combines financial and nonfinancial information into an investment solution. In the end that's what we think is the future of investing, because you went from active to passive and now you go from passive to almost autonomous.

Does identifying sustainable outperformers necessarily lead to a better financial investment or share price?

I don't want to make it too complicated, but I think that there are two ways to think about ESG in investment decisions. One is you define outcomes. So, you say, I want to optimize my investment strategy for a certain outcome and the outcome can actually be a financial outcome but can also be a sustainability outcome.

As an example, I want to build a portfolio that is aligned with net zero pathways. That is a fairly complex exercise, but essentially you build a portfolio of companies that have a pathway that gets close to net zero by 2050. There you don't try to pick companies that will deliver better performance because of sustainability, but you pick companies that deliver a certain outcome.

The alternative approach is that you use ESG data to predict outperformance—and models and machines can deliver both for you. Many investors want the former rather than the latter. They want to use data models to make sure that we deliver certain outcomes. The track record on companies delivering better share price performance is still very young.

Explain how your quantitative model works, the research behind it, and how algorithms are selected.

That's the really interesting bit here because essentially you move from quant to artificial intelligence and what artificial intelligence does is it builds patterns. It recognizes patterns and it learns all the time. We have 30 data engineers that are all Imperial PhDs. Essentially, you don't build a single quant model that runs an engine with the processing power of 20,000 machines. You actually allow a machine to recognize patterns and to change patterns.

On the AI platform, we now have the first funds live. They outperform the market at the moment. We take all the information—analyst forecasts, weather patterns, and you look for patterns and pattern recognition.

How does Arabesque incorporate the S-Ray data into its investment process?

It's included in two ways. What the team has built is essentially an artificial Chief Investment Officer. We call it autoCIO. It allows you in the first step to customize your investment strategy. You go through all the different investment choices you want to make: long only;

long- short; you want to do global equities; you want to do all the sectors. And you also in that process define what your sustainability criteria that you're going after are. And that's the first place where our data comes in, so you define the boundaries.

Step two is where the artificial intelligence platform actually runs your strategy. Given that it's not managed by a portfolio manager but by a machine, you can run as many strategies as you want to because it's infinitely scalable. That's where the machine forecasts 30,000 equity prices every day. If you want to, it gives you a daily signal for how you should change your capital allocation. And again, that's the second point where the S-Ray data comes in, because sustainability information is just another data point where you look for patterns. But it's not just sustainability data, obviously. It's all the fundamental data that you have in the market. It does your portfolio construction and it aims to generate alpha by taking information into account that is quite hard for the human brain to digest.

In the long term, will it be more profitable to provide this technology, data, and scoring than actually managing assets yourself?

Our view is, that the financial service industry is the most fragmented industry in the world. There are thousands of banks, thousands of insurance companies, thousands of asset managers, thousands of asset owners. Very few of them will be able to develop their own tools, data sources, and data models. So, everybody will need help and I think that is really where we want to go. We want to be the engineers behind the industry that help others achieve sustainability outcomes. You also know that the entire industry is facing incredible cost pressures. So, people will need to look at technology to replace essentially what today people are doing, and therefore bring better data and better technology in to solve quite a fundamental problem. All this while you have to deliver on your sustainability commitments. You have to manage future risks. You have to comply with regulatory solutions. Everybody will need help.

Describe the process of how you go from sustainable goals down to actual stock selection?

Maybe we should start with how you actually assess a company for sustainability, because I think that's the first important piece. Obviously, sustainability means many different things for different people.

We start with two data sources. We start with information that companies disclose, so we collect about 450 ESG data points on more than 8,000 listed companies in the world. That ranges from your greenhouse gas emissions footprint to the number of women you have on the board. We then build that up into a data model that gives you scores. It gives you an ESG score and a Global Compact score. An ESG score is commonly used to identify companies that do things well, whereas a Global Compact score is often used to identify companies that are exposed to certain risks such as labor malpractices or human rights risks.

We also create indicators such as the Temperature Score, where we combine all of that information with temperature models, where we take the International Energy Agency scenarios and essentially model which company is actually aligned to it, along different pathways. And you can work out if a company is actually aligned with a three-degree world, a two and a half-degree world, a two-degree world, or a one and a half-degree world.

Then we use that information to help investors get transparency in their portfolio, but also to construct portfolios. We build indices for certain investors; say that if you want to build an index portfolio that is aligned with one and a half degrees, what stocks do you pick? And then you let it run. We essentially take a universe of 150 million data points, build it up to company level indicators, and use that to inform investment choices.

How does Arabesque Asset Management buying and selling shares on the secondary market change corporate behavior?

There are three ways that we and other investors deal with this. The most traditional way is exclusionary approaches. You just say, "I don't buy certain activities," and with that, you restrict access to capital. You've seen a few industries that went through this; the tobacco industry certainly did. You currently see coal going through this and increasingly the broader fossil fuel industry. That is a concern for companies because it actually means they're really restricting the access to liquid markets.

The second approach is stewardship engagement. You use your ownership power to express preferences at AGM's. That's why all the proxy voting companies are increasingly important and look at real data. That's why shareholder stewardship and engagement are increasingly in focus from the largest investors in the world.

The third approach is, let's say, positive discrimination. You build investment products that overemphasize companies that have certain characteristics. It's the opposite of the exclusionary approach. It allows you to funnel more capital and therefore, in an ideal world, increase the share price of companies that have certain characteristics.

How does S-Ray differ from competing ESG data providers?

I would say it differs in three areas. One, sustainability is all that we do. We have 250 people; we just do sustainability. With that, we believe that we build better analytics. We build better insights into sustainability, like the Temperature Score, which was a thing that we essentially invented—now the entire industry uses it.

Secondly, we have a more transparent approach. The big criticism of some of our competitors is always that the ESG score is essentially a black box. It's very heavily driven by controversies. It's very heavily driven by negative news and therefore for a company to actually understand what drives their ESG score is very, very hard.

The third reason is we deliver a better technology. Our technology is built in this decade; it's built in the Cloud. It's flexible. It is very different than if you built your business model 30 years ago. We all know legacy business models are great, but also much harder to change and bring along. So, it's a combination of better insights and really market leading analytics with more transparency and better technology.

Do policy makers have the most important role in driving market behavior, or can the markets allocate capital sustainably to get to net zero?

It will only work if you have both. The role of policymakers is twofold. One is to harmonize metrics. It's a bit like in the 1930s, when a P&L wasn't a P&L and it's very hard to compare profit if you don't have a standard definition of what is profit. I think harmonizing disclosure is really important. If you look at TCFD (Task Force on Climate-related Financial Disclosures) reports of two companies today, even in the same industry, they say completely different things. As an investor, if you don't have good signals, it is very hard to reallocate capital. We're doing some of that job for investors by harmonizing data. But it would be much easier if you actually had standardized data sources, and people like the

IFRS Foundation (*International Financial Reporting Standards Foundation)* are now picking this up to increasingly include such standards.

The second rule for investors, for central banks, and for policymakers is to ensure that the financial system appropriately prices for risks. That's where Mark Carney's "Tragedy of the Horizon" came in. The Bank of England evidenced that the financial system is mispricing future risks, because it finds it hard to price risks that haven't historically occurred. And that's when climate stress tests and the like come in. It's not trying to make judgments of whether a financial actor is doing the right thing or not; it's trying to take a belief into something that they can actually run as a scenario, put into numbers. If you're not prepared for it, hold more capital.

Sticking to the climate discussion, if we believe that we want to and that we have to reduce the carbon footprint by 50 percent in this decade, you probably need policy signals. Just investor commitment will probably not make it. You need a combination of both.

What do you know now about ESG investing that you wish you knew in 2017, when you became the Global Head of Sustainable Finance at HSBC?

Mostly I think how long it takes to take a senior level commitment through an organization. What we're really talking about is system change. You can only change the system if you change every moving part of the system, the way you measure, the way you incentivize, the way you report. And the complexity of integrating ESG properly in the system is something that I think we all underestimate. In most organizations, that started as a side department that was doing ethical investing and sustainable investing. Now everybody is moving that side department into the core. But to get into the core, it's a fundamental change where you need to change every part of the system.

If someone wants to get into the sustainable finance space, how would you advise them?

First of all, it's everywhere now; it's no longer a little side activity. You have it in your sustainable supply chain teams, in your bond teams, in your asset management teams. The first important recognition is it's not something where you need to join a certain team, but it's increasingly part of every line of business.

The second is, it's bringing together financial know-how and sustainability know-how, which not many people have. You can approach it from either end, but you need to build the other capability. You can be the best sustainability expert, but if you don't understand financial markets there's no chance that you can be a better investor. But if you don't understand sustainability, you will also fall short. The key is bringing in that combination and building your skillset through academic experience and real-life experience.

Third, frankly, this is still such an evolving field. One just needs to get started.

Chapter Five

Fixed Income

The other core asset class in most investment portfolios is Fixed Income. Examples of Fixed Income securities can include sovereign bonds, municipal bonds, or corporate bonds. Bonds are securities similar to a loan agreement, except the borrower is a government, city, or corporation. In general, the issuer of a Fixed Income security is obliged to pay interest (referred to as a "coupon") at a fixed interest rate and over a specified period of time until the original principal is repaid.

So, with Fixed Income securities, investors receive a fixed and predictable return, unlike with equity security investments where there is no obligation to pay any type of income to stockholders.

ENTER GREEN BONDS

In 2008, the World Bank issued a new fixed income instrument for institutional investors, the first "green bond,"—today also referred to as "climate bonds." These specifically target environmental projects, and raise money for such things as energy efficiency, pollution prevention, sustainable agriculture, fishery and forestry, protection of aquatic and terrestrial ecosystems, clean transportation and infrastructure, clean water, and sustainable water management.

Since their debut, the market for these bonds—which are typically backed by the issuing entity's balance sheet—has grown substantially. The total volume of climate bonds issued in 2016 (the same year Apple became the first tech company and Poland the first country to issue a green bond) was estimated to be $82 billion.[1] By 2020 that figure had more than tripled, approaching $270 billion.[2]

RINGING IN A GREENER WORLD

The attraction of SRI Fixed Income securities is that the proceeds of a majority of issuances are "ringfenced," which means that investors are assured that their funds are earmarked for only a specific "green" use, which is referred to as "use-of-proceeds" in bond parlance. In the case of green bonds, that could be anything from purchasing renewable energy generation assets to investing in energy efficiency interventions across a real estate portfolio. This obviously differs from the issuance of equity shares where investors have no granular usage visibility.

The rapid growth in the size of the green bond market over the last few years has been partially fueled by their familiarity—their similarity in structure to traditional bonds—so investors have been able to participate without a steep learning curve. They remain risk-weighted, credit-rated, and tradeable on secondary markets in the same way that conventional bonds are. (This chapter refers to public debt, and we will consider private debt later in chapter 7, titled Alternatives: Private Debt.)

This growth has been particularly beneficial since it has signaled to both governments and companies alike that when seeking to finance the low carbon transitions that are urgent and necessary to address climate and environmental challenges, there is an appetite for risk and available capital. This has, in turn, led to an increase in the number of companies seeking to raise money for those purposes and, it could be argued, corporate behavioral change.

GREEN USED AS CAMOUFLAGE

Of course, with eco-conscious goodwill and public relations incentives to "go green," someone will inevitably exploit that opportunity with misleading marketing. Add to that the powerful financial incentives like reduced coupon rates, and its game-on for those hoping to game the system. This practice is nothing new and, in fact, became so prevalent back in the early days of SRI, that in 1986, environmentalist Jay Westerveld dubbed it "greenwashing."

Greenwashing in the SRI Fixed Income space is the practice of misleading investors by issuing so-called green bonds but then channeling the financial proceeds from green bond issuance into activities that have a negligible, or even negative, environmental impact. One notable example was the issuance of a €500 million green bond by the giant Spanish oil and gas conglomerate Repsol in 2017, on the pretense of reducing carbon emissions by 1.2 million tons within three years. Ultimately, the proceeds were instead used to upgrade Repsol's refineries in order to expand their fossil fuel production. Similarly, green bonds were issued by the operator of the Three Gorges Corporation in China, which has been frequently called out for polluting water and damaging ecosystems. In 2014, GDF Suez used proceeds from its green bonds to build the Jirau Dam in Brazil, a project that flooded a rainforest.

The phenomenon of greenwashing has certainly tempered the growth of green bond investing, because it undermines investor confidence. Unfortunately, there are no universally accepted governance regulations in the green bond market, and current conventions to accredit green bonds are not universally adopted across the wide-ranging, geographically diverse market. In the absence of universally accepted standards and oversight, companies may tout bonds as green without publishing reports and metrics to support and verify the legitimacy of their "green" labeling.

To overcome greenwashing in Fixed Income SRI strategies, it is imperative that investors carefully scrutinize the alignment of the bond's use of proceeds (or the investment manager's scrutiny . . .) and ensure transparency and verifiability by using one or more of the green bond and reporting frameworks (explained below).

CREDENTIALS, INCENTIVES, AND PERSPECTIVES

The rapid growth and market evolution of the SRI Fixed Income market has resulted in lots of labels that may have been intended to clarify but inevitably can lead to confusion. You've got "green bonds" and "blue bonds," "sustainability bonds" and "social bonds"—each often targeting slightly different, but sometimes similar, impact. The introduction of formal certification bodies, which insist on third-party verification requirements, has attempted to resolve the issue by verifying and specifying the bond issuer's green credentials, or an issuance's green credentials, most often on an annual basis. Examples include ICMA's Green Bond Principles, Climate Bonds Standard, EU Green Bond Standard, ISO 14030, ASEAN Green Bond Standard, and the Green Bond Endorsed Project Catalogue, among others. But questions remain about whether not only the use of funds from bond offerings should be considered, or also the sustainability profile of the issuer itself.

There are similar concerns with more recent "sustainability-linked loans" (where the interest rate an issuer pays is dependent on their progress toward specified sustainability metrics). Corporations may set easy targets to ensure they are certainly met—as a way to reduce the interest rate they pay. Or investors may be perversely incentivized in the hope that the corporation issuing the bonds fails to meet their sustainability targets and has to pay lenders a higher return.

Investors have different opinions on all of these compelling issues that have prompted discussion and exploration—and in this chapter our interviewees will share their own perspectives.

"It's pretty clear that over the last couple of years, if you compare a green bond portfolio to a traditional, fixed income portfolio, the green bonds have been doing better, not worse."

GREEN BONDS
BRAM BOS
NN INVESTMENT PARTNERS
LI: linkedin.com/in/bram-bos-4623a3
NNIP.COM/EN-INT/PROFESSIONAL

Bram Bos is lead portfolio manager of the green bond strategies at NN Investment Partners ("NNIP"), part of NN Group, one of the largest insurance companies in the Netherlands. He has built the green bond franchise at NNIP since its inception in 2015. Today it includes four dedicated green bond funds with total assets under management of €3.8 billion. Bos has over 20 years of portfolio management experience, including previous roles at Unilever, APG Asset Management, Nomura, and Fullerton Fund Management.

Please describe what you do.

We manage funds and mandates for institutional and retail investors, predominantly in fixed income. As a firm, a lot of the focus has been on responsible investing. I think that really changed about five years ago, although we have been active in sustainable finance, funds, and mandates for over 20 years. I set up the green bond strategy in 2016, when we launched our first green bond fund—at the very early stage of the green bond market.

Since then, we have been growing the strategy and now we have four dedicated green bond funds. We are also managing several mandates for pension funds, and the total assets under management in the dedicated green bond strategies is currently around €4 billion. So, it has grown from zero in 2016 to close to €4 billion.

Just to give you a little bit more color, every month I get an overview of all the RFPs from all clients across NNIP. Green bonds are the highest product in demand at the moment within NNIP, by far—even when compared to other regular, traditional strategies. So, this is very typical of how demand for sustainable finance is currently really growing exponentially. That is the case for green bonds and also other strategies in this space.

Can you provide an overview of NNIP's green bond funds?

The first was launched in 2016, and it's an aggregate green bond fund combining corporates, covered bonds, supranationals, agencies, and government bonds. It covers the whole fixed income space.

We have a second green bond fund which is similar—the only difference being that we hedge the duration to only two years. So, it's a short duration variation. I think in the current environment, where people are very worried about rising interest rates, that is very attractive for many investors. The third green bond fund, launched in 2020, is focusing only on corporate green bonds.

Then, on the other side of that is the fourth fund, launched on the 31st of March 2021. It is a sovereign green bond fund which focuses mainly on sovereign bonds. It's also a unique fund, because there's no other government bond fund in the world focusing and measuring impact yet. So, it's quite innovative.

Describe your green bond investors.

There are largely two different groups. One group is banks/wealth managers. For example, if you have a lot of money and you go to your bank and you say, "Hey, I want to invest in a sustainable portfolio," they will offer you a portfolio of different sustainable investment funds. One of those investment funds is quite often a green bond fund. So, banks/wealth managers are a very big part of our client base, predominantly in Europe.

Next to that, there are a lot of pension funds who increasingly are allocating a part of their assets to a separate green bond portfolio or mandate. We have at the moment several pension funds invested in our funds, but also several mandates, and these types of mandates are gaining quite a lot of momentum at the moment. That's because we are seeing more and more pension funds allocating money to bonds.

These two groups comprise about 80 percent of our investor base, maybe even a bit more.

Are they investing with you because of passion about environmental outcomes or are they looking for solid fixed income strategies that look green to the public?

In the end, everybody investing in sustainable finance is welcome because it all helps. I think the first group of investors we saw in 2016 to 2018 clearly had the passion and the belief that "I want to be green and do good"—because at that moment there was no proof whatsoever that you could get a higher return from green bond investments. I think a lot of people were arguing at that moment that investing in ESG and "green" means sacrificing return. That was clearly happening. So, it was a very conscious choice for those investors.

I think since 2019 we are seeing a new group entering the green bond space. These are investors who maybe are not that convinced about the "green" part but are just saying a little bit, the green bond space seems to be hot. And maybe it gives a bit of window dressing to show under their hoods. But most importantly, it's pretty clear that over the last couple of years if you compare a green bond portfolio to a normal fixed income portfolio, the green bonds have been doing better and not worse. That is something that more and more investors are starting to see and they start to include in their thought process. When deciding what investments to make in general, green bonds do pop up.

What is a green bond and what makes it "green"?

First of all, it's very important to realize that green bonds—in terms of liquidity, legal status, credit rating, and the way they trade—are exactly the same as a normal bond.

Where does it differ? It differs because with a green bond the issuer commits to separate the proceeds of the bond from the rest of the company and use those only for predefined "green" projects. And those predefined projects can be a lot of things, right? So, these must be documented in advance. I think that's very important. It has to be very clear what they are going to use the money for.

The most important part of the green bond structure is that once a year the issuer reports back to the investor how the money has been used, what types of projects are being financed with the proceeds, and what the impact is of those projects. Reporting back to the investor is the most important part of the green bond structure. So, in the end, it is a commitment to the investor and as an investor you can make sure that is really happening. That's why the impact reporting is a very important part of the agreement structure.

What are some examples of "use of proceeds" that would qualify as a green bond?

If you look at the definition of green projects, of course, there is sometimes a debate about what exactly is a green project, but there are some good international guidelines. One is the Green Bond Principles from the International Capital Markets Association (ICMA). We also have the Climate Bonds Initiative Taxonomy, and currently the European Union Green Bond Standard is being developed. So, there's quite a lot of guidance for investors and also for issuers, to figure out what is really a green-eligible project for green bonds. These are things which we use at NNIP to determine if a green bond really meets international standards. Examples of projects that the majority of green bonds are funding include renewable energy projects, green buildings, or clean transportation projects. Eighty percent of green bonds issued are financing these types of projects.

Renewable energy is rather straight forward. Most of the time, when a utility company issues a green bond and they finance a windmill with it, there's not much discussion about the "greenness" of those projects. Sometimes it can be more tricky, like with big hydro projects or maybe with gas or nuclear—is it green or not? There's always a bit of a gray area in some of these discussions. But for NNIP, renewable energy is a rather straightforward project category.

One other example is the Dutch government, who issued a green bond in 2019. As a country, the Netherlands is below sea level and a big part of the green bond proceeds is being used to build higher dikes and to make sure that all the dams are being well maintained, which makes a lot of sense for us as a country. The Belgium government also issued a green bond. They have mainly used the proceeds to upgrade and build new train infrastructure. And trains have already been around for a long time, but I think the reality is still that the more trains there are, the more cars you indirectly take off the road.

In your opinion, how good is the ringfencing of the "use of proceeds"?

I think that the ringfencing of the proceeds and allocating to the right projects, etc., is all okay. I don't think that there are a lot of unexpected things happening. Most of the time what companies or treasuries are doing is very predictable. But the question still remains because, for example, an oil company invests €20 billion in fossil fuels. They have a €1 billion windmill park and now they're going to issue a green bond to finance this windmill park while still spending €20 billion on fossil fuels. How credible is that? I think that is really where it becomes more challenging, and that's also why I think I have a job. Because that is what our green bond strategies are trying to do—we try to avoid greenwashing in the end, right? We want to make sure that whenever a green bond is being issued, there's alignment between the projects which they are financing and the broader strategy of the company. That's crucial.

So that's also why we are saying that the greenness of a bond is not only determined by the projects which are being financed, but also by the broader ESG strategy of the company, their transition story, and their targets. So that part is really very important. Again, that's why we think we have a role in the markets to play, to protect that green bond label. That also means that we are rejecting some "green" bonds because we think they're not green enough or not credible. I would not necessarily say that these bonds are greenwashing, because in every country they have different standards and in emerging markets, standards are different. We're just saying that we have high standards.

When I think about all the green bonds which we are monitoring globally, I think currently that's around 800 green bonds, and up to 20 percent are not meeting our standards. Again, that does not mean that they are necessarily greenwashing, but they're just not meeting our dark green approach.

What is the attraction of green bonds vs. traditional bonds for investors?

I quite often get the question, "Why would a company issue green bonds in the first place, because they would do those projects anyway?" The way I see green bonds is that they are the ultimate proof of what a company is doing. It's a transparency to a product. For example, a company can say, "Hey, I am a very green company. I have the highest ESG rating in the world." But that could also just be because I have 20 people working on writing papers, policy papers. The question is what are they really doing?

With a green bond, you really get transparency on the balance sheet of the issuer or company. You get insight into the projects and the way they work. I think that is really the main function of the green bond market: proving what companies are really doing and saying. That's also why, in my view, blindly looking at ESG ratings does not make sense at all. It's not going far enough; you have to go further. That's why the whole "use of proceeds" concept for green bonds, and actually also for social bonds, is very powerful and makes it very tangible for a lot of investors—because they can almost touch the projects. They really get the idea that they're contributing positively to those projects. They can almost find them on the map and point at them and say, "I'm financing that project." I think that is also what makes it very attractive for a lot of businesses.

Are green bonds more attractive from a transparency perspective or is there a performance aspect or other dimension to it?

I think, in the end, more transparency means lower risk. And specifically for green bonds, you know that if a company has credible green bonds it is looking very seriously at climate risks, trying to adapt to that, and will have less risk of being involved in, for example, stranded assets. I think the companies and issuers who are active in the green bond markets are more forward-looking, more innovative, less exposed to climate and ESG risks, and therefore, from a risk point of view, more attractive. But I would also say from a return point of view they should perform better than companies who don't. So, I think that's really how we are seeing green bonds and the quantitative proof is starting to become more and more in line with this philosophical view.

What do you mean by "quantitative proof with regard to performance"?

So, if you look at the green bond index and compare that to a regular fixed income index in Euros—because that's the biggest part of the green bond markets—over the last seven years on average, the green bonds have performed 40 basis points per year better. For corporates it's even as high as 60 basis points. I think this is also triggering less green-focused investors into the market, but I think we should not care about that. In the end, we just want the green capital market to grow, and we also need the regular investors for that.

Do you see an advantage to green bonds versus other sustainable impact asset classes?

I think one of the advantages, of course, is that it's very liquid. If you look at the impact investing space and you have some alternative products in the form of loans or private equity, you can maybe go in and out once a month, if you're lucky. Green bonds are tradable every day, and a lot of pension funds have very big allocations to regular bonds.

So, switching out of regular bonds into green bonds for them is low-hanging fruit. The liquidity aspect is very important here, which is why this is such an attractive instrument compared to those other forms of impact investing.

Are there any inherent risks or downsides to investors with green bonds?

It's a self-labeled market, so there's no formal law at the moment. The European Union is trying to implement regulation for that, but it's not there yet. So, any company can issue green bonds if they have one small green project somewhere. Some additional work must be done to make sure that those green bonds really have a positive impact. For example, there are airports issuing green bonds. Poland's government, heavily dependent on coal and refusing to get into the European Union green deal, has issued quite a lot of green bonds. Also there, a railway company has issued green bonds, while most of what they do is transport fossil fuel. So, that's also one of the risks, that there's greenwashing and you need to allocate the additional resources to be able to filter those less-green bonds out of your portfolio.

So how do you evaluate and quantify the social or environmental impact over the holding period?

Well, I think the challenge is that, in terms of impact measurements, there's not one way of doing it at the moment. There's still quite a lot of debate going on how to do this. I also really want to emphasize that quantitative proof is not the only thing you want as an investor. Because if you look at France, for example, which runs exclusively on nuclear energy and you go to build a windmill there, your CO_2 savings is in general being calculated against the average energy electricity in the country. Nuclear is emitting zero CO_2, but still by building this windmill, I think you're doing something good. We try to quantify as much as we can in our monthly reporting but there's more than just the quantitative proof. I think most investors really want to see the projects. Also, for example building dykes, what we're doing in the Netherlands, it's climate adaption.

Do you have a way you analyze impact that you apply fairly consistently, but that differs from other investors?

So, we have our screening process. At the moment, we buy a bond based on international standards, for example the Climate Bonds Initiative or EU Green Bond Standards, and we apply that as much as possible to select projects which we think are really green. Then, once we have invested our portfolio, we report to our investors what the impact is, based on all the impact reporting we are getting from all those green bond issuers. We aggregate them on the portfolio level. We look at all those numbers critically and align them as much as possible.

But there are lots of challenges, because if you build a windmill, for example, some issuers are calculating the CO_2 savings against an average in a country. Some others are calculating the CO_2 savings compared to, for example, fossil fuels or coal electricity generation, which always looks much better of course. So, there are different ways of calculating it. We always try to streamline them and only include those numbers and methodologies which are credible in our view.

Do you use the same standards each time or do you require that they meet one or more or two or more, or does it depend on the project?

Our own green bond framework is based on all those standards. We pick what we think are the best parts from these standards and put these in our own framework. So, we have parts of the Green Bond Principles, parts of the Climate Bonds Initiative taxonomy and also parts of the EU taxonomy in our framework. But we do not agree with everything that's in those taxonomies. We sometimes have our own views on top of that, and that's how we have created our own green bond framework.

What is greenwashing for you and how does it affect the sector and how do you deal with it?

I think it's really crucial to avoid [investing in any kind of] greenwashing. When a new green bond is being issued and we see from day one that it's not meeting our standards, we flag it as not green and we are not allowed to buy it. Sometimes it also happens that we have a bond in our portfolio which finances windmills, for example, but the company suddenly starts to do something non-green. That can happen. It doesn't happen too often, but the risk, of course, is always there, and a company can also change course. When that happens, we have a formal process in place to start first engaging with the company. If this doesn't help, we downgrade the green bond to non-green and we sell it from our portfolios. You have people screening those green bonds, not only at the moment you're buying them, but also while you have them in the portfolio. You have to remain critical. You have people monitoring how those proceeds are being used, but also what the company is doing.

How do you define whether a company is doing good things? You refer to your standards but what are they? For example, would a generation four nuclear power plant be considered green energy or not?

There are also different views on this, so we work with different external providers to give us input. For example, we work with Sustainalytics, ISS, and MSCI. We use all those sources of inputs for our analysis. By combining all these pieces of information and meeting the issuer in person, we get a fairly good impression of how credible the green bond is and what direction the company is heading. In terms of nuclear energy, it's a bit of a mixed view. We do not invest in companies building new nuclear plants—that is fully excluded from our green bond portfolios. But I would also say that nuclear isn't really bad by definition. I'd rather phase out all coal than shut down all nuclear and build coal plants instead.

How do you actively engage with bond issuers?

I think we have close to 100 meetings a year with green bond issuers. We try to meet all of them at least once every two years, sometimes more often. So, it's a crucial part of our investment process. Meeting them and being able to ask more than just formal questions over the phone or through documentation, you always get a lot of information.

There are a multitude of fixed income labels: green bonds, social bonds, sustainability bonds, sustainability-linked bonds etc. Do you think this increases a risk of confusion or dilution for managers?

Sometimes it's really a nightmare, with all those regulations in Europe coming up. Last year, for our sustainable funds, we had to apply for the Belgium Febelfin label. As an asset manager, it was a lot of work to apply for this label. Now in France we're going through exactly the same exercise. In Europe you have the SFDR classification for funds, so we try to align with that, as well. It almost becomes such a big burden operationally that yes, it takes so much of our time and effort. In the end you can wonder, "Hey, why do we have to be in line with all those different regulations? Can't there be more centralized regulation?"

On top of that, I fully agree with all the different things thrown at us. How do you know what's real and what's not, that could be a risk for the sustainable finance market? So, I've also tried to push back some of the labels which are being invented at the moment. They have the green bond label; but you also have many other sustainable bond labels like a transition bond label. It's ridiculous. So, we also try to stay in the market a little bit in the direction of okay, it's good, but let's not over-innovate because then you push investors away. We have to balance between the two, I think.

What do you see as the most important challenge right now in the green bond space?

It's what we discussed before—the "label mania" as I call it, the over-innovation in the labeled bond market.

"I can't invest in corporate bonds without doing credit analysis. In the same way, I can't invest in them without doing ESG analysis. It's almost like two sides of the same coin, and you shouldn't really detach this."

ESG FIXED INCOME INVESTING
MARK DOWDING
BLUEBAY ASSET MANAGEMENT
BLUEBAY.COM

LI: https://www.linkedin.com/in/mark-dowding-88968b28/

Mark Dowding is Chief Investment Officer of BlueBay Asset Management, LLP. He joined BlueBay in 2010, having previously occupied roles as Head of Fixed Income in Europe at Deutsche Asset Management and Invesco. Dowding, a macro fixed income specialist, meets regularly in that context with global policymakers and has been actively involved in sovereign ESG engagement. He began his career in 1993 as a fixed income portfolio manager, after earning his economics degree at the University of Warwick.

Please provide an overview of BlueBay Asset Management and your role there as CIO.

We're a manager who's running $80 billion in assets. We're owned by the Royal Bank of Canada, RBC, and all we do is fixed income. They're just fixed income strategies and we're distributing those strategies to institutional investors or investors in what we'd call the financial institutions channel, the FIG channel. Our clients are largely corporate pension and wealth managers.

In terms of our geographic footprint of the $80 billion, the vast majority of that is from European clients and to a lesser extent clients in Japan. By contrast, we have about $4–$5 billion of AUM in the USA.

We're running global and regional products. We have strategies that target corporate bonds and government bonds, and others targeting aggregate strategies where we're putting those together. But, in terms of how we break our business up more formally, just north of $50 billion of the total $80 billion is in what we call investment grade fixed income.

Obviously, to generate strong investment returns, you need to have an investment edge. For us that is coming through our proprietary research.

So, our individuals who are working in different sectors are meeting with corporate issuers and the senior management there. Or they're meeting with the policymakers on the sovereign side, in order to discern the future direction of travel and of the intrinsics within what we're trying to uncover within our investment process. ESG analysis is an important part of the analysis that we're doing on all of these alpha sources.

How many funds do you have?

We have something like 120 to 130 funds.

Some of your funds you categorize as "ESG aware" which are not necessarily constrained by ESG factors, and you have other funds that are much more ESG oriented and incorporate more exclusionary practices. Can you explain this?

The way that we've approached this is that we fully embraced ESG integration a number of years ago. We're incorporating ESG analysis as a formal part of our analysis of every investment decision. When I speak about these alpha sources, you'll see 1,500 to 1,600 of these alpha sources across our platform. These are individual investment decisions that we can make. You can think of these as very granular components that we can then apply to different products that we manufacture using different product designs.

For all of these alpha sources, there is a full ESG analysis undertaken on all of the issuers that we're investing in—a full ESG checklist and an audit on everything that we do in this space. That's because we believe passionately about the role of ESG in every investment position that we're taking.

Now when it comes to taking those decisions and then building investment products, those products are built around product designs. We can say that any BlueBay product is fully incorporating ESG integration within it and is adhering to a minimum list of exclusions, including things like bans on controversial weapons. But then, in terms of where we are imposing additional constraints, this is really more of a case of what we want to incorporate into this particular product design that we have.

We have some strategies that stop where I've just left it, where we've just done the ESG integration. And we don't have additional constraints which are embodied, all the way through to other strategies, where we are imposing constraints at a sector level.

So, for example, in investment grade most of our strategies will be Article 8[3] and here we don't have any tobacco [company bonds in the portfolio]. The way that we rank all of our issuers on a proprietary basis is on a scale from very low ESG risk to very high ESG risk. We're formally excluding anything that screens as very high ESG risk from those Article 8 funds that we have in investment grade. Here we are also imposing constraints in other areas like emerging markets, because so many of the issuers that we have as part of the benchmark actually come out as very high risk. It's actually difficult to have that same methodology apply to those emerging market funds because you couldn't really manage to that particular benchmark. In this case, clients have said, "We'd like you to demonstrate, on average, if you've got a better ESG profile than the benchmark has got." We've got other requirements [and considerations] that we're seeking to deliver there.

I can also extend this all the way through to what we're doing in terms of ESG-focused products, where we're incorporating far more exclusions—whether it's sort of a Paris Climate Accord list and various other criteria that we're signing up to in ESG labeled products, all the way through to our impact strategy which is a true Article 9[4] strategy where we obviously try to measure the impact that we're delivering to investors who are motivated by making those differences and a change.

I think the philosophy here is we want to be able to deliver any fixed income product to any client in a way that meets their needs and requirements. We're wanting to make sure that ESG thinking is part of every investment decision, because we think that we'll make better investment decisions. But when it comes to the individual product design itself, this is really a question for a client. If a client wants to exclude certain things, they're at liberty to do so. We are aware that it's not a one-size-fits-all approach.

So, you view ESG risk as an essential risk across the board?

I can't invest in corporate bonds without doing credit analysis. In the same way, I can't invest in them without doing ESG analysis. It's almost like two sides of the same coin, and you shouldn't really detach this.

I'd also say that philosophically it speaks to how we've set ourselves up at BlueBay. When we started in ESG, the dedicated ESG team doing the ESG audits and coming up with the ESG framework that we were applying to issuers was actually set up as a separate function that reported within the risk team. There was almost a philosophy that you were thinking about ESG risk.

But, a few years back, we actually said, no, this is actually the wrong way of thinking about ESG. ESG is an investment function. It needs to be treated as an investment function and be completely and fully imbedded and intertwined within everything you're doing in the context of your investment process.

You invest in all kinds of bonds and not necessarily just green bonds?

I mean green bonds do have a place; they're an interesting issuance. But we think they're only interesting issues where they are being effectively used to finance projects and initiatives which otherwise would not have taken place if that issuance had not taken place. So, if we're able to ringfence proceeds, if we're able to identify the projects that are being financed as a result of green bond issuance, we think that they're valid investments. But when you have certain large, developed countries issuing green bonds, we actually feel as if that's a real dumbing-down in a disappointing way of what green bonds are. Because if you're a government borrower like the UK or Germany, you could issue a green bond. But all you're really doing is you're making the rest of your issuance more brown. It's not clear to us that the green bond issuance in and of itself is actually driving you to deliver a policy that otherwise wouldn't really have occurred.

We think it sort of dumbs-down the asset class and we've spoken out against this. We think that this is massively missing out on the really big opportunity in ESG and sustainable investing, which is intrinsically for us as stewards of capital to really use our influence in order to drive an agenda of some change both at a corporate and a sovereign level.

So for me, a lot of this is what you achieve through engagement. I think that a proactive engagement is something that interests us a lot more in the context of ESG. What really should matter more is what is in store in terms of future behavior.

BlueBay unusually uses the power of shorting to drive corporate behavior change by aggressively selling against an issuer and shorting their bond. How are you doing this?

Ultimately, we don't own the equity and we don't have voting rights. But we are able to make clear our thoughts to borrowers in terms of issuer performance in ESG. We can really articulate how we feel if, for example, there are issuers who are paying no attention to their ESG performance and they take a somewhat arrogant approach to this. And, as well as having the carrot to reward those issuers doing the right thing, by buying their debt and allocating capital in their direction, we also have the ability in a number of our strategies to actually use a stick as well as a carrot and to actually express our displeasure at what we see as poor ESG performance. When we identify truly bad ESG performance, we think that is going to be a catalyst for that issuer to underperform its peers and there's an opportunity for us actually to generate investment performance by looking at spreads going wider for those issuers who are performing poorly from an ESG perspective.

An example of this is a couple of years back we were meeting with Saudi Arabia as an issuer. At the time Saudi Arabia was not a very common issuer in bond markets. Saudi has always had lots of assets and lots of money, and no need whatsoever to raise debt. As reserves became depleted with low oil prices and large fiscal deficits, they needed to tap the markets and they conducted investor meetings.

When they did, one of the things we were quizzing them about was their performance from an ESG perspective, in terms of their carbon-based economy and based on their treatment of minorities within the country, the issues of women's rights and other concerns that we had. At the time, I think it was fair to say that it felt like we were given very short shrift and we were laughed out of the room. The intrinsic message was "Who do you think you are? We're Saudi Arabia, you're just BlueBay. Who are you to be giving us a lecture?"

As we left that meeting, our reflection was that if that was the message that other investors were going to be hearing, we questioned whether there would be as many people queuing up to buy the debt of Saudi Arabia. We thought that there would be a real opportunity for the credit spread to move wider. At the time, we could buy credit default swaps (CDS) on Saudi Arabia at a spread of 65 basis points on a five-year maturity. We purchased close to a billion dollars' worth at 65 basis points and closed that less than a year later at a spread of 165 basis points. We'd made a gain with the credit spread moving wider by 100 basis points, through that particular period.

That generated a positive investment return for us but it also led us to have subsequent meetings with Saudi Arabia as an issuer who came back to us and said "Actually, a lot of people are talking about this ESG thing. Can you educate us a bit more? We want to listen; we want to engage. We will have a dialogue."

I think it's fair to say that what we've seen over the course of the last few years is quite a material change in behavior on the part of Saudi as an issuer and as a country. Although I would discern that looking through my eyes, it still has a very long way to go, the delta in terms of the change [we've witnessed] in the last couple of years has been quite material. It's actually gone quite a long way in quite a short space of time in the grand scheme of things.

And so, having given Saudi at one point the very worst ESG rating, more recently we've actually lifted it up in terms of the internal ESG score we'd be allocating to Saudi. So, we would be more inclined to be long of Saudi rather than short of Saudi, as an issuer at this particular time.

I think it's an interesting anecdote, and I don't want to overstate our influence on their behavior. But I think it speaks to how we can identify opportunities to seek to educate, change issuer behavior, and generate returns for our investors in the process.

Describe how you engage with sovereigns.

We're having a dialogue with all sovereigns, large and small. But your ability to have more leverage obviously applies much more readily to smaller sovereigns than it does very big sovereigns. Clearly, if you have sovereigns where borrowing costs are more stressed or more elevated, they're more likely to listen to what you have to say, than those where their borrowing costs are very cheap.

In the context of how we're engaging, I guess the first thing to say is we will be meeting the issuance agencies with one-on-one meetings. They'll have road shows but we'll have one-on-one meetings with the representatives of different sovereign issuers as they're bringing bonds to market, so we have a regular dialogue here.

Secondly, that leads to ad-hoc dialogue and exchange of information. For example, we write quite a lot of content at BlueBay, and policymakers are on the distribution list. They'll ask us questions and we'll give our views and thoughts and opinions. There'll be an active two-way dialogue around themes that we see.

Thirdly, I'd say that where we might want to lobby, we're doing so in public media, in the press, or by signing up to bond holder groups or action groups to bring attention to certain issues. Last year for example, we joined a group which was protesting deforestation and treatment of indigenous people in Brazil, and we wrote an article on this which was published in the FT (*Financial Times of London*). We're also putting articles in the Brazilian press on the back of that. So, I was sitting in my garden last year and I got a call from the Deputy Governor of the Central Bank of Brazil saying, "What is BlueBay doing criticizing us in the press? We want to have a dialogue. We're going to set up a task force to look at deforestation and indigenous people's rights." A number of the visiting cabinet members were going to be part of that task force and they wanted BlueBay to participate on that task force. There were other stakeholders they invited as well.

It's an example of how by taking a public position, by speaking out on issues that you feel matter, you can punch above your weight. And you'll get a bit of a hearing which will get you access and give you the opportunity to be part of the dialogue.

Can you point to any concrete result in this case of Brazil?

It's still ongoing; there are certain measures that the Brazilian authorities are still working on. Let's be honest with ourselves, we're talking about a big, big problem here and we're not in a position to be able to fix it. Part of the view here is if there's enough pressure in the right direction then we will see change take place over time. If we're the only voice who's trying to do this, I'm not sure we will get very far. The more investors that are pushing this sort of agenda, the more we have the opportunity to deliver this change. Obviously with smaller sovereigns, some of this is, in a way, easier to affect.

Can ESG sovereign ringfencing really exist within the treasury of a country?

In some cases it may be ringfenced. But the question with the green bonds is whether the green issuance, even if it's being ringfenced, are you financing a project which would never have taken place if they hadn't had the green bond issue? I tend to be fairly skeptical about this, but I think that most of these projects would happen regardless of whether you had issued a green bond or not.

I'm not sure whether the green bonds themselves are really playing the role that you'd want to see them play. A lot of time, I see that when you've got clients who want to invest in green bond funds, green bonds will trade at a premium—lower borrowing costs than traditional bonds.

Obviously, investment banks will speak to issuers and say, "You need to have a green bond and you can look good by being green and have lower borrowing costs. You've got to issue a green bond." And someone says, "Oh yeah, that's a good idea. I'll have some of that," and the ringfencing of any proceeds is an afterthought.

I'm being a little bit damning here, partly because people are allocating green capital to those sorts of issues when that capital should be going to things that make more of a difference.

Give an overview of the first impact-aligned bond fund that you launched this year.

This is an Article 9 strategy fund that we've launched. The framework was mapped out of the UN SDG framework. From that, we've tried to hone down into specific themes and specific assets which we can measure.

We see a real demand on the part of investors to be able to invest in strategies which are making a measurable difference and change. One of the problems with a lot of the impact bond strategies to date is that they are investing in employment markets and they're not particularly scalable in terms of what they can deliver. They're more of a niche and don't really fit the needs of a lot of investors who need to invest in open-ended, UCITS type strategies.

We thought that in terms of looking at things like the UN SDGs, we can pick out specific themes that we want to be able to manage to and deliver, and then map individual assets in terms of their ability to meet and attain those themes. For example, we've got themes like enabling a circular economy, ensuring clean and plentiful water, promoting clean and safe energy, or promoting sustainable mobility and infrastructure. These are themes that we might have, and then we're looking for individual assets that we can map to that particular theme.

So that's what we're looking to do in this particular strategy. It's a corporate bond strategy and it's not managed to a particular benchmark. It's investing in high-yield issuers as well as investment grade issuers. That's because often, some of the smaller companies which are up and coming in some of these developing areas of technology tend to be companies with less robust balance sheets—which will sit more within the sub-investment grade space.

We feel that we've built a very strong and robust ESG framework. And, in terms of mapping assets in this way and measuring the output that they deliver, we have a very credible, very interesting impact-aligned strategy that can meet the needs and requirements of a growing number of investors that we have.

"No one asks, 'Do you do ESG?' anymore. They don't even say, 'How do you do ESG?' They want to know what's the carbon footprint of the portfolio. Where's it going? All these SDGs . . . which one does this tick in the questionnaire? Investors are much more sophisticated."

SUSTAINABLE FIXED INCOME
MITCH REZNICK, CFA
FEDERATED HERMES
HERMES-INVESTMENT.COM

Mitch Reznick is the Head of Research & Sustainable Fixed Income and Co-Manager of the Federated Hermes SDG Engagement High Yield Credit Fund. He has over 23 years of specialized experience in the corporate credit industry, was previously Co-Head of Credit Research at Fortis Investments, and worked in the leveraged finance group at Moody's Investors Service. He has a Master's in International Affairs from Columbia University, a Bachelor's in History from Pitzer College, and is a CFA® charterholder.

Reznick is Co-Chair of the Federated Hermes Sustainability Investment Centre; a founding member of the Executive Committee for the European Leveraged Finance Association (ELFA); Co-Chair of the Credit Risk and Ratings Advisory Committee at the UN Principles for Responsible Investment (PRI); and serves on the CFO Taskforce for the United Nations Global Compact (UNGC). He's also a member of the Target Setting Workstream at the Institutional Investors Group on Climate Change (IIGCC), and a member of the Technical Working Group (Communications and Technology) for the U.S.-based Sustainability Accounting Standards Board (SASB).

Formerly, Reznick was Co-Chair of the Capital Markets Advisory Committee of the IFRS Foundation; a member of the Sovereign Working Group (PRI); a workstream member of the UK-China Green Finance Task Force; and served on the Green Finance Advisory of the City of London.

Are ESG principles applied across everything Federated Hermes is doing?

For us at the international business, if you break things down into the EU's Sustainable Finance Framework (SFDR) articles, everything starts with Article 8 where there's a demonstrable and credible ESG integration. That's everything that we do. From there, we create sustainable-themed strategies by layering social and environmental objectives onto traditional financial objectives. As such, seeking a combination of financial and social/environmental outcomes governs these sustainable-themed strategies—like our SDG Engagement High Yield Fund. It's cumulative, right? Everything [at the international business of Federated Hermes] is Article 8 and then you take that extra step of an additional nonfinancial objective. For us, that is the transition point where ESG-integrated pivots at the union of these two investment objectives.

Can you explain to me why ESG results in improved credit spreads?

Well, to begin, through quantitative studies, we observe a statistically significant relationship between credit spreads and ESG strength. However, before jumping to that, let's discuss the investment philosophy that led us to run the quantitative studies. We believe these nonfundamental factors—just like fundamentals such as operating and financial factors—impact cash flows. As such, they therefore have an impact on enterprise value, and thus have an impact on the credit risk of a business. Therein lies the direct link between nonfundamental factors and credit risk and thus credit spreads. This implies that as credit investors we are compelled to fully integrate ESG factors into the investment process.

Before we launched the first quantitative study, we observed this anecdotally, but wanted some quantitative evidence because we wanted to create some precision around pricing ESG risks. At the time of the first study, we didn't see anything in the market that provided this information, so we decided, "right, let's do it ourselves." We have in-house a quantitative assessment of ESG quality, they're called QESG scores. Using this QESG score as a reflection of ESG strength and credit spreads as a reflection of credit risk, we ran a historical study to understand the relationship between the two. What we use for credit spreads is credit default swaps (CDS), because CDS allows you to sterilize the credit spreads from the effects of bond math: convexity and duration. It's a pure five-year credit spread that rolls every six months. We applied regression analysis, to see that a relationship existed between ESG quality and credit spreads. The weaker the ESG factors, the wider the credit spreads. Well, one could say, "okay, maybe that's just a coincidence, the fact that companies who happen to be higher quality credit companies just happen to be good on ESG factors."

To deal with that concern, we controlled for credit quality as per credit ratings, to assess whether a correlation exists between ESG concerns and credit ratings. We found that although a significant positive correlation existed, there was also a very wide dispersion of QESG scores or ESG quality in each rating bucket, meaning that the credit ratings alone don't sufficiently explain ESG quality. So, the results compel you to look at ESG factors in addition to traditional fundamental analysis. Investors should be mindful that an issuer's ESG performance could look very different from its credit rating.

We took the results and created an innovative and pioneering pricing model, where we built an implied credit curve based on ESG quality, helping investors to price ESG risk.

So, ESG analysis matters because of credit risk. But credit risk—default and recovery—can vary greatly within a company. This is because companies often have multiple credit securities to choose from, and each of these will have a different default risk and recovery profile because of where they sit in the debt capital stack; what the maturity profile is and what type of security it is. The more precision we have when making that decision about security type—i.e., volatility contribution to any given fund—the better informed we are when making that investment decision. The integration of ESG factors provides a little bit more information and precision. We can have a better sense of uncertainty and if we feel good about it, then we can take more volatility contribution and more risk than we normally would. It's not just own the name or don't own the name.

A question often asked, is how can we show that this analysis has an impact on returns for our clients? This was an issue we debated about seven years ago in our internal Credit Committee. We understood from academic and meta studies and anecdotally that this all matters, but we questioned whether anyone had tried to price this risk. We went out to the market and didn't see that anyone had really made an earnest attempt to price ESG risks. We thought, okay, well, let's just try to do it ourselves.

So, does this mean everyone is now pricing in ESG risk like you? Or are they coming to the same conclusion from a more traditional risk assessment perspective?

I think it's difficult for me to comment on how much of the market is pricing ESG risk in the way we have. There have been a handful of studies that have been done mostly by the sell-side and academics and us. Deploying that in a practical way can probably be more challenging if you don't have everything in-house.

However, it's quite clear that ESG integration is now mainstream. No investor who's serious in the market is not going to have a pretty robust ESG integration approach. We have our own scores in-house, but there are a lot of vendors externally scoring companies on their ESG performance and there are many ways for investors to use those scores and build their own analysis.

The reality is that our clients want this, too. I mean, no one asks, "Do you do ESG?" anymore. They don't even just say, "How do you do ESG?" Clients and prospects are much more sophisticated. For example, many want to understand what the carbon footprint of the portfolio is and where it's going. That's what's driving investors, us, and our competitors to being demonstrably more sophisticated about ESG integration. Clients care about these non-financial factors and outcomes because they know that at a minimum, the impact on returns is neutral, but they more than likely make you a better and more informed investor. That's what our studies show.

Introduce the SDG Engagement High Yield Credit Fund that you co-manage.

The fund was launched in October 2019. It was a global launch as a 40 Act in the United States [registered under the U.S. Investment Company Act of 1940] and UCITS [Undertakings for Collective Investment in Transferable Securities Directive, a consolidated EU directive allowing collective investment schemes to operate freely throughout the EU on the basis of a single authorization from one member state]. It started out at about $125 million and now in Q3 2021, it's just shy of $1.6 billion.

From an investment point of view, the fund is straightforward. It's a long-only, high-yield credit fund with an investment objective to outperform a mainstream high-yield index. In addition to that, its objective is to invest in companies that will deliver positive change in society and the environment, with engagement being the catalyst to facilitate that change. In that sense, it has a Laggard to Leaders feel to it. It's an impact fund and classed as "Article 9" in SFDR terms. The leaders are already well on their way, and we think that there's a link between performance and delivering into those sustainable objectives.

So, what we love about the Sustainable Development Goals is they are becoming a *lingua franca*, a normalized taxonomy for us to reclassify the myriad of sustainable environmental and social issues. You can pour water over these issues, and they'll drop into any one of these 17 goals, which makes it a lot easier to have discussion and discourse and to assess, measure, track, and report on sustainability progression. They're incredibly useful from that point of view. You can remap sustainability issues, the environmental and social of ESG, into these 17 sustainable goals.

What kind of issuances are you investing in?

The great thing about this fund is we are not a forced buyer of any security, because it is not tied to a specific security theme. From a technical point of view, in the high-yield space, there isn't a plethora of those labeled securities [i.e., explicitly labelled "Green Bonds" or "Sustainability Linked Bonds" (SLB)] at this point and the ones that do come to market can be questionable in terms of the use-of-proceeds. Having said that, we do own a handful of those labelled securities in the portfolio, but only insofar as they make sense from the two investment objectives: deliver financial returns and facilitate a company delivering into the SDGs.

For us, what really matters is how a company is performing at the corporate level as it affects the entire capital structure. For that reason, we like ambitious sustainability-linked bonds because they keep a company on track to hit overarching sustainability objectives. Whether or not we own that specific security in the capital structure depends on factors such as its value, liquidity profile availability.

Are there inherent risks to your investors apart from the market risks that any traditional bond fund is exposed to?

There are two key risks or downsides to all sustainable investors: "greenwashing" and "greeniums." A greenium is a pricing advantage to the company of a security that is derived from the labelling of the security. It's a pricing advantage over non-labelled obligations of identical profile for which the credit risk is the same as that labelled security. Greeniums exist in the market; they have been observed in different credit markets and at different levels. One could argue that investors are willing to pay for the greenium because labelled securities have some additional benefits to mainstream securities, for example, they tend to be less volatile and therefore have a relatively better risk-adjusted return profile and, if credible, the labelled security should be financing positive change.

Currently, the greeniums that exist are very small. I don't believe that there is a holistic repricing or even alarming repricing of credit risk at this point.

The discount becomes a little bit wider when you are looking at carbon-intensive businesses. However, this can partially be explained by the fact that within a diversified portfolio, access to a fossil fuel company might only be via the green bond of a fossil fuel company. Also, carbon-intensive businesses are typically a lower credit quality, triple B. So, the six basis points in a triple B is about as meaningful as maybe one or two basis points for a double-A. Investors have to look at these greeniums in a relative way rather than notional. Either way, it's important to avoid being a forced buyer of any security.

Then there's the greenwashing component. It runs the risk of destroying the credibility of the market itself, but most are well aware of that. In my view, the challenge centers around the authenticity of a company's transition implied by the green or sustainability bond. With greenwashing of an issuance, investors can be led to believe a company will succeed and the transition is beneficial to the credit risk of the business. However, they could be at risk of loss because greenwashing has misguided them as to the credibility of its sustainability objective which was bought into as an alpha story.

The sustainable investment universe is in its nascency, but with many companies rushing to declare net-zero or sustainability, investors must assess the probability and timeframe of those objectives being achieved.

When it comes to green bonds and greenwashing, it is important for investors to understand that some green bonds issued haven't been specific use-of-proceeds bonds. Some have been used to refinance mainstream bonds and therefore the capital raised was not directed toward a specific green project. However, in some cases, the company itself had strong, green credentials.

How do you guard against greenwashing?

Internal investment frameworks are an important tool to protect from greenwashing and allow investors to assess specific labelling in a sophisticated way. Skilled managers will also know the right questions to ask management and where to put pressure if necessary. Managers need the knowledge and expertise to test the credibility and credulity of the issuers that are in the market. That's driven by human capital, passion, training, and experience.

How do you judge whether the penalty step-up mechanisms are correct?

So, a step-up is a feature of sustainability-linked bonds, and it refers to a mechanism whereby the coupon payment on the SLB "steps up" if certain sustainability goals are not met by a certain date. In SLB terms, they are referred to as KPIs (key performance indicators) and SPTs (sustainability performance targets). At present, the step-up components are very diverse, however some norms are forming.

For example, an investment-grade issuer, high-yield bond issuer may have a bond with a 25-basis points step-up on a bond with a coupon of sub 1 percent. So, the question we ask is whether 25 basis points is an appropriate step-up for a bond with a 4 or 5 percent coupon that you might see on a high yield issuer. In my opinion, relative to the size of the coupon, that 25 basis points on a high coupon bond is not punitive enough. It doesn't convey the level of confidence that you would expect to see from a company.

We're observing all sustainability-linked bonds that come into the market to better understand what the right coupon size should be. In my own view, I think a floor should be established relative to the base coupon which can vary because of the prevailing level of interest rates. The market seems to be consolidated around 25 basis points in total, not even per KPI, but I believe that step-ups should rise as coupon size rises.

Can these SDG related step-ups effectively create perverse incentives for investors betting that the issuer isn't going to hit their SDG targets?

Cynically, you could argue that investors would want companies to miss their performance targets in order to earn more from the step-up. I would argue that if the company is failing on the sustainability targets, they have bigger issues that could have an eclipsing and negative effect on sustainability progress and credit risk.

What's your opinion on transition bonds?

Transition bonds were created, like many financial instruments including the sustainability-linked bonds, in some engine room of an investment bank. They are, essentially, green bonds issued by "brown" or carbon-intensive companies. Like green bonds they are "use of proceeds" in character, but it is hard to sell a green bond from a carbon-intensive company, even one in transition.

Labelled bonds are an important part of the market, but they're neither entirely good nor entirely bad. In this continuum between credible and substantial labeling, where do they sit? For me, I don't have a strong view but again, what I care about is a company's intention and authenticity. Understanding a company's objectives and trajectory is of much greater importance than the label of the bond.

With such secular change in the economy, particularly in response to the climate crisis, there will always be winners and losers. Stimulus such as the European recovery plan and President Biden's infrastructure bill have demonstrated that change is being driven from the top-down at the policymaker level as well as bottom-up from corporations and investors. Companies with the willingness and ability to transition in this environment will be the ones that benefit.

Who are your primary investors, and have you observed any changes in the investor mix over the years, not just in the SDG Engagement High Yield Credit Fund but also in your ESG fixed income funds?

Over time our investors have changed from being ESG aware to ESG focused to ESG determined. One driver behind this is the elevated media focus on ESG, whether it's from a financial performance or an allocation point of view. Additionally, we see changing demographics contributing to this shift and the recognition that ESG factors are an enhancement to the investment process, from both a risk management point-of-view and as a performance driver.

Many exogenous forces are having a real impact, such as regulation, stewardship codes, and what I would call trade groups. For example, the Net-Zero Asset Owners Alliance—one of many trade groups creating momentum particularly in certain thematic areas such as climate change and biodiversity, demonstrating a shift from ESG integration to purposeful capital.

What's the most important challenge facing the sustainable fixed income space at this time?

Greenwashing. I fear that is rising because sustainability is "hot" right now. There are some in every corner of the capital markets that take a superficial approach to sustainability to exploit the opportunity. If these shift from the few to the many, it could undermine the credibility of those with substance in their approach to sustainability and ESG.

Data is also a major challenge. The reality is that for smaller companies and private companies there is a dearth of data to quickly and efficiently build a sustainability profile for a company. The data is dated and a little bit stale, whereas investing is forward-looking. The variation in ESG assessments for any given issue can vary widely, which is why overreliance on these services could lead to suboptimal outcomes.

Also, most sustainability data is mapped to equity tickers. This probably sounds a little bit esoteric, but it is sometimes tough to map that data to the actual bond-issuing entity. For example, sometimes climate data of a private, high yield company is mapped to the private equity fund that owns the company. That is the wrong connection to make but the PE firm is not the issuer of the data. This is why it is really important to have a proprietary, credible approach. Human capital is required.

What do you know now about sustainable fixed income investing that you wish you had known in 2010, when you showed up at Federated Hermes?

How to create more precision in the risk assessment process and to assess what the most material factors are in each sector. To not be spoon-fed but to know these factors from my own experience. Understanding the materiality of factors, knowing the right questions to ask and how to weigh those in an investment framework. Having a much better feel for what are the most important, the most material factors, by sector, and knowing how to convert that into investment thinking.

"The tenets of *Shari'ah* compliance are where SRI began; it was an awareness of aligning investments with a values approach. It covers the 'S' part of ESG, incorporates governance, and has an explicit financial component. So, it's like 'ESGF.'"

ISLAMIC FINANCE
PATRICK DRUM
SATURNA CAPITAL
SATURNA.COM
LI: https://www.linkedin.com/in/patrick-t-drum-cfa-cfp-mba-a000354/

Patrick T. Drum leads the Environmental, Social & Governance investment research at Saturna Capital, a private investment management firm with $5.5 billion in assets under management.

He is the portfolio manager for Saturna's Sustainable Global Fixed Income Fund; the Amana Participation Fund (the oldest and largest family of funds in the United States following principles of Islamic finance), and the firm's institutional subsidiary, Saturna Sdn. Berhad in Kuala Lumpur, Malaysia.

Drum holds a BA in economics from Western Washington University and an MBA from Seattle University Albers School of Business and is a CFA® Charterholder and Certified Financial Planner®. Previously, Drum was Chairman of the United Nation's Principles for Investment (UNPRI) Fixed Income Outreach Subcommittee and an adjunct professor of finance for the Sustainable MBA Program at Pinchot's Bainbridge Graduate Institute.

What is your role at Saturna Capital?

I'm the portfolio manager of the Amana Participation Fund which is a *Shari'ah* compliant bond fund. I also run a multicurrency sustainable conventional bond fund which doesn't adhere to Sharia compliance standards but does have some similar characteristics such as not investing in companies that derive more than 5 percent of their revenues from alcohol and the industrial military complex.

Approximately half of your investors in your *Shari'ah* compliant Islamic investment funds are non-Muslims. What attracts them?

It is really the performance and, interestingly enough, a bit of happenstance—the by-product of the tenets of the faith, meaning low leverage and strong governance. These attributes lead us to invest in industries that demonstrate strong performance and then running the fund's sustainably aligned investment selection. So, for example, everybody seems to own Apple, but our cost basis on Apple is below a dollar because we bought it so long ago. That's because *Shari'ah* compliance leans us toward certain industries such as technology, healthcare, and other industries that have strong balance sheet characteristics, such as low leverage and fiscal flexibility in conjunction with a strong earnings outlook.

And as a result, those industries have been experiencing favorable and strong performance over a long period of time. Our funds have thirty-year track history, and we tend to have less draw-down during the equity [market] pullbacks. It's a little bit less volatile because of the lower leverage, and these attributes have screened favorably among consultants and advisors.

What percent of your AUM is Halal (run according to Islamic principles)?

Of our $5.5 billion AUM, it's about 90 percent. It's the bulk of our businesses. We're a no-load mutual fund that was launched in the 1980s. Because of its low cost and easy access, it's always been an easy venue for investors.

How does SRI fit into this?

Through the Western lens, ESG was founded by the Methodists, in particular John Wesley. He was a Methodist clergyman who started that very first venue into sustainability through negative screening by avoiding certain industries. But interestingly, I would tend to argue that the tenets of *Shari'ah* compliance are really where early SRI began, because it was an awareness of aligning investments with a values approach. Among some of its basic tenets are that you can't own pork, pornography, or any sort of the *haram* (forbidden) behaviors that adhere to that faith. There's a modesty/prudence type of aspect to it.

What are the principles of Islamic or *Shari'ah* compliance investing?

Shari'ah compliance includes both negative screens with a soft positive screen. *Shari'ah* compliance is that you can't make money off of money, also known as *Riba* or *Gharar* (uncertainty, hazards, risk). But also, you can't have too much leverage, so we use the debt-to-market cap for anything and that has to be below 34 percent. So, essentially the approach is [a universe of] large companies that are not levered and we do a kind of management review that incorporates the tenets of the *Shari'ah* compliance.

One of the key tenets of a positive screen is the alignment of interests, so *Shari'ah* compliance is heavily bent on what is known as risk-sharing. What I mean by risk-sharing is that there's both a sharing of the profits but also the losses. And philosophically, that's where the usury aspect comes into it, or *Gharar,* which reflects gambling. That's *Haram*, meaning it's prohibited. *Halal* is approved or appropriate and consistent with the faith. So, usury or earning interest off interest or using money for money growth has always been an adverse attribute to the Islamic faith. From an equity screening standpoint, that's why we have companies with low leverage. You can have leverage and we use the mark which tends to be standard, which is about 34 percent. So, debt to market cap has to have on the equity side less than 34 percent on a trailing 12-month basis.

You can't have large cash excesses earning interest. So, we look at those types of aspects but also we are looking at the negative screening, meaning certain industries that we know that are excluded, like pork and so forth that we cannot own. And then we've extended that to industries like the military/war complex, very much in similar lines to the Methodists; the sustainable attributes that John Wesley was pointing to, "what we should not do." The Islamic faith had that normative aspect, but then also incorporated a financial component.

Those are the basic tenets. It incorporates a social element that I've highlighted, the governance, the considerations of what is appropriate to make a profit. But it also considers how the investment impacts that community as well.

Can you summarize how *Shari'ah* compliance aligns with SRI?

The tenets of *Shari'ah* compliance are where SRI began; it was an awareness of aligning investments with a values approach. It covers the "S" part of ESG, incorporates governance, and has an explicit financial component. So, it's like "ESGF." That's why I would tend to argue that the Islamic faith has a much longer history of the sustainable attributes that John Wesley was pointing to; that norm of "what we should not do." The Islamic faith has that normative aspect but also incorporates a financial component, and this all goes back to the Koran.

I am not a *Shari'ah* adviser. My job is to honor and adhere to these principles. I look for guidance when in doubt, but more importantly, my job is purely portfolio management and to be that steward.

What's the difference between traditional bonds and the Islamic fixed income equivalents?

A *Sukuk* is an Islamic financial certificate, similar to a bond in Western finance and it provides an undivided ownership in an asset. It can be a hard asset or it could be services, but you're having an ownership interest in this asset and you are sharing the risks as well as the profits.

There are four tenets that qualify and distinguish a *Sukuk* from a fixed income instrument. The first is a risk sharing component, meaning you're sharing the losses as well as the profits. Under the *Shari'ah* standards, there is a pass through of losses to the holder and that is a structuring tenet that adheres to the faith. The bonds are structured and look and act like bonds, so that they get that broad distribution and acceptance by typical bond holders like ourselves. It has a typical credit rating and stated maturity just like a bond, but *Sukuk* are structured to act and look like fixed income.

The second thing is that you're actually an asset owner, not a debt obligator. So as an investor, you are an owner of an asset and typically there is specific identification of what assets you're owning.

Underlying that, the third tenet is that there can't be any guarantees, and this is a really important aspect because even though we have a stated coupon, the issuer cannot make a guarantee of the coupon payment or a return of principle. That ties back to the very first tenet of risk sharing. Even though it's structured as such, it's not a promissory legal contract and the aim and convention is that it works as such, but it can't be guaranteed by the issuer.

Lastly, and what's a distinguishing aspect, is that it has to go through what is known as a *Fatwa* which is a formalized religious review by *Shari'ah* scholars. In that review, they go through a discerning process of making sure the structure, the issue, and the issuer's activities are considered *Halal*, meaning they're in the alignment with *Shari'ah* standards and principles. That in itself is what distinguishes it. And to most it's like, well, that's soft and not profound in difference. But those subtle details because of that religious review, the sharing of principles of the assets, and no guarantees is what makes *Sukuk* separate from bonds.

How do you screen *Sukuks* for *Shari'ah* compliance?

Because Saturna Capital has been involved in *Shari'ah* screening for a long time, we built our own proprietary screening process nearly three decades ago, which we still employ today. This was before any kind of quantitative modeling had been employed from an investment standpoint and is what's been our driving source in process.

On the equity side, we have to make that discernment of whether that issuer meets those standards of *Shari'ah* compliance by a quantitative approach, the soft approach, the social aspects, and the normative of exclusion that I highlighted. With a *Sukuk*, it's a bit different in that I'll look at the prospectus and the very first thing that I'll look for is whether or not it's gone through a *Fatwa*, and whether that *Fatwa* says it's compliant, which to me is good.

Even with our long-standing Shari'ah screening processes, Saturna Capital employs the services of a Shari'ah adviser to provide a review, a *Fatwa*, for added assurance of compliance to Islamic principles.

What is *Murabaha*?

Murabaha has all the attributes of a certificate of deposit, but it doesn't pay interest. It's a cost-plus markup with a negotiated rate of return. It's like a bank deposit in every form and fashion. But it's *Shari'ah* compliant so that upon maturity, I get a certain markup in return of capital that represents an implied interest rate, which typically is very close to conventional benchmarks, such as a LIBOR rate plus some added spread based upon the offering institution.

I've heard references to green *Sukuk*. In what way does this differ from traditional *Sukuk*?

Green *Sukuk* can be described as a faith-based investment with ESG. So, it's covering three zones because a green bond appeals to an investor with an alignment to the environment, but a *Shari'ah Sukuk* represents a trifecta of attracting and appealing to a faith-based element, an investment-based element, and an environmental or ESG sustainable element. So, they're actually kind of attracting three different market priority participants that extend beyond just investment, or investment in environmental, to investment, environmental, and faith.

But it's a very small market . . . like 1 percent of the entire *Sukuk* market. I own a few in my Sustainable Bond Fund and what I found is that the Malaysian Ringgit-denominated green *Sukuk* do not experience the "greenium" performance characteristics that we see currently observed in other green bond markets, such as the euro or U.S. dollar. But the U.S. dollar denominated green *Sukuk* tend to exhibit both primary and secondary enhanced performance metrics.

How do your returns compare with a traditional bond fund or fixed income?

When I go against the world bond, in the way I manage the fund in this prospectus design, I am either number one or number 99. It's because I'm [competing] against emerging markets that tend to be highly levered, high yield, non-U.S. dollar and U.S. dollar. For example, the Amana Participation Fund earned a five-star rating right after the pandemic lock-down started and was ranked number one for about six months out of my universe of 200 funds. And then the recovery trade occurred, and I slowly lost that.

Philosophically, I'm not really trying to aim for the fences in returns. I'm aiming for singles and doubles, I'm aiming for capital preservation, competitive rates. I tend to typically underperform that benchmark quite dramatically during certain periods, because of their duration and concentration differences.

Is there any kind of consensus among Muslim investors on climate change?

Consensus among any community is going to be hard, but my observation is there has been a transition. 2014 was a warning shot across the bow to that entire Middle Eastern community about the importance of diversification—in particular because their entire economy is oil dependent. From 2014 to 2015, the price of oil got as high as $107 a barrel and as low as $26 and their economics changed materially. Following this collapse of oil prices, GCC members turned to the capital markets as a means to supplement government funding gaps. So, they've emphasized diversification and also from an energy perspective. Because with their population growth they can't keep up with the energy consumption, so diversification has been a high priority.

Part of that is an economic and social restructuring, to move their economies away from heavy dependence on hydrocarbons. I would argue there's always going to be an emphasis on hydrocarbons. The Muslim communities tend to be highly populated among the resource economies of the world, many of which were colonized and each of these region's resources were extracted for their oil, or for their agriculture like palm oil. Over time, colonized regions were able to nationalize or formalize their own countries and they are resource dependent economies, whether it's agriculture or hydrocarbons. And I kind of find it's interesting, because they went through this colonialization period, and now I see a bit of Western standard reverse-colonialization occurring.

Clearly these economies are always very dependent upon these resources which the world has wanted and has needed. So, they were overtaken and were able to form their own identity and export these. Now, through sustainability finance, what I somewhat controversially refer to as the soft dark side of sustainability, we're placing a normative standard that all of a sudden, their industries are bad. But yet, we in the West went there to exploit that, build it up, and take it away.

You have such a large part of their population dependent upon these hydrocarbons or resource extraction industries. To pivot and appeal to a normative play coming out of Western Europe, I kind of find it's a little bit of the dark side of ESG. The Middle East is moving in that direction because they have to, and we want them to move quicker. They're trying to modify their economies at a rapid rate. There is a bit of historical and cultural context that takes time, that is going to be moving at a different rate. I applaud the Western standard priority of climate first. I don't question that. But I observe it through a different lens, by saying that there are some flavors of re-colonization here and a bit of a double standard being applied to them.

How are you able to help them navigate this complicated transition?

So, it provides us the opportunity to come together and recognize a large part of these countries' need for financing and to help move them to that transition. In the sustainable bond fund, we own holdings that are facilitating the development of sustainable agriculture, sustainable energy sources or, for example, green financing with the green *Sukuk.*

I intentionally own controversial companies because they're in a tough fight to make these transitions. I mean, 85 percent of the world does not live in the developed world, and a large part of them live on a very small income. If we're able to make changes for 85 percent of the world's population, we're elevating the game for everyone. Some of the companies [I invest in] I'll get a lot of comments like, "Well, their track record isn't great." And I'll say, "Well, yeah, that's right, but they're trying to do this and that to make these differences." I want to own those companies that are fighting the tough fights.

I don't know if you've heard of the term, the "spirituality of imperfection." What that means is we all aspire for enlightenment to navigate life with a sense of purity and faith, but as humans we're stuck in the mud and we live with the weight of gravity. The reality is we have to kind of navigate through a conventional framework of best-of-class and say, that while we're aspiring, we're going to have to walk a bit through the mud and get a bit dirty in that process. That's the "spirituality of imperfection."

"One of the preconceptions people have of impact investing is that you have to sacrifice financial returns. We're trying to disavow people of that preconception. You shouldn't need to sacrifice financial returns in order to do good. Also, you should be able to put money in today and take it out tomorrow. That's what the Threadneedle Social Bond strategy is providing, and this should be mainstream."

SOCIAL IMPACT INVESTING
SIMON BOND
COLUMBIA THREADNEEDLE INVESTMENTS
COLUMBIATHREADNEEDLE.COM

Simon Bond is Executive Director of Responsible Investment Portfolio Management and the portfolio manager of the Threadneedle UK Social Bond Fund and the Threadneedle (Lux) European Social Bond Fund at Columbia Threadneedle Investments. It is the asset management arm of Ameriprise Financial, which has total assets under management of $593 billion (as of 30 June 2021).

Bond has over three and a half decades of experience in the fund management industry and is a recognized specialist in corporate credit. A Fellow of the Chartered Institute for Securities and Investment, he holds the Investment Management Certificate and the General Registered Representatives Certificate.

In December 2013, Bond conceived of and launched the Threadneedle UK Social Bond Fund, which was the first daily liquid fixed income impact fund in the UK, designed to deliver social outcomes and financial returns. It does so by investing in a diversified portfolio of fixed income securities with social impact criteria and currently has total assets under management of approximately £361 million (as of 17 August 2021).

In 2017, Bond launched the Threadneedle (Lux) European Social Fund, targeting social developments and projects with positive outcomes for individuals, communities, and society predominantly in geographical Europe—with total assets under management of approximately £397 million (as of 17 August 2021). Both funds apply traditional corporate bond investment acumen to an innovative approach to social investment.

Why do you view bonds as a particularly powerful mechanism to deliver social and environmental impact?

We manage our impact funds by taking a bond market expert's view on how the bond market can best deliver for society, rather than overlaying Responsible Investment on to existing ways of managing funds.

The bond market has a very wide spectrum of opportunities and entities that are doing good for society. They include charities, not-for-profit organizations, housing associations, local authorities, and special purpose vehicles for infrastructure projects all the way to supra-nationals and agencies. They should be focused on doing good for society by their very nature, but you can't invest in those entities through common equity, but they all issue bonds. Therefore, the spectrum of opportunities to do good in the credit market is so much greater.

Another advantage of the bond market is its much greater ability to target social impact by enabling you to follow the money through to the use of proceeds. That's the point from which the impact assessment starts, and from which we can determine the good that the use of proceeds does for society.

How do you ensure that social impact considerations are integrated into your investment decision-making?

We have an independent social partner, Big Issue Invest, who defined the eight areas of "positive social outcome" that we are targeting. We also established an oversight committee called the Social Advisory Committee, which replicates what you would expect to see from a risk committee on the financial side. If you've got a risk committee holding your feet to the fire on the financial side, you should have an equivalent entity on the social impact side and for us that's the Social Advisory Committee. It verifies the delivery of the promises we make to investors on the social credentials of the fund. In addition, once a year the social partner produces an independent social impact report on the fund.

The social analysis is an evidence-based approach to ascertain the social intensity of each and every bond in the portfolio and is very much Columbia Threadneedle Investments' central role. Our philosophy for managing the fund is based on our expert knowledge of how the bond markets can best deliver for society. When I initially described our approach to The Big Issue, I didn't even know that this was called "impact." I just knew how my asset class could be used for the benefit of society.

This approach is very different to most other funds in the market but whilst it is innovative, it is a corporate bond fund after all, a conventional asset class targeted to optimize the delivery of social impact. That's why it's not a Responsible Investment or ESG overlay. We have a positive inclusion philosophy, not a negative exclusion philosophy and so we are actively looking for investments that will deliver both a financial return and deliver for society.

Explain your screening and investment process.

Our first pillar is positive inclusion, however we do have minimum standards. We avoid alcohol and tobacco for example. Nevertheless, we would engage widely with companies so we're not excluding whole sectors of the economy.

Our second pillar is our evidence-based analytical approach. Social impact can be difficult to measure because there is no one-size-fits-all equivalent to carbon footprint, carbon emissions, or carbon transition, for example. The evidence for an educational outcome will necessarily be different to a health outcome. But that doesn't mean that you can't build those evidence measurements into a similar consistent analytical approach to determine the social outcome we can then deliver—this is what we call a Social Intensity Score.

Engagement is the third pillar. If we can't find the evidence we're looking for, we engage with companies and start asking difficult questions. For example, we will ask about the treatment of vulnerable employees. How have you treated them during furlough? Have you laid off staff? Are you paying a living wage? Are you training? The answers to these kinds of questions form part of the analytical process.

One should bear in mind that when investing in the bond market you're a stakeholder, not an owner. Therefore, your ability to access management is key.

We focus quite heavily on the impact achieved through the new issue market. But as a daily priced, daily liquid fund we also buy secondary issues. Overall, we have an outcomes-based, evidence-based approach and we are focused on maximizing impact within the remit of the fund to achieve "social alpha."

You only invest in investment grade bonds?

The Threadneedle UK Social Bond Fund is a typical investment grade corporate bond fund with an average single A-rating but as such we can buy up to 10 percent of high yield.

In the UK Social Bond Fund, 80 percent of the outcomes/impacts must be domestically focused within the UK. For example, let's say Iberdrola (a Spanish multinational electric utility company based in Bilbao, Spain) issues a green bond: Iberdrola is a Spanish company, Spanish domiciled with a Spanish head office. But 100 percent of the use of proceeds of one of their green bonds is to fund wind farms off the coast of Norfolk in England. So, the domicile might be Spain, but the impact is the UK. Similarly, in the European Social Bond Fund, 80 percent of the impact needs to be within geographical Europe.

Explain how your funds seek social outcomes as opposed to outputs?

The objective of the process of assessing bonds and buying bonds first and foremost still is the financial criteria. Ultimately, if you get that wrong, you're neither going to deliver the financial return nor are you going to deliver the impact. It has to be the primary consideration, which is founded in the basic traditional financial rigor, the bottom-up fundamental stock picking that we're known for.

The second stage, which we describe as the ESG stage, is effectively assessing the internal management practices. We like to quote PGGM, a big Dutch pension fund, who have said: "ESG is doing *the thing right*, and impact as doing *the right thing*." So, in terms of doing *the thing right*, we look at the internal management practices and culture. What are their environmental credentials, their employment credentials, their governance? How do they go about managing their business within their own four walls? We also set great store by the analysis of controversies, not the incidence of controversies but management reaction to controversies. Have they mitigated, compensated, and adjusted policies to make sure it doesn't happen again? This gives us an impression of the culture and confidence that they will behave with integrity in the future, or not as the case may be.

Only if we pass those first two stages will we then go on to the third stage, which is the impact assessment stage. This is where we drop from the company level assessment down to a bond-by-bond assessment, looking principally at the use-of-proceeds and the good it is likely to do for society through the bonds that we're buying.

For example, Natwest issued two ICMA (International Capital Market Association) branded social bonds. The first social bond was use-of-proceeds specifically targeting SME lending in more deprived areas of the UK, to address deprivation and provide additional lending. However, the second social bond they issued was completely different: It was funding loans to affordable and social housing providers. So, with the same issuer and same structure, they are both social bonds, they can target completely different outcomes.

We look for a "focus on deprivation" and "additionality," that is to say benefits to a deprived section of society and additional benefits through more infrastructure services and general benefits to society as a whole. This is the criteria we use to filter down a large number of bonds and select the ones that are more likely to do good for the portfolio and for society.

Are all of the use-of-proceeds ringfenced in every bond in your portfolios?

The Threadneedle UK Social Bond Fund is a fund that is aiming to do good for society through all the bonds it buys. Its framework allows us to buy general corporate purpose bonds as well as green bonds with social benefits, not just Social or Sustainability Bond issues. Therefore, in operation, it is different to an ICMA compliant social bond fund.

For example, we look for additional social benefits in green bonds such as when we engaged with Transport for London (TFL) who are regulated to be green. This bond was to fund upgrading transport infrastructure in a crowded and polluted capital city. That was very beneficial to society through the provision of transport infrastructure. So, the additionality of this bond would be a social one and was bought on that basis rather than just its environmental credentials.

On the other hand, there may be green bonds without social benefits, which we wouldn't invest in. However, it must be stressed that if we don't address the climate problem it is likely to create tremendous social problems as a consequence, and so one of our eight areas of social outcome is Utilities and the Environment with this in mind.

Why was it important for you to partner with Big Issue Invest?

We believe in the partnership model and have a long and successful history. This includes the Big Issue Invest for the Threadneedle

UK Social Bond Fund but also the Threadneedle Carbon Neutral Real Estate Fund which partners with the Carbon Trust, a leading adviser to businesses, governments, and the public sector on carbon reduction. For the European Social Bond Fund, we have a pan-European social partner—Inco as well as gaining from the international expertise of Oxfam who are an independent member of the Social Advisory Panel for the European fund. We recognize that we are well known for our financial acumen through rigorous fundamental stock picking and research on the financial side and are looking for an equal partner whose expertise and reputation is on the social side.

We developed the UK Social Assessment Methodology with The Big Issue for our UK Social Bond Fund and then went on to develop the next generation methodology for the European Social Bond Fund. However, both funds also map every bond to the United Nations Sustainable Development Goals. In fact, we don't map to the 17 UNSDGs, we map to the 169 targets that underly them, because they're much more precise and relevant for developed markets.

Similar to a sharp ratio which allows you to compare an equity fund manager, a fixed income fund manager, and a property fund manager on an equivalent risk adjusted basis, you can also compare by using the common language of the UN SDGs.

Equally, on the impact side we're also starting to adopt the ABC criteria and methodology of the Impact Management Project: The first one is "Act to avoid harm," the second is "Benefit stakeholders" and the third is "Contribute to solutions."

We think this might develop into the "common language" of the impact community and also map each and every bond we buy to these categorizations to allow comparison with other impact managers.

How do you balance your portfolio's construction between financial and social intensity?

The three focuses for our portfolio construction are social intensity, the return for the risk that you're taking, and liquidity.

We believe if you take a corporate bond risk, you should expect a corporate bond return. Beyond this we look to optimize the social intensity of the fund and use the liquidity that the bond market provides through trading to provide a daily liquid, daily priced fund. A misconception some people have of impact investing is that it's illiquid, meaning that your money is put away for a long period of time, and you can't have access to it. We want to disavow people of this assertion. We want to bring social investment into the mainstream.

What are the risks to your investors beyond those inherent to all bond funds?

We clearly have a style bias which is social. Therefore, when the oil, gas, or tobacco companies and brewers do well with their bonds, we might underperform. On the other side, when housing associations do well or when utilities do well, when social bonds do better than conventional bonds, then we might outperform. We're a little bit less cyclical and we're a little bit more conservative by being social.

Provide a real-world example of an investment that fits your mandate.

The Charities Aid Foundation met with us when we were first marketing the fund. Six months later they were doing market soundings on recapitalizing their charity bank and asked for our perspectives as a social bond investor. We were able to point them toward Retail Charity Bond Platforms, recently launched by Canacord and Alia, so they could consider widening the investor base from, for example, a loan structure.

A year later I was invited to the roadshow of their inaugural Retail Charity Bond which after due diligence we bought at new issue.

Through their on-lending by the Charity Bank, we gained access to the types of small- and medium-size charities that wouldn't otherwise be big enough to issue bonds in their own right.

Does the concept of greenwashing ever come up in social impact investing?

Yes, indeed in addition to greenwashing I have also heard the terms "social washing" and "SDG" or rainbow washing." We are big advocates of transparency in the market and are therefore recommending the concept of second party verification. This currently tends to be verification that the process is being followed, and the monies have been disbursed to the right kind of projects.

We are also encouraging the concept of "confirmation" as well as verification. That is confirmation that the target population are benefiting from the use of proceeds. We're normally looking for a sample survey of the target population as part of the standard impact reporting.

Other perspectives of the greenwashing debate, in addition to the question are: is it actually doing any good? Would it be adding anything new? Is it benefiting more than would have happened without it? To answer this, we look at three things: additionality, focus on deprivation, and the quality of impact reporting. These are the fundamental areas that our analysts look at to determine the social intensity.

Chapter Six

Alternatives: Private Equity

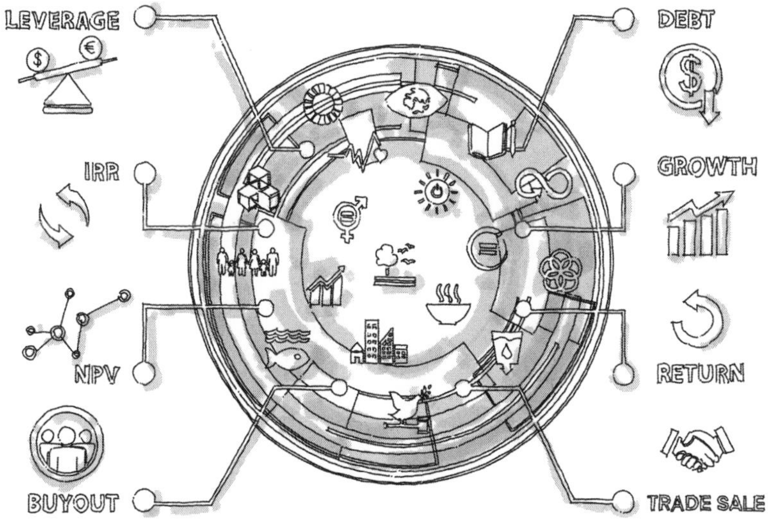

The Private Equity (PE) asset class involves investments in private companies that are not publicly listed or traded. PE investing entails direct investment into a company and generally requires a significant capital outlay. In almost all cases, such investments are made by institutional investors and large private equity funds, and these funds and strategies are not accessible to the average investor. For that reason, and because public disclosures are not required, they differ considerably from Public Equities and Fixed Income investments covered in previous chapters.

Typically, funds have a $250,000 minimum entry requirement, although others can require $1 million or more. PE funds typically invest funds with an investment horizon of between four to seven years, and investments in these types of funds are not liquid in the short-term. Nevertheless, there are some PE firms that do offer publicly traded stock in business development companies. That can provide the average investor with the opportunity to gain some investment exposure to the PE market.

There are various types of PE strategies, and PE firms have a range of investment preferences that define their risk-return profile. These are delved into in this chapter's interviews—and can include leveraged buyouts, mezzanine capital, distressed or special situations, and venture capital (which we'll consider in more detail as a separate asset class in chapter 8). But the majority of SRI investors focus on Growth Equity, which provides working capital to companies in order to finance future growth. Growth can mean different things to different companies: expanding operations, increasing market share, launching new products, or entering new markets either organically or through acquisition.

SRI PE RETURNS: NO LONGER A ZERO-SUM GAME

Investors have historically placed money with PE funds with the intention of earning financial returns that are substantially better than what can generally be achieved in public equity markets. But when it comes to SRI investors, this hasn't always been the case.

Sustainable and responsible investing in PE historically evolved from values-based investors. These were mission-oriented government-backed Development Finance Institutions (DFIs) or philanthropic innovators such as High Net Worth Investors (HNWIs), venture philanthropists like the Acumen Fund, and charitable foundations like the Ford Foundation. Program-related investments (PRIs) from foundations initially experimented by disbursing funds to for-profit companies that delivered on particular charitable objectives. These foundations did so in return for a concessionary rate of return (relative to the inherent risk). Then they began developing Mission-Related Investments (MRIs), often made from their own endowments, into mission-driven companies that were expected to generate a commercial market-rate financial return.

This represented a key psychological transition which continues to gain momentum—that PE impact investing can be deployed by institutional fiduciaries such as pension funds and insurance companies, that follow a strict profit-maximizing mandate. Doing good and doing well is no longer considered a zero-sum game.

VALUE CREATION BY ACTIVE ENGAGEMENT

Central to this thesis, and a way in which PE also differs fundamentally from public equity, is the idea that investors expect to play an activist role in the oversight, management, and strategic direction of the investment. They will often demand nominee directors on the boards of investee companies to grant them sufficient corporate oversight and control. This differs from public equity investors who—while they may proactively lobby for behavioral change through management engagement or by introducing shareholder resolutions (see chapter 4), they have no power to force or implement those changes directly. Depending on the terms and size of each PE investment, the investor may be able to dictate, and certainly veto, certain strategies and policies as they wish—to align the interests of company management with those of the PE firm and its investors.

Consequently, PE investors are well-placed to direct capital to impactful structural growth themes, unrestricted by a necessity to track an index benchmark (e.g., focused strategies targeting low-income healthcare, renewable energy). They can also work with existing management (leveraging their experience, networks, and bandwidth) to implement the ESG policies and impact strategies they want to achieve, regardless of the industry in question.

TO ESG AND BEYOND

ESG has existed within private equity for many years. As early as 2006, the United Nations launched their Principles of Responsible Investing (UN PRI), where signatories were required to adhere to six principles, the first being "We will incorporate ESG issues into investment analysis and decision-making processes." Impact investing within private equity moves beyond that expectation and, adopting the Global Impact Investing Network's definition, demands a level of intentionality to proactively seek and improve social and environmental *outcomes*.

Given the volume of specifically labelled impact-oriented fund launches over the last few years, the International Finance Corporation (IFC) published their Operating Principles for Impact Management in 2019, to avoid "impact-washing" and serve as a guide for those actively considering the asset class. The publication articulated nine principles that provide a robust framework to ensure that impact considerations, not just ESG, are integrated throughout the investment life cycle.

ESG LEADERSHIP FROM LIMITED PARTNERS

In a similar way that companies need to raise money from PE investors, PE investors must also raise money for their funds from Limited Partners. These are asset owners like sovereign wealth funds or insurance companies, who invest via intermediary asset managers to achieve their target asset allocations and required investment returns.

Today, studies show a strong positive correlation between impact and ESG funds and financial outperformance. A recent Bain study of 450 funds in Asia-Pacific showed that impact funds returned a median multiple on invested capital of 3.4x, vs a traditional 2.5x—and with lower variability (risk) of returns.[1] Therefore, Limited Partners are demanding that these "non-financial" elements are prioritized, no longer just to reduce risk but to actively deliver better returns. For example, Japan's $1.5 trillion Government Pension Investment Fund (the world's largest) now require all of its investment managers to become PRI signatories. It also announced in 2017 that it would be allocating at least 10 percent of its funds to sustainable and responsible investments.[2]

The interviews that follow are from innovative investors whose funds stand out in a crowded marketplace to practically demonstrate that this trend has powerful momentum. They provide keen insight into why the current momentum is likely just the tip of the iceberg for impact and ESG funds—as the performance and relevance of the traditional approach gradually loses ground and Sustainable & Responsible Investing is no longer peripheral but mainstream.

"Your fiduciary responsibility to your future pensioners is that there's still a world for them to live in 40 or 50 years from now. Stop looking at purely financial returns and start investing in true scalable solutions."

EMERGING & FRONTIER MARKETS IMPACT INVESTING

JEAN-PHILIPPE DE SCHREVEL
BAMBOO CAPITAL PARTNERS
BAMBOOCP.COM
LI: https://www.linkedin.com/in/jean-philippe-de-schrevel-9418b569/
TW: @JeanSchrevel

Jean-Philippe De Schrevel is Founder and a Managing Partner at Bamboo Capital Partners. He has dedicated most of his career to the development of the impact investing field, within which he is considered a global pioneer. He has launched eight investment funds and raised over $1 billion across a variety of asset classes and sectors.

De Schrevel's 20-year journey in professional finance stems from early personal exposure to extreme poverty while traveling, working, and living in Eastern Europe, Africa, Asia, and Latin America. His work objectives are driven by deeply rooted faith, values, and an ambition to contribute to solving at scale some of the most critical problems of our planet.

He co-founded BlueOrchard Finance in 2001 and previously worked at McKinsey & Co., the UN, and for various NGOs. He holds an MBA from the Wharton School of Business and is fluent in French, English, and Spanish.

What led you to found Bamboo Capital Partners?

In 2007, six years after starting BlueOrchard, I had the instinct that just doing micro-finance was great but was not enough. The financial institutions we were serving were progressively becoming more regulated, bigger, and needed to capitalize themselves. We needed private equity, not just private debt. Also, if we could do that in financial services, then there was no reason why we would not be able to find sustainable businesses in other sectors that would serve the same population.

I mean, when you think about it, it's great to give very poor people in India access, as small micro entrepreneurs, to some sort of finance—

and it's impactful. But their families need access to education, healthcare, clean energy, and housing. You don't solve the poverty problem if you don't take a holistic and ecosystem approach.

I thought I'd love to try and invest in other sectors, in companies, risky companies, non-proven companies, that are trying to bring essential services to those very same people we're serving through microfinance. I was really convinced of that, although it was not a proven business.

The board of BlueOrchard said, "Jean-Philippe this is too soon, too early, too risky. We need to focus on microfinance debt and that's what we're going to do." I said, "Well, then please allow me to start Bamboo on my own, with my own money, and I promise I will not bother you too much with that and I'll do my best."

They said yes and I started it and raised my first fund, mostly from private wealthy individuals that believed that if I was able to do that for microfinance, then maybe I would be able to do that for other sectors. They trusted me and I was very frank with them. I said, "Look, I don't know what sector, I don't know what geography, but I'm going to do my best. For sure, we are going to have some serious, positive impact. But financially speaking, I don't know. That's risky."

We went on and raised what I called the Oasis Fund, which was a very pioneer prototype fund with more than $50 million from very wealthy individuals who trusted me. I still owe them a lot for allowing me to start Bamboo.

Introduce Bamboo Capital and its mission.

First of all, I think it's important to understand what we mean by impact investing. Many people talk about responsible investing. Responsible investing is basically saying "I'm going to invest by excluding things I believe are harmful. Drugs, weapons, oil, maybe. And I'm doing something good because I'm responsible." The next step is "I'm doing not just responsible investment, but sustainable investment. I'm going to invest in companies that behave quite nicely—for the environment, for social reasons, for governance. They're transparent, pay their taxes, and treat their employees and suppliers well."

Then, not only do you have the responsible investors and the sustainable investors, you have the impact investors who are saying, "Not only do I want to invest in companies that are behaving well, but I want to solve a problem that I have identified. I'm going to proactively and intentionally direct my capital to those companies that I believe will be solving that problem." So, it's a more active way of investing for impact.

What do we do? We are globally emerging market investors. We invest in Asia, Africa, Latin America, and have offices in Bogota, Kenya, and Singapore—[they] are our three regional platforms. We are also a regulated alternative investment fund manager in Luxembourg and have an office in Geneva. We have a team of 40 people and so far have deployed roughly $500 million in companies active in different sectors.

The companies in which we invest are usually early-stage small companies, SMEs. Typically, the investment ticket size would be between $250 thousand and $5 million. In equity they would be either a seed stage or series A and B, so we are really focused on what is called the "Missing Middle" market segment. We are not investing in growth stage companies, or the $20 million or $50 million-dollar tickets. We are really focused on the SME segment of emerging markets.

I had experience in microfinance, so we started with microfinance private equity, and we raised the first fund there. Then I raised the Oasis Fund on the side, to explore pioneer investments in other sectors.

We learned a lot of things, made many mistakes, and did a few good things. And there was one sector we realized was very impactful and worthy of financial investments: the access to energy sector, specifically access to solar energy in off-grid markets. So, we created another fund for those markets, specifically in Africa, the BEAM Fund, and that has been doing great.

Then we were invited by the World Bank saying, "Well, you seem to be having a decent experience and expertise in managing and investing for access to energy. Will you compete in a public request for proposal for electrification of Haiti?" We loved the idea of actually pushing the boundaries and going to Haiti which is, as you can imagine, one of the toughest places to do business on the planet—but well worth the effort. We won that mandate and then won another similar one in Madagascar, where we are also electrifying the island.

I was moving out of BlueOrchard and remained by myself as the owner of Bamboo. Then I realized that I was becoming a bottleneck to my own growth, because keyman risk was always flagged by investors. "This is Jean-Philippe's business. What if Jean-Philippe goes?" For that reason and many others, I decided to open up the business to different partners and my key partner, Florian Kemmerich, joined me in 2016.

That was an opportunity to rethink the positioning of Bamboo and we thought we could position Bamboo as a platform open to partnerships.

Effectively, we started responding to requests for proposals from international organizations, because we felt that they had value to bring to the table, and we had the experience of managing investments in difficult environments for early-stage companies, which is exactly what they were looking for. We answered, for example, the International Fund for Agricultural Development request for proposal and won that tender, by the way, against BlueOrchard, to manage a fund lending money to small-scale holders in Africa. We won another request for proposal from the United Nations Capital Development Fund, to manage an SME fund for the least-developed countries. And we have structured a partnership with the International Trade Center and Care USA, to do gender investing.

Then we were selected by the Smart Africa network, a group of thirty-one African states, to manage their Tech For Impact fund in Africa. We're now talking to many different UN agencies and international organizations willing to come to the field of impact investing, bring their technical assistance, knowledge on the ground, feet on the ground, thousands of employees, and their deal sourcing abilities. But with the rigor and discipline of the private equity process of investing. That's a very strong and very powerful association, when you can make it work.

That's the shift that happened with Bamboo business development. We still have our other funds. But have also now embraced projects with the World Bank and partnerships with UN organizations—specifically in blended finance structures.

What are the different problems that you're trying to solve with each fund?

When we see a problem in an emerging market that is important to solve, we look at whether there are business solutions to that problem. If we believe that there are enough investible solutions in the markets we're targeting, then we structure the investment proposition ourselves and we present it to investors. It's not an investor coming to us saying, "I'd like you to do this."

Now, when we respond to requests for proposals, those are institutions saying, "We'd love to do this for small-scale holders or for the least developed countries and we're looking for a manager." Then it's our decision whether to apply or not and compete to get that mandate.

Is the Haiti off-grid energy fund open-ended?

It is a fully funded fund by the government of Haiti and the World Bank so there are no third-party private investors.

You're managing the deployment of capital for these institutions. Is that the same for the Market Development Fund?

That one is a mandate from the World Bank and the government of Madagascar to manage investments and grants to really grow the sector of access to solar energy across the island.

So, the rest of your investments are in the UN sponsored SDG 500 Fund?

That's true for the moment. That's because a whole range of international NGOs, organizations, and UN agencies are realizing that the pure grant making business is challenged and is probably not sufficient to meet the SDG goals by 2030. That said, they have a ton of experience and knowledge and presence in those emerging markets, so they are fantastic partners.

The second trend we're seeing is this evolution toward blended finance. Basically, blended finance is structured finance using different types of capital into one single pool of assets. That allows us to remain in this missing middle segment, the early-stage SMEs, but de-risking such investment for the private sector with the use of first loss tranches. Essentially we're saying, instead of having plain vanilla funds where you take the full risk, maybe there's an intelligent way of combining catalytic capital, public money capital, subsidy or risk-taking capital, and put them in the first loss tranche that will take the first hits on the portfolio.

Then, on the senior tranches, on the senior notes that we would be issuing from those funds, private sector investors looking for a decent risk-adjusted return will be incentivized to come in because they are de-risked, they are protected, and the return is okay for them on a market basis. That allows for those private investors to take part in truly impactful investments, not doing impact washing or greenwashing by paying lip service to some ESG. That's really being impactful where the money is most needed, while being protected.

For the catalytic capital—the public money—it's a way of being really efficient. For every dollar you're putting in the first loss tranche of the fund, you know that three or four dollars of private sector money is going to come on top. So, you truly catalyze private sector money to the problems you want to solve, as a philanthropist, as a public organization. That's very powerful. Our association with those UN agencies and international NGOs are allowing us to put this together. That's the most fascinating trend I've seen over the past 20 years in impact investing and has the potential of becoming really scalable.

What's the idea behind the SDG 500?

Large institutional investors, the big guys that really do have the power to move the needle, will never look at our funds; we're too small. The total size of our funds is the minimum ticket they would write, and they usually may not represent more than 10 percent of any fund they invest in. So, if we want to remain true to our mission of being an early-stage SME investor in tough markets, how do we get to scale? Well, by bundling. And that's the idea behind SDG500, to say, okay, we are going to bundle the funds we have—small scale agribusinesses, SMEs, gender with International Trade Center and Care USA, tech for impact—and instead of raising the senior tranches of each of those funds separately, we are going to raise for an SPV for $360 million dollars.

To raise that money, we are going to actually have a small equity mezzanine in the SPV and issue notes. We could structure senior notes or subordinated notes. Let's enable private, large institutional investors to actually get an instrument that they can put in their asset allocation. It's a fixed income instrument, a note that has been issued by an SPV, and that has a certain coupon. That is fully protected, not only by the equity mezzanine but also the first loss tranches of each of the underlying funds. We are going to place that quickly to institutional investors willing to take bite sizes of 30, 50, 100 million dollars. So, money would be flowing to the underlying funds in a very diversified way and actually, when you think about it, eventually down the line they will be funding hundreds of SMEs in over 30 or 40 emerging markets in a very diversified way—but without taking the pain of going through all those investments individually. It's just one note purchase at the top.

And when we started this exercise, COVID hit, so that's not been the best environment to raise money, but the concept remains. Now the funds have been launched separately with their own investors and first losses. We have not succeeded yet in launching this SPV and the series of notes, but in my opinion, that's the way to go to get to true scale without abandoning our mission.

And will these notes be across all the SDG funds?

That's the goal because we can actually leverage each of our individual funds. I mean, we are actually receiving money from Development Finance Institutions, lending to specific funds if they want to. But the real breakthrough, in my opinion, is if we get a single note issuance to the institutional market and that's what we're trying to do. That's the way to go, in my opinion.

There are six of these SGD funds within the platform. Is there a plan to create more?

I see these mandates as being extremely promising, in terms of their scalability and impact, because those partners bring a footprint that would take us a century to build. When you team up with Care USA, for example, you team up with 8,000 employees in more than eighty-five emerging markets—and we bring them the discipline of investment.

What are your target returns?

It's difficult to give general numbers, but roughly, if you talk about the private equity fund, we are in the 15 percent net IRR target. I mean, not much different from any private equity funds. If you talk about private debt, if it's pure private debt microfinance, you're probably in the high single digit net return. If you do early stage investing in private debt in tough environments, we are not capable of charging the interest rate that would reflect the true risk that we're taking. This is where blended finance comes in. If we can charge 10 or 11 percent dollar equivalent in a hedged loan to an early-stage SME in Kenya, but you're protected by a first loss tranche that represents 20 percent of the total AUM of your fund, then I believe that getting a 5, 6, or 7 percent net return to the U.S. dollar is a very decent return on your investment, given the fact that you're protected by the first loss and the impact you're adding.

And if you're leveraging those funds on top of the equity in the funds, on top of the first loss and the senior tranche, with loan programs to development finance institutions or whoever would want to buy those notes, you're in the 2 or 3 percent net return. That's because you come first in the waterfall and you're protected by all the equity tranches, senior, mezzanine and 1st loss below you.

How do you identify and screen your investment targets?

Each time we set up a fund, we actually start with our Theory of Change. What is the problem we're trying to solve? How is it that investing in those companies is going to solve or contribute to solving that problem? What criteria do we need to check to make sure that they contribute to solving that problem? This is embedded in the investment process, so it's very thorough. It takes us weeks and months to prepare that Theory of Change.

When it gets put into practice, then we have this desktop research. If we believe at our internal risk committee meetings that this company is worth drilling down further, we do. There's another risk committee that then decides whether an in-person visit to that company is worthy or not. Then we have our investment teams go in and kick the tires, on the ground, with the team, with the company, in the field, and then they come back with their findings. When the risk committee, which is composed of our most senior fund managers, decides that we are ready to present to the investment committee, then we talk to the investment committee that makes a decision. It's yes, no, maybe. If no, it's no. If maybe, then we go back to the drawing board. If it's yes, we proceed.

If at any point in time we believe that the company is not truly impactful, or not aligned on the social mission that we have established for the fund, we're not going to do it—even if it's an exciting financial investment.

How do you avoid greenwashing or impact washing?

Greenwashing and impact washing happens at the larger size tickets, not at the small size tickets in the trenches in emerging markets that we do. And when you look at the theories of change and the impact assessment criteria and reporting that we're doing on a daily basis and the reports we're sending to our investors, I would dare say that we're exemplary.

We integrate impact due diligence all along in our investment process; that's the first thing we check. We're an impact investor, with a fiduciary responsibility to our investors. In the past, fiduciary responsibility meant I need to deliver the return I promised. Well, in impact investing fiduciary responsibility means I have to deliver the social impact and the financial impact that I promised. And if I'm not equipping my investment process and my teams to actually deliver on those, then I'm a liar.

So how do you verify your investments?

We're on the ground and visit those companies, see the clients, and talk to their clients. Also now, with the partnerships we have with international NGOs and UN agencies, they do verify that.

But how do you measure it?

There are two things in impact as you may know, what we call the output indicators and then the outcomes. The output indicators are really the measurable things that you can count. How many solar units installed, how many households served, time of usage of those appliances? Then, by each unit that is being placed, how many liters of kerosene are not being burned every day? How much CO_2 are you removing in terms of emissions, for example, and do we have a decrease in household fires? How do you decrease the hospitalization of households because they have not inhaled fumes from kerosene inside their huts, through clean solar energy?

Of course, the problem is not in the output tracking, because that's something we do easily—just like financial reporting. The problem is when you want to infer what has been the long-term outcome of your action and how you link that with the causality effect, with the output indicators that you're measuring. That's tough and tricky.

But if you lend $100 to a micro entrepreneur needing money for his grocery shop, when no one else would lend money to them, that's impactful. You put a solar panel in a village in Africa that was chopping wood or burning kerosene for their energy needs. You've provided them with a clean source of energy that is renewable, cheap, can replace kerosene or wood and deforestation. I think you're having an impact. It doesn't take a PhD to understand that.

How important is proactive technical assistance to your portfolio companies?

Well, first of all, it's not only technical assistance, but also active portfolio management. We sit on the board of each company in which we invest equity; we have monthly reporting from our private debt assets. We visit them very regularly. We take part in the strategy decisions and the governance of the company. We contribute to the best of our knowledge. We can help with recruiting, financial discipline, many different aspects of a business life. And that's what we do on our equity investments. On the external financing on private debt, you have less of an interaction. But given the fact that we have relatively shorter maturities of lending to those companies, we are in constant interaction with them, and we know what they need, and we keep visiting them. That's our daily job of asset manager.

On top of that, what we call technical assistance are side pockets of money, usually provided pro bono. Those are grants managed not by us but by specialized technical assistance consultants and providers. The trick is we need to have the manager of the technical assistance be very much in sync and aligned with the fund manager of our portfolio, because you want to use that grant money for technical assistance to benefit the portfolio companies of your fund. You want them to address either pre-investment or post-investment weaknesses that you have identified in your due diligence, and that's very powerful. But that's on top of our daily job of being an active fund manager.

It's got to be more expensive to do due diligence on a small company in Mozambique, than one in Denver.

Yeah, that's what people who criticize our 2 percent or 2.5 percent management fee don't realize. I'm going in the trenches of Mozambique to land or to invest a million dollars. It's expensive. But the management fee covers everything. That's why Bamboo is never going to get rich and that's okay.

Who are your funds' typical investors?

Before, we were really focused on private sector investors and very wealthy families that were very supportive. We keep talking to family offices and institutional investors, but we have added discussions with, as I mentioned, UN agencies, international NGOs, and multilateral organizations.

In the past, I thought that this would have been a mistake. Today I believe that it's the way to go. We can address, through blended finance, different pools of capital with the same goal. There's no exclusion. We can deal with public money and private money and align them in a very coherent way.

Another thing I should mention is that there's a regulatory bottleneck that is to me a pity, and that's the access to the retail segment for specialized impact investors. Because honestly, I believe that we would be managing more money if I were able to collect one-hundred-euro investment sizes into my investment funds, rather than to go to the ultra-high net worth individual institutional investor. This regulatory system that protects the retail investor from risky funds is something that I feel is a huge bottleneck on the growth of the impact industry.

When I talk to friends of my young sons, they get it immediately. Even if it's 50 francs, they would invest. It takes forever to convince the gatekeeper of a family office when you're doing the right thing. But it takes me 20 minutes to the younger generations. They were born into a world that is having those problems and they know that they need to do something about it, and the new generation of wealth owners are getting it much faster than the older generations. If we were able to access those younger generations more easily and broadly and even on a retail basis, I'm pretty sure it would be a landslide.

What's your total AUM right now?

Roughly $350 million.

Are the capital markets sufficient to deliver the $2.5 trillion per annum SDG funding gap that the UN has cited?

I don't know how that has been calculated. All I know is that we have big problems all over the globe. I'm bringing my contribution to that, and I do believe that we are doing our part as best as we can. What I'm really saddened by is that people who do have the means of accelerating that movement are actually not doing it. You look at the sovereign wealth funds and those huge pension funds that hide themselves behind their fiduciary responsibility to their pensioners or future pensioners. I'm tempted to say, well, your fiduciary responsibility is that there's still a world for them to live in 40 or 50 years from now. Stop looking at purely financial returns and the risk of avoidance and start investing in true scalable solutions, for God's sake. That's your fiduciary responsibility, not chasing the 20 percent IRRs that everybody knows you're not achieving anyway.

What can technology enable over the next decade in the industries you're working in?

Technology is increasingly central to impact investing, like with artificial intelligence, remote control batteries, mobile wallets, mobile payments, and pay as you go systems. Technology is bringing you the accessibility to services. In times of COVID, we've seen that telehealth and telemedicine could be extremely useful in many of those markets. The second thing it brings is affordability. Because usually if you get to scale, you can price the entry point, the price point, quite low—so that it becomes attractive and feasible for people.

If you have accessibility and affordability thanks to technology, then that's the way to go for access to energy, education, healthcare, and finance. I think we are at the very beginning of something I cannot even imagine, that technology will be the driving force of the scalability of impact in many sectors. I'm convinced of that, and that's why we're launching two tech-for-impact funds in Latin America and Africa. We see that this is the next way to scale impact, and those are potentially great financial investments, as well.

Why are we so excited about the access to clean energy and solar energy in off-grid markets? It's because once you have energy, you can have access to content. You have access to the worldwide web. Suddenly you unlock populations, and you open the world to them. You open entrepreneurship, knowledge, participation, and inclusion—and that's fabulous. Once you have opened that access, there's no way back. It's a very positive snowballing ethic for the younger generations.

When you launched Bamboo, what did you think was really important that now you know isn't?

We believed that what we were trying to do could not have any relation to philanthropy, or to the traditional cooperation work or social work. We wanted to stay clear of that. We didn't want to talk to development finance institutions, to NGOs, and we felt that being pure private investors would go a long way toward our potential scale-up.

When I now see the potential of blended finance and actually a way of not excluding any sort of capital but combining their strength into coherent structures and investment strategies, I think that was a big mistake. Now, since we did that, we are able to bring to the table the private investor relationships we have cultivated over the years. In retrospect, I wish we had embraced those collaborations earlier to learn from them.

Can you give me an example of an investment that at the time you made it, you were convinced that it ticked all your boxes, but in the end didn't work out? What was the lesson learned?

An investment that I was really proud of, and I was really believing in, was one we made in India in a chain of primary care hospitals. I really admired the CEO and the founder, a really charismatic leader. He had founded, at the time we invested, four hospitals in a state in India and two of them were break-even. The other two were about to break even and we invested what was, at the time, a significant amount of money to help him scale that business. They started launching new units, new hospitals across different states, too quickly, eagerly, and ambitiously. At the time we felt that the footprint was a driver to the value of the business, as opposed to the per unit economics of the business. That was a huge mistake because, in the end, the follow-on investors and buyers look at the unit economics as opposed to the footprint.

The lesson learned is that you can have a charismatic leader and founder. But if this guy is not followed by a very solid, bigger management team—whoever he is, and whatever his ideas and however fantastic they are—it's not going to be put into practice. The execution and the solid middle management of a social company is essential.

If you could sit down and pick anyone's brain, who would it be?

I would love to have a conversation with the CIO of a sovereign wealth fund and just understand why they're not doing more in impact. To ask how they are not capable of being innovative and taking risk, even for a micro fraction of the assets they have under their management. What is their justification? Generally, the minute you start managing over $500 billion dollars and you tell me that you will put the whole institution at risk because you test something on $300 million, I have a hard time believing that. I would love to understand that.

"This is not something we're doing like old-fashioned private equity and then just giving it some 'impact lipstick' at the end. The impact analysis is just as serious as the financial analysis. It has to be a good financial investment and it has to help us to reach our impact objectives, which involves reaching millions of low-income people."

EMERGING MARKETS IMPACT INVESTING

STEWART LANGDON
LEAPFROG INVESTMENTS
LEAPFROGINVEST.COM
LI: https://www.linkedin.com/in/stewart-langdon-65a14015/

Stewart Langdon is LeapFrog Investment's Partner and Co-Head of South Asian Investments. A private equity specialist with expertise in mergers and acquisitions, IPOs, restructuring, disposals, and debt raising, Langdon combines his technical experience with deep knowledge of emerging financial services markets. He leads financial services investments primarily in India and digital financial services across Asia and Africa, with a focus on deal sourcing and execution.

Langdon oversees those deal teams and has led LeapFrog initiatives including the successful exits of Mahindra Insurance Brokers, Magma Fincorp, and BIMA. He also chairs LeapFrog's deal review committee, is an investment committee alternate member, and sits on the boards of a number of portfolio companies including WorldRemit, BIMA, and Cignifi.

He previously worked in corporate finance, investment banking, and capital markets advisory as a vice president at Rothschild. He specialized in the insurance, banking, and telecom sectors across Asia, Africa, and the Middle East. A member of the Emerging Markets Private Equity Association, Langdon is also a trustee of the Asia Scotland Institute and chairs its business advisory council. He holds a Bachelor of Laws degree from the University of Aberdeen and is a chartered accountant.

Please provide an overview of LeapFrog Investments.

We see ourselves as one of the world's leading impact investment firms, and we define impact investing as profit with purpose. This is a fully commercial activity; we don't believe in trade-offs at all. We believe that it's possible to build big businesses that are serving low-income people and helping them get access to the services they need—while at the same time building big organizations and making money for investors.

Our theory of change is to provide essential services to emerging consumers. It's all about the idea that if you look at poverty and what is really happening there, you have a large group of low-income people who don't have access to healthcare, financial services, insurance payments, etc. If we can help them gain access to these essential services that everybody else in the world takes for granted, that will reduce poverty and help to lift that group up toward the middle class. There is so much social good that you can do by providing these services to people.

That's where we get both our profit, because we're building businesses that do that, and our purpose.

What geographies do you focus on?

So, for us, a really important theme has always been scale. We were never very interested in the idea of funding projects where you could help 1,000 or even 10,000 people. We always asked, "how can we invest in businesses that are helping to lift millions of people out of poverty?" And if you want to do that, you need to think about the markets where there are large numbers of low-income people.

For us there are three clusters. There's Southeast Asia, where we're very active in places like Vietnam, the Philippines, and Indonesia. Then you have South Asia, where India is our single biggest market, accounting for about a third of our portfolio. Finally, we're very active in sub-Saharan Africa.

But we're certainly not global. We're not in China or Latin America. We're just very intentional about this handful of large low-income markets that we invest in across Asia and Africa.

Describe your investment activities in India.

We invest across financial services and healthcare in India. This includes insurance businesses that protect low-income people and lending businesses not dissimilar to some of the micro-lenders.

Of course, none of these countries are easy places to do business. But, oddly enough, we've never had a really difficult exit challenge in India. Actually, most of the time, investors are pretty excited about India just because the total addressable market there is always absolutely massive, and the growth potential is always enormous.

I think in a funny way we are quite fortunate that strategic investors who are largely oriented in say, Western markets, or maybe in Japan, kind of sat there in sectors like insurance and healthcare saying, "Oh my goodness, where's the growth going to come from?" And the answer to that I think is perhaps partly now in changes in technology. But I think the big part of it is in countries like India. If you're running an insurance company today, it's going to be very tough to grow in Germany or the UK, but India is always an exciting growth opportunity. So, we've usually done quite well by selling our investments in India to strategic investors who want to take the business to the next stage.

Explain your transition from investing in insurance products to healthcare and finance.

So, we started in insurance, and the theory there—and I think this played out very well—was that insurance penetration was very low in all these countries. Yet the people who lived there lived risky, vulnerable lives. People were constantly suffering and slipping backwards economically, because of adverse health events. Or maybe the father or the mother of the family dies, or they have a key livelihood asset that goes missing like a vehicle or livestock. But nobody had any way to formally protect themselves against those kinds of risks. So, the first fund was all about that theory of "how can we help the insurance sector to expand and serve more low-income people and help to protect them against those risks."

We had all sorts of success stories with that, including a health product that we did with a company called Mahindra that reached two million people. We had a company we invested with called BIMA, which I think sold around 30 million policies in the period that we were invested there. BIMA's distribution was completely digital, which is the reason we were able to scale so fast.

In our second fund, we said, "Well, that's worked really well, how do we take this into other areas of financial services?" So, we started investing in credit businesses and we invested in a few you would have known as NBFCs (Non-Banking Financial Companies) in India, as well as across Africa. Finally, in our third fund, we expanded that again to include healthcare, which was a natural adjacency to the health insurance expertise that we already had.

Even today, although we have expanded from where we were in terms of just being in insurance, we're in financial services and healthcare and that's it. We don't do anything else. We've never been about investing in every kind of impactful business we can think of. We're not impact generalists. We're very specialized. We know how to do financial services, and we know how to do healthcare, and that's it. We don't go outside of those tramlines. What we're doing is still very carefully defined and very intentional.

Describe your funds.

We have four. Three standard, typical GP/LP private equity style funds. We have one separate managed account which is with Prudential. The U.S. Prudential put some money into a vehicle that we use to invest just in life insurance, in Africa.

They are all closed-ended funds. The original idea, when LeapFrog first started, was we wanted the funds to be as close to standard as possible. That's because at that time, the whole impact investing story was so new and so different that we didn't want to have too many wacky things in the structure. We just went for a vanilla private equity structure.

Right now, our average ticket size is anywhere between $10 and $17 million. Our most recent fund, for example, was $740 million. Our AUM is about $2 billion at this point. We benchmark ourselves against the private equity peer group. We see no good reason why we should be underperforming our private equity peers, just because we're investing for impact. In fact, we think if anything it enhances returns. The impact investing lens, which draws our focus to purposeful businesses solving major problems, is also a commercial lens. These businesses address critical needs and can quite naturally scale and grow. So that's how we benchmark ourselves.

Describe your investment strategy.

The first thing to say is that everybody who works at LeapFrog is very specialized in terms of country and market. Everybody's either a financial services specialist or a healthcare specialist. All of the investment people are very, very close to their sectors and their markets and spend all their time there. They're so specialized that they just go around meeting CEOs of companies in that sector. That's all they do. They're very close to what is going on in these places. So, very practically, the key to deployment is that kind of localism.

All these companies are usually growing, so sooner or later they have some capital need. Usually, we'll try and have a proprietary conversation with them about whether we can be the capital provider. We don't like auctions. All private equity firms say that, but we really don't like participating in auctions. We like to go and do proprietary things with people who we feel are really values-aligned.

In terms of how we make the decisions, typically two partners will get together to look at a deal. We have an investment committee, which has effectively three stages that you have to go through to get approval. And to get that approval, the deal team will write up a long paper, which includes the usual commercial due diligence around the market, the company, the other shareholders and so on, alongside rigorous impact due diligence which outlines the current and future states of the business, and how the lives of emerging consumers will be dramatically improved through the investment. The really critical thing is that the valuation section and the impact section are equals in the decision-making process.

Again, there's no trade-off, this is not something where we're basically doing old-fashioned private equity and then just giving it some "impact lipstick" at the end. The impact analysis is just as serious as the financial analysis. Each investment has to meet both bars. It has to be a good financial investment and it has to help us to reach our impact objectives, which at this point involves reaching millions of low-income people.

Describe your investment screens, both financial, and nonfinancial.

Essentially, the financial metric is private equity standard returns. The impact metric is that we will set ourselves a goal for the number of low-income people we want to reach for each fund. The latest one was 100 million people, and then each investment has to make a material contribution toward that. If I come along with an investment and say, "Hey, this thing's going to do 30 percent return" everyone will say, "That's great, what's the impact metric?" If I say, "Well, unfortunately, it's only reaching 5,000 low-income people" they'll say that's not good enough, that's not giving us a good enough impact profile toward our target. Both are taken just as seriously and measured just as seriously.

LeapFrog uses its in-house measurement framework, FIIRM (Financial, Impact, Innovation, and Risk Management), to set goals and track portfolio company and fund performance. This covers four metrics: Firstly, Financial, which drives toward top-line growth, bottom line profitability and profitable products. Key Performance Indicators (KPIs) include revenue growth, EBITDA and/or NPAT (Net Profit After Tax) margins, or product contribution margins.

Secondly, Impact which drives toward emerging consumer scale, quality products (client protection), good governance and policy. Example KPIs include the ratio of underserved customers versus overall people reached, a product quality index and LeapFrog's Good Governance & Policy Index.

Thirdly, Innovation which drives toward more appropriately priced products, scalable or alternative distribution, improvements in productivity.

And finally Risk Management by which we ensure effective risk management with KPIs like solvency ratios and other risk categorizations.

How do you vet targets and how do you do ongoing due diligence once a company is in your portfolio?

Since the beginning of our first fund, we have always been well supported by the development finance institutions. People like IFC and CDC and TEG, and that group of organizations, DFC, now OPEC, as it used to be known. Legally, we've always been absolutely insistent on all of our companies operating to the highest possible standards. When we do investment agreements with people, it is always essential that they sign up to a very, very stringent set of rules around issues like corruption and bribery and anti-money laundering.

LeapFrog has developed a rigorous sourcing and investment process incorporating best-practice ESG principles that it implements with respect to investment activities. First, LeapFrog has a Responsible Investment Code (RIC) which is formally adopted by each portfolio company. The RIC outlines material ESG risks and serves as a basis to discuss these risks openly with each portfolio company since the beginning of the process.

Second, as part of its FIIRM Framework, LeapFrog has developed an ESG questionnaire that deal teams and companies complete during due diligence which provides a clear report on the current status in ESG and opportunities for improvement.

Third, LeapFrog has worked with specialized independent consultants in higher-ESG risk investments to fully analyze potential risks and opportunities.

We talk a lot about partner selection, which means that we try very hard to find businesses that are operating to world-class standards in terms of governance around these issues. A good example of that is the Mahindra Group, which was one of our first partners in India. We invested in their insurance business, which was a fantastic outcome for us both financially and from an impact perspective. We want to find the people in these countries where the governance is absolutely top notch.

Provide two real-world examples of investments you've made that capture your strategy.

One example is a company called BIMA which is this mobile insurance business in which we invested in 2013. Essentially what it did at the time was partner with mobile operators to sell insurance to their customer bases. The mobile operators are very dominant. They have incredible data that is very predictive and very easy to use. They have payment mechanisms that you can use easily to collect a payment for the service that you're providing. They're fantastic brands, which really matters a lot in insurance, because insurance is all about trust. For many people in the developing world, their first experience of insurance was being scammed by somebody.

So, BIMA had developed this means of partnering with mobile operators and selling life and health insurance to their customer bases, and this grew incredibly quickly. When we first invested in them, they had a million dollars of revenue. By the time we exited, there was $30 million of revenue and they'd gone from maybe three or four markets to being present in nine markets across Ghana, Tanzania, Bangladesh, Indonesia, Sri Lanka—a lot of big places. So that did incredibly well for us. At the same time, because they were using all of this mobile infrastructure, they brought the cost of providing insurance down to a dollar a month and sometimes less, for coverage of a few thousand dollars. Around 80 percent of the BIMA customer base had never had insurance before.

The health insurance piece was incredibly new to the customer base. So that did well for us and, eventually, I think in 2018, we ended up getting an approach from Allianz and sold our shareholding to Allianz. First of all, they were fascinated by this company that was selling insurance digitally and doing so successfully and scaling quickly. They felt there would be a lot of lessons from the core business. Secondly, the impact story was incredible. I think the business reached 30 million low-income customers over the period that LeapFrog was invested. Finally, it's just a lot of growth and Allianz, as we're seeing, they're very worried about digital disruption and finding growth in Germany and other markets. For them, this was really an appealing prospect to buy into a company growing so quickly.

Another one that I'm personally very close to is a business that is now known as Zepz. Zepz is a holding company. They were set up to own WorldRemit and another business they acquired called Sendwave. WorldRemit was started by Ismail Ahmed, a migrant who left Somaliland at the height of the civil war in the 1980s and made it to the UK. He went from that to launching a remittance business, which in a way does something very simple. It transfers money from people in Western markets back to their families, usually in lower income emerging markets. There are two interesting things about it. First, it's very large. I think in the formal market something like $600 billion gets transferred every year. In the informal market, it's probably the same. You're talking about something like a trillion dollars total market size that historically was dominated by traditional players.

What Ismail did was to figure out that using digital technology you could bring the cost of this service down dramatically, which he did. Two things happened: first of all, he grew this business to an enormous scale, in the hundreds of millions of dollars. But he also slashed the costs of sending money home for migrants. It means there's much less leakage to the migrants, much more money makes it back to their families, and that has a huge impact at home.

So, it's very consistent with our strategy, both on the profit side and on the purpose side, because about two-thirds of the money they send goes to Africa. The latest round of investment has done a $5 billion valuation. So, obviously, we were in that in the relatively early stages, and it's been a very good outcome for us.

Are most of your exits to acquisitions trade sales?

I think increasingly the equity markets are doing so well that I expect we might see one or two businesses come to market relatively soon. But historically, yes—selling to Western strategics has been our forte.

How you verify an investment's impact?

Our FIIRM Framework (discussed above) is our quarterly reporting mechanism that all of our portfolio companies report through every quarter. I think there are a couple of unusual things about it: First, it includes both financial and impact metrics. It says what your revenue is, what's your profit, what your balance sheet looks like—all of that kind of accounting stuff that's normal enough. But it also says how many low-income people you are reaching.

It depends a bit on the company, but we always try and understand the quality, relevance, and affordability of every service that we provide so on the quality front, we might say, "What was the claims ratio?" to make sure people are getting value out of this product. We might say, "What is the affordability like, what is the average price point? Let's make sure that people can actually afford these essential services."

How do you avoid green washing or impact washing?

I think we have two inherent advantages here. One is that we are investing intentionally around a very particular problem, which is poverty. And we've got a way of defining our theory of change around helping low-income people to access essential services. We are not a generalist. I think if you're an impact generalist, if you just say, "Well, we invest in companies that have an impact," then it's very easy to become engaged in impact washing. Because you can figure out some way to say that just about any company has some sort of impact.

The second thing is that we have been impact from the beginning, which means the impact piece, the requirement to produce large scale social impact, has always been in the DNA. Every investment we've ever done has this. We're so specific about the impact that we want to try and have. At this point we've been working so hard in our markets, for such a long period of time, that we feel like we know who the good people are.

What expertise do you bring to an investment beyond the board level?

The fact that so many people on our team come from operating backgrounds rather than financial backgrounds is really helpful around this. All of the companies that we invest in are oriented toward lower-income consumers. You have to design products and services in a very affordable, very straightforward way, so we've developed a lot of competence around designing those sorts of products.

For example, in our first fund, one of the things we tried to do was expand the reach of health insurance via the portfolio companies. We partnered with Mahindra Insurance to design a health insurance product in India, a very simple cashless hospitalization product. If you are hospitalized, you're covered for a certain amount. And that was very popular.

We've developed two other areas of competence, both based on feedback around what would be helpful from management teams that we've backed. The first is something called the Customer Experience Launchpad. We have a couple of people who specialize in how to develop products to overcome barriers of access and affordability that are specific to emerging consumers. This team has developed apps, CX (Customer Experience) dashboards, retail concepts, and other tools for portfolio companies that help them build products and services around the real lives of emerging consumers. That's been a big success. We did a big project around that in Ghana with a company called miLife Insurance that we invest in there.

The final one is the Talent Accelerator. That was really created around the idea that for all these companies that we invest in, retaining and motivating talented people is a constant challenge. We often found the companies we were investing in weren't necessarily of the size that they could offer really exciting development opportunities. But if we pulled them all together, we could set up interesting leadership courses and do interesting things with leadership teams at the LeapFrog level. So, we put that together as well.

These are the kinds of things where there's the product design piece or the customer experience piece or the talent piece that we're doing that we think make us distinct from other people.

Describe the typical profile of your investors.

What is really interesting is that it's changed over time. In our first fund we had a number of wealthy people and institutions who were committed to impact. Pierre Omidyar, the founder of eBay, George Soros, and a lot of development finance institutions like IFC and EIB and people who were interested in development. That first fund was $135 million. Then, as we started to do more in insurance, we found we got more interest from insurance companies. So, in our second fund, we had different insurance companies come in, as well. Our third fund has broadened our Limited Partner base again to include commercial investment institutions. That's because as we proved the experience out, as we delivered on the returns on both the financial and the impact side and impact investing became better known, we started to get a lot more interest from pension funds, big investment institutions, and other traditional asset managers.

Are there any downsides or risks that are unique to your investors?

The risk they worry about the most is the reputational risk. They all worry about something going wrong at one of the portfolio companies, particularly portfolio companies dealing with low-income people.

Currency is a huge problem for us, so we've had one or two investments where we've done pretty well, local currency-wise, and had it all wiped out by devaluation. It's also true that regulators in the countries we work in are much less predictable than they are in Europe or the United States, so we've had a couple of times where regulatory interventions have caused our businesses problems. Those tend to be the big two market risks that we face: currency and regulation.

What impact do you see technology having in the developing world over the next decade?

At the heart of all this is the fact that smartphone penetration has just rocketed over the last few years, even among low-income people in Asia and Africa. And, as you and I know, smartphones can radically alter the affordability of key services and allow you to totally reimagine the way that services are delivered. Added to this, in healthcare many of the next generation of cutting-edge interventions like genomic-based precision medical care, advanced diagnostic imaging, and telemedicine are becoming more affordable and are on the cusp of being scaled in emerging markets. This will have an incredible impact on health and quality of life across these regions.

Can you give me an example of an investment you made that you were convinced at the time ticked all your boxes, but in the end didn't turn out?

I think the most obvious example was one where we made a bet on a company that had really good technology, but unfortunately the execution wasn't quite there. I think the learning was that you can have the best idea in the world, but unless you can execute on it, it's just hopeless. And so, ever since then, execution has really been at the top of my list—rather than having a good idea or a good technology.

Have you ever passed up an investment that later you regretted?

I passed on an insurance investment in India which I really regret. I met the company in 2012 when the entrepreneur was raising money. I think the valuation was $50 million and it had kind of just got off the ground. I remember he had a big lead over any of his competitors, but the company was still very small. I just couldn't quite see how technology would change the way insurance was bought and sold in India. Anyway, he will IPO his business in the near term. People are talking about, I think, $3 billion or $5 billion.

It was before the smartphone thing happened and I just couldn't see how that would change everything, so, unfortunately, I passed on that one. The lesson learned on that was again, technology—underestimating the ability of technology to change things quickly.

"You need to bring the investors on the journey with you. In the past, we have declined investments despite a very good return profile because we could not prove to ourselves, and to our investors, that they were environmentally sustainable. In our pursuit for environmental sustainability, we discovered a number of concerning issues and they discovered them together with us."

ENVIRONMENTAL SUSTAINABILITY SME INVESTING

STEFANO BACCI
AMBIENTA
AMBIENTASGR.COM
LI: https://www.linkedin.com/in/stefano-bacci-63b9a224/

Stefano Bacci is a Partner at Ambienta and its ESG Manager. Based in London, he joined Ambienta in 2012 and has been involved in a number of transactions including Tower Light, Calucem, Oskar Nolte, IP Cleaning, SF Filter, and Namirial.

Prior to joining Ambienta, he was a Partner at Palamon Capital Partners (London) for nine years and spent seven years at the Boston Consulting Group (Milan, Stockholm, Helsinki) focusing on European industrial companies. He started his career at BASF in Basel, first in the R&D division and eventually in the stabilization of recycled plastics.

Bacci graduated from Politecnico University of Milan with a degree in Chemical Engineering and holds MBAs from both the Helsinki School of Economics and Boston's MIT. He also completed postgraduate studies in physical chemistry at the Technische Universität Darmstadt.

Please introduce Ambienta and its mission.

Ambienta is a purpose-built asset manager pursuing environmental sustainability across industrial sectors and/or economic sectors. We measure resource efficiency and pollution control to invest in models where you use resources more efficiently. As such, we strive for a reduction of pollution, waste, and landfills—and cleaner water and air.

We raised about €230 million for the original fund back in 2008. Then, in 2013, we raised Ambienta II which was around €330 million. In 2018 we raised Ambienta III, which was €635 million, and is currently still investing—plus some co-investment vehicles. That brings the raised amount in private equity to over €1.2 billion, making us one of the largest environmental specialist private equity investors in the world that is entirely and exclusively dedicated to environmental sustainability. From the beginning we have done nothing else other than environmental sustainability.

What is your public market fund, Ambienta X?

In order to really understand sustainability, we needed to create an internal research capability, which is now actually quite large. We have a team of six highly qualified individuals who are engineers and have MBAs. In the past, we used to sell an environmental advisory service to other managers in order to optimize our investment. Eventually we realized that our knowledge could serve more asset classes than just private equity and created a long-short strategy. This product is quite recent, only 18 months old [at the time of this interview].

What are your private equity funds' target return?

I think the entire market is probably going to give you the same number, which is usually an IRR of nearly 20–30 percent. Now the real question is how many can deliver it. Many Limited Partners in the world publish the returns of the funds where they have invested, so to a certain extent, those numbers are public, though contractually by agreement with the investors they are secret so I can't tell you!

I can tell you that according to our placement agents, for our Ambienta II we are well into the top quartile funds in terms of returns. And our Ambienta III, which is the current program, is probably going to be at the same level. I think that's interesting because it proves that to pursue an environmentally positive thesis, you don't have to compromise on return expectations. On the contrary, our portfolio companies generate higher returns because of sustainability.

If you look at our investor base, you might imagine that because Ambienta is so green, all investors are focused on sustainability as well. But no, only one part of our investors have green-labeled or thematic vehicles with some sustainability element or environmental sustainability. The others are just traditional institutional investors who are attracted by our returns.

What is your target investment size?

If you look at Ambienta III with the co-investment vehicles that are attached, we can call it a €700 million program and we are looking at doing about ten investments out of that fund. So that gives you an equity ticket on average of about €70 million, with a ticket size range of €40 million up to €100 million.

Imagining a 50–50 debt-to-equity ratio, and understanding that we do majority share investments only, it means we can chase up to a couple of hundred million euros of enterprise value.

You only do majority share investments?

According to the rules of the fund, we can also do minority investments. But in the journey of Ambienta, Ambienta Fund I was 50–50 minorities/majorities. Ambienta Fund II had less minority investments and Ambienta Fund III doesn't have any minority investments. You can very easily correlate returns with control, and where you have less control, returns are way more volatile. I'm not saying you're not going to make money, but the returns will be more volatile.

What is Ambienta's theory of change?

At this point, the logic in my head bifurcates, because ESG and sustainability are two different things. You can have very good ESG management, even in nuclear bomb shells, but in terms of sustainability we cannot invest in nuclear bomb shells.

So, we have an investment strategy which is focused on sustainability—resource efficiency, and pollution control. We have developed a number of tools, particularly our proprietary Environmental Impact Analysis, which is a quantitative methodology to assess environmental impact. That guides how we invest the money or guides us to stay away from greenwashing. And that's sustainability.

We started many years ago to work very actively in ESG but ESG is not [the primary] part of our investment strategy. We will never decline an investment because it scores low on ESG. Our philosophy is that in our five years [invested in the company] we will improve whatever ESG management level we get, whatever we start with.

With sustainability, that's not possible. If a business model is not sustainable, there is nothing you can do in five years. It's probably going to die because it's not sustainable or it's not interesting because it's not sustainable. But we don't have the ambition to change these business models. The ambition is to identify business models that have a positive environmental impact and help them grow faster, bigger, and more international.

How do you select your investments?

The first thing we do is check sustainability because in private equity the bottleneck is really your time and people, not your capital. You always have more capital than is reported on your books, because if you find an incredible investment your investors will give you all the money you want to do a much bigger investment.

The problem is not the money. The problem is to find the investments. The problem is your internal resources, the people you can mobilize, and the people that you have. You don't want to waste a minute on an investment that you cannot do because it's not environmental. So, the first thing we do is to analyze a certain business and convince ourselves it is in an environmentally positive position. We go and we measure how environmentally positive it is and if it passes thresholds, we say, "Okay, let's proceed to a non-binding offer. Let's begin due diligence. Let's branch out in the industry." But if we don't convince ourselves it is positive on the environment, then it's not a business for us.

ESG comes much later in the investment process. Once the investment is in proper formal due diligence, then we do a separate ESG due diligence. That will reveal certain risks and opportunities and low-hanging fruits. We will then do a materiality analysis and an ESG action plan and implement it, etc.

As I said before, we are not going to decline an investment because it's poor on ESG. We will improve it with time. But sustainability is not curable. If you do cigarettes, just to use a silly example, we don't have the ambition to buy a producer of tobacco and turn it into . . . I wouldn't know what, in five years. Because even if I knew what, it's probably not going to happen in five years, which is our average holding time.

Is it better to have your own proprietary scoring methodologies for ESG and sustainability or to have a convergence across the industry?

Sustainability is more defined, because if a business model, like digging coal, doesn't have a positive environmental impact it's very difficult to argue that it's sustainable. Because there is science, there is work, there is a certain thinking that goes in a certain direction. We don't manipulate the thinking. We simply measure the impact.

For example, how much CO_2 do you get when you burn a ton of coal? If we dig coal, we know it's going to be burned. It will have a negative release of so many thousands of tons of CO_2. So, we've quantified how negative that is.

Conversely, if you invent a type of fuel that doesn't release CO_2, then we would say, "Okay, this fuel offsets for each ton. Or for each caloric output of this fuel, it offsets the equivalent caloric output of so many kilos of coal that would have released so much CO_2. We quantify what is the CO_2 savings of this new technology, compared to an incumbent technology—like coal, in this example.

I think sustainability can be quite numerically defined and you can follow it. You just need to have a number of metrics that cover all sustainability. For example, the world has very much been insisting on [reducing emissions of] CO_2. I certainly agree that's important, but CO_2 is not everything. We will have businesses where you save CO_2 and you measure how much CO_2 you save. Great. Then, for example, we have businesses where you measure clean water. It's got nothing to do with CO_2, but you take dirty water, you remove all the contaminants, and you dispose of them accordingly. Then you release within the system fresh, uncontaminated water. This is also a positive environmental impact which has got nothing to do with CO_2. Another one of our environmental metrics is biodiversity. You have certain business models that foster biodiversity but have nothing to do with CO_2.

We use 11 environmental metrics because we think you need that many to really cover all the aspects of what an environmentally sustainable business is. And that, I think, is our uniqueness. A few managers try to do the same, only a few, but they only use CO_2.

Provide an example of the type of investment that you prefer.

We have an investment that produces additives for the cement industry, which is very much under the microscope right now because of its CO_2 emissions. The cement industry has done a lot in terms of evolving their technological processes to save CO_2, and they have achieved results.

Now you can blend grey cement with more intelligent binders. You also have multicomponent mixes that offer better performances than cement. Thanks to this, you use less cement in terms of quantity.

For example, there are certain combinations of acidity and temperature like you often have in Asia that pit cement. Sewage pipes made with cement are cheap, but they become pitted and start leaking and you have to dig everything out and repair them. But, for example, you make them out of pure calcium luminous cement, which nobody does because it's very expensive. Calcium illuminate cement is an oddity for cement and we own a company that does it. If you blend it with cement, you have a pipe that lasts, even under the most aggressive circumstances, over a century. Accelerated lab tests prove that. You would never have to dig a city out to re-pipe sewage.

There you have an environmental impact. You don't have leakages of dirty water. You don't have all the emissions that are associated with digging those pipes out, recasting them, and replacing them. This is an example of a type of sustainable business we like to invest in.

Another one we invested in many years ago is the European leader in water-based pigments in coatings for wood. With solvent-based pigments you release a lot of compounds which are usually toxic and at least cancerogenic. Or you can use water-based pigments. It's a different, more complicated technology and a bit more expensive. In Europe now the share of water-based wood coatings is almost 100 percent, but in Asia it's almost zero, because in Asia the cost is still prevailing over the environment.

How do you measure impact?

For example, in the case of the coatings, we know in what application sectors we sell how many tons of what. And we know what other technology we are going to displace with our sales. We know how many tons of what kind of solvent-based coloring systems we are going to replace.

For example, specific to wood coatings, we knew our product was going on front and back coatings of wider panels. You replace different kinds of paints, because what you use for painting the front is more glossy and usually more expensive than what you use to paint the back. We have product for both lines, and we know what we compete against. We can calculate how many tons of solvents we eventually replace with all the tons of product that we sell. We can calculate how many tons of solvents we eliminated. So, it's a fairly precise calculation of the environmental impact. We can also calculate the savings in terms of CO_2, because solvent-based coating systems are heavier—so they have higher transportation costs.

Do you have this level of precision in calculating impact for most of your investments?

What we declare to our investors, first of all, is that the methodology we use is proprietary. But it's not secret. Our LPs have it. It is agreed upon with them, so they are happy with the methodology. We told them very clearly that we are not an academic institution, so our ambition is not to be perfect, but to make sure we are not investing in greenwashing. Our goal is to be reasonably accurate in order to verify that we are putting money into something which is environmentally positive. This is key for us, because if we can prove this to our investors, they will continue to invest with us and others like us, in environmentally positive propositions.

How do you provide proactive value-add to your portfolio companies?

We help them with ESG and we also help with operations. We have the investment team, and then we have operating partners that dive into the operations of our portfolio companies and help management find what we are looking for, which is different company by company. Sometimes you look for output. Sometimes you look for efficiencies.

For example, this company was doing components for tractors, and it is a manufacturing company, not a service company. The challenge was they needed to double sales within 18 months. Now, doubling a manufacturing company is not as easy as in a service company. In a service company you sell more, but in manufacturing you've got to produce double the widgets that you sell.

You can't double the plant and the workforce of 500 people in 18 months. So, we needed the help of the entire organization, working in a different way. So, we went down to the individual employee and created a bonus system that included the entire firm. We created WhatsApp groups where every shift was communicating the level of productivity to the incoming shift, so that the incoming shift knew whether they were starting from an advantage or disadvantage against the budget or production scheduling—and whether there was something they needed to recover. We created an internal kindergarten for all the employees that have problems with childcare, so they could bring them to work. In that case, we made our business plan by striking a pact with the entire workforce, not just with the CEO and the CFO.

Who are your typical investors?

Our current investors are the usual suspects—global institutional investors. Some are investors with programs that focus on sustainability, so they're thematic investors. Most are actually generalists who are focused on financial returns.

Now in Ambienta IV, which we will probably be raising at some point soon because we are three years into Ambienta III, I think this will change. That's because most generalist investors, though they may remain generalists, are becoming ESG activists and are developing an interest in sustainability. With sustainability taking a center stage in the global debate against climate change, investor demand for our investment strategy is increasing, from generalist investors from all over the world.

What impact will technology have on sustainability and visa-versa?

Every six months we publish something we call the Ambienta Lens, and the last one actually discussed the impact of technology on sustainability. Of course, the understanding in the imagination is that yes, technology is going to be positive and this is probably 90 percent true. But there are exceptions and it's important to have an analytical frame to figure out what these exceptions are, so that you don't fall prey to them.

What do you know now about sustainable investing that you wish you knew in 2012 when you joined Ambienta?

I think the rigor of the approach is the most important thing. You need to have a methodology that you apply in what you do that is shared with investors, because you need to bring them along on the journey with you. Where I think Ambienta has been successful against other funds is that we start and complete the journeys. We have been able to continuously communicate with our investors and bring them along as we have discovered a number of things, and they have discovered them with us. We declined investments that investors loved due to the fact that these were good investments. But we proved to ourselves and to our investors that these investments were not environmentally sustainable. For example, the sustainability aspect of palm oil is very debatable. In terms of resource efficiency, palm oil is great. It's the best edible fat at the cheapest possible price. But in terms of biodiversity, it's going to kill the planet. We decided not to invest in palm oil, and we had to prove it to our investors.

"There's risk in the person you're backing, there's risk in the market, there's risk in the product. But I think investing in the circular economy, at least today, is a way of actually de-risking your investment because you're investing in the direction of major industry."

CIRCULAR ECONOMY INVESTING
RON GONEN
CLOSED LOOP PARTNERS
CLOSEDLOOPPARTNERS.COM
LI: https://www.linkedin.com/in/ron-gonen-807a49

Ron Gonen is the Founder and CEO of Closed Loop Partners, a New York-based investment firm comprised of venture capital, growth equity, private equity, project-based finance, and an innovation center that's focused on building the circular economy.

Prior to Closed Loop Partners, he was New York City's Deputy Commissioner of Sanitation, Recycling, and Sustainability, during the Bloomberg administration. Gonen oversaw public policy in that regard, and the collection and processing of NYC's paper, metal, glass, plastic, textile waste, electronic waste, organics, and hazardous waste. In 2013, the Natural Resources Defense Council and Earth Day New York named him the city's Public Official of the Year.

Throughout his career, Gonen has earned numerous business and environmental awards, including recognition as "Champion of the Earth" by the United Nations Environment Program. He was awarded a Medal of Excellence by Columbia University, where he earned his MBA and later served as an Adjunct Professor in its business School from 2010–2018. He was also the 2021 recipient of the Social Enterprise Center Award for Excellence in Teaching.

Earlier in his career, Gonen was the Co-Founder and CEO of RecycleBank and his career started at Deloitte Consulting. A former member of the Council on Foreign Relations and Henry Catto Fellow at the Aspen Institute, he holds multiple recycling industry technology and business method patents.

Please provide an overview of Closed Loop Partners.

Closed Loop Partners is an investment firm and innovation center focused on the circular economy. We're structured to be able to invest along the growth trajectory of a solution. We look at bottlenecks and supply chains, identify solutions and the right type of capital for them, and then focus on solving that bottleneck. We try to do it in industry verticals where we have deep expertise, or where our corporate LPs are prominent. So that's in consumer products and packaging, food and agriculture, fashion apparel, and electronics. We have a venture fund, a project finance fund, a growth equity fund, and a private equity fund.

I don't necessarily view myself as an investor, but I'm using an investment platform to build out the circular economy—and I find all of those asset classes interesting.

What is the circular economy and how does it differ from the linear one?

The linear economy is structured where extractive industries like oil and gas and mining, and the landfill industries dominate in terms of value creation. In order to manufacture anything, you need to extract a natural resource. It's usually designed to be used once and then disposed of in a landfill. The next unit you manufacture, you have to again extract the natural resource and dispose of it in a landfill. And that type of system, while it's in the best financial interest of the extractive industries and the landfills, it is not in the interest of taxpayers, consumers, consumer products, companies, or municipalities. What is in their interest is a circular economy, where you're constantly reusing material in a sustainable loop.

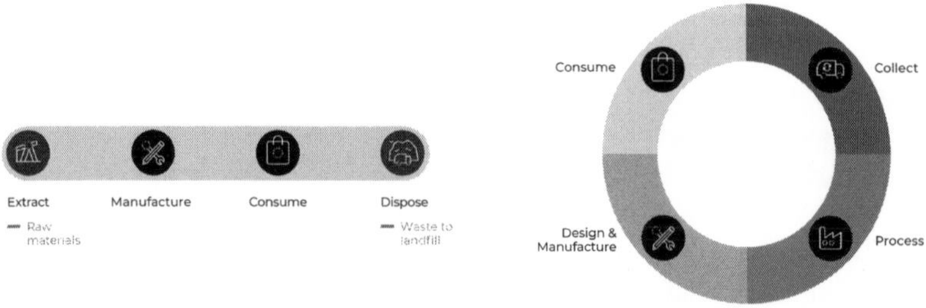

Transition from a linear economy to a circular economy. *Source:* Closed Loop Partners

Why are your funds a more attractive investment compared to traditional or even environmentally focused VC or PE funds?

It's because we believe that we're investing in where the market and the economy is moving, and that we have proprietary insights in terms of that direction because of our corporate Limited Partner base. Why invest in us? Because we provide financial market exposure and the ability to invest in products and services that are beneficial to your community in the world. That's very, very important to me, that people begin to recognize that by investing in either a circular economy or in sustainable products, the combination of financial market exposure and community benefit places the investor on a parallel path with the future of investing.

It's my view—and I think the data backs this up—that you are going to end up investing in companies that have a strong chance to outperform the market. But, even more importantly, you're going to screen for, and disregard, companies that are going to lose significant value in the long term. Either because of something they're doing that they're not exposing in the market, or are trying to hide, or because they just don't recognize where the world is going and have not planned for it.

Explain how you identify your investment targets and the screening processes that you use.

I'm a big believer in value investing. We try to ensure that each one of our funds is a very strict price-to-value discipline, as opposed to just "Hey, this is a cool company. Let's try to see if the valuation is correct." We try to say, "Within this asset class, this is our price-to-value ratio that we're comfortable with to make an investment."

Sometimes we see investments where we really like the companies, where we really like the CEO, but it just doesn't fit our price-to-value discipline. So, the first thing we're always looking for is, does it fit within our investing model? That doesn't mean that we don't miss investments sometimes. But it means we optimize our time and our focus on our expertise on specific market segments and sizes within those markets.

At the same time, we have nonfinancial screens that involve how circular the company is, what impact it's having, how many tons is it ensuring don't go to a landfill, and how many tons of greenhouse gas emissions it's reducing. So, we definitely screen for the social and environmental impact of the company at its core business and not in an esoteric way.

What are the companies that you don't invest in?

On the venture fund side, probably the biggest screen is that we'll only invest in a company where the post-money valuation is below $10 million when we invest. It may be an interesting company, but it just doesn't meet our investment model and the price-to-value ratio that we need. The next screen is generally whether a technology can be advanced to the stage where it's a business.

So, we're always asking the question, "what problem is this solving for somebody that would pay to have the problem solved?" Because there are businesses or governments that have problems, but they're not motivated for whatever reason to fix them. You have to make sure that the solution is good enough that the buyer—whether it be a business or a family or an individual or a government—says, "Wow, that really solves a problem for me."

Provide a couple of examples of circular economy investments you've selected.

We were the seed investor in a company called HomeBiogas, based in Israel, which has since gone public on the Tel Aviv stock exchange. It's a company that has developed household anaerobic digesters, appliances that go in your home or backyard. You put food waste into it and it converts it to gas that you can use to heat your water to cook. This was a solution that I had been looking for and had actually been writing about, and, in a parallel universe, the founders and CEO were developing it. As luck would have it, we got connected. We became their first investor and they've done a great job.

Another cool company from the early stage was Mori, who developed an odorless, tasteless, edible silk protein that goes around fruits, vegetables, meats, etc. to create an oxidization barrier and reduce spoilage. You can't see it, can safely digest it, and it eventually evaporates into the atmosphere. It's a perfect example of using material science to get rid of the unnecessary plastic packaging involved in supply chains and storage of foods.

What does impact mean to you and how do you measure it?

What we're looking for in terms of impact is the ability to reduce extraction of natural resources and disposal in landfills. Any investment we look at, whether it's an anaerobic digester, material science company, or a recycling facility, we're always looking at it through that lens.

In terms of how we measure impact, we have certain criteria that we ask our portfolios to report on in the areas in which we think they're having impact. It may be how much recycled material did they use so that we can measure natural resources then that weren't extracted. Or, if you're a recycling company, how much are you recycling—which represents material that could have gone to a landfill, but instead went back into the supply chain.

Who are your typical investors and why do they invest with you?

We have a lot of corporate investors, and they obviously look at their returns, but they're also interested in making sure that our investments are creating supply chain solutions for them as we can offer a multi-tier benefit for these investors. Other investors include family offices, financial institutions, and foundations. They also seek a combination of attractive financial returns and the assurance that their money is invested in something that's creating some type of benefit without causing harm.

What is an example of the supply chain solutions that your investments create?

Sometimes we're developing innovative new solutions; sometimes we're just getting solutions to scale. We invested in a company called rPlanet Earth, which is a bottle-to-bottle recycling facility in California. It was $150 million financing: Oaktree, Citi, the State of California, and us. Our corporate LPs really care about that facility getting built because they want that material. They're just not in the business of financing manufacturing facilities, so it doesn't get built if someone else doesn't step in. They look to us to help with that.

Are your investors exposed to any risks unique to the circular economy versus a traditional PE or VC fund?

What makes what we're doing unique is that we have the brands giving us insights in terms of their future direction and the evolving market landscape. Our thesis might be idealistic and aspirational that we want our investments to do better for the world. But by the same token, maybe we're not idealistic or aspirational—maybe we're just realistic about where the world is headed. Our corporate LPs and the largest consumer packaged goods companies tell us where they're trying to go, and we're trying to put money behind that direction.

There's risk in the person you're backing, there's risk in the market, there's risk in the product. But I think investing in the circular economy, at least today, is a way of actually de-risking your investment because you're investing in the direction of major industry.

What is your Innovation Center for the Circular Economy and what led to its development?

Pretty early on in the formation of our company, our corporates started asking us for advice and recommendations and suggestions on different challenges they faced. We started offering insight and the demand for this started growing and growing. So, I recognized that we have a business here where we could leverage our subject matter expertise to offer advisory services, research, and development. That really became the seed for the Center for the Circular Economy.

I got somebody that I worked with very closely in the Bloomberg administration, Kate Daly, to join me and lead that, which helped significantly. Since the business had an ongoing platform to jump into, it's been able to take off and do really well.

Does it give you a competitive advantage?

Definitely. You can think about where things are going and what's happening without the pressure of "Am I investing or not?" They're just evaluating it from a pure industry analysis scenario.

The center has been very helpful to us because you have this internal group that's working on bottlenecks where there aren't yet investment grade solutions. The center works on why there isn't a solution, what's required for there to be a solution, or if there's a solution that just needs a little tweaking.

Having that type of innovation and insight group within an investment firm is really helpful, because it tells us where some of the biggest opportunities are—as well as some of the challenges.

To what extent are companies off-loading their environmental costs onto the public?

It's a really big issue. Just to give you an example, the fossil fuel industry, which is the maker of plastics, receives $20 billion a year in local and federal subsidies. When you're giving an industry that much money, it can artificially keep its price low and make sure there are no other alternatives that scale.

If the U.S. government took the money it gave to dirty industries in tax subsidies and other subsidies, and shifted that over to sustainable and circular industries, you'd see tremendous growth. Over the following five years they could say, "We're going to spend $100 billion on sustainable solutions and renewable energy and the circular economy, and it doesn't cost taxpayers a cent. All that would be doing is shifting that money from petrol over to another industry.

What about changing the accounting rules for these costs?

It'll drive some toward circular. Some will fail. But the bigger problem is a lot of these industries have only been profitable because they've been subsidized by the public.

Are you up against powerful forces who have vested interest in the traditional economy?

There's definitely some opposition. They used to be winning, but I think the tide has turned and now they're fighting an uphill battle. There is definitely opposition from the extractive industries and the landfill industry. Those are the two industries that don't want to see this change happen.

I wouldn't think that they're applying resources directly against us, but that in most cases, they're just trying to keep growing the legacy footprint that they have. In that sense, we compete and we butt heads, but not because they're trying to do what we're trying to do, or we're trying to do what they're trying to do. We're both going after the same pie. Right now, they have the largest piece of the pie by far. But every time we just take another small nibble out of it, and the bite's getting much bigger because now it's the government that's biting.

Tell me about the book you recently released, *The Waste-Free World: How the Circular Economy Will Take Less, Make More and Save the Planet*[3] and what motivated you to write it?

The book is a chronicle, in a fun and interesting way, of modern U.S. economics and manufacturing and production, and how decisions were made in the best interests of certain industries, like extractive industries, that were not to the public's benefit. But it's the public that ends up having to pay.

The motivation behind it was that I had wanted to write about these ideas for a really long time, and the right situation came along where I got an offer to do so.

Chapter Seven

Alternatives: Private Debt

The Global Financial Crisis of 2008 began with a downturn in the U.S. housing market that triggered an international banking crisis. The economic devastation quickly spread worldwide, through interdependencies in the global financial system and became what many consider the most serious financial crisis since the Great Depression. Insolvencies reached a climax with the bankruptcy of Lehman Brothers on September 15, 2008 and financial institutions around the world had to rely on government support to avoid the same fate as they suffered massive losses.

Following that meltdown, new global banking regulations took effect. Known as the Third Basel Accord, these were in response to the revealed deficiencies in the international banking system. They increased minimum capital requirements and decreased bank leverage, making it more difficult for banks to grant loans to small and medium-sized enterprises. The stricter regulatory environment and risk aversion caused many banks—the traditional source of company debt—to retreat from the market, creating an opportunity for specialist lenders of private debt to step into the sector. At that time, private debt was considered a relatively new alternative asset class. Today, $812 billion is invested in private debt—representing between 10 and 15 percent of total assets under management, with a market of at least 4,000 active investors.

Private debt strategies essentially involve investors purchasing the debt of private companies. This can be senior secured instruments, mezzanine, high-yield debt or even microcredit and can be extended to both listed or unlisted companies. But, unlike public debt (i.e., fixed income, see chapter 5), the debt is not tradeable on liquid secondary exchanges.

BEHIND THE ATTRACTION

The increased demand from investors for private debt over the last decade has been driven by a number of factors. Institutional investors have had to hunt for yield in a historically ultra-low yield environment while companies have simultaneously needed capital to grow. Demand has also been driven by investor's desire to diversify from other asset classes given private debt's low correlation, predictable and contracted cash flows, and floating rate solutions that can protect against rising rates. It also has a lower risk than private equity, given private debt's position in the capital structure in the event of insolvency.

Another attraction is the breadth of industry and the capitalization and risk/return profiles that it can offer. Private debt can be extended to everything from higher-risk, emerging market, small- and medium-sized enterprises to lower-risk, developed market real assets—such as airports, toll bridges, and real estate.

IMPACT PUNCHES ABOVE ITS WEIGHT

Interestingly, despite its status as a relative newcomer, private debt is actually the largest impact-oriented asset class by AUM. According to the most recent GIIN survey,[1] it represents between 20 and 30 percent of total impact assets under management. Historically, that has been concentrated within microfinance funds—which we explore with BlueOrchard later in this chapter, and which have been in existence since the 1990s. But now it increasingly includes ever more specific and impactful themes.

This demand has not been exclusively driven by financial considerations. Private debt can enjoy a similar level of control to private equity, in demanding certain terms attached to a loan. Loans increasingly include a commitment by the company to assess and report on specific social or environmental impact, either for a discrete project being financed or for the company's entire operations. Since most private debt transactions are bilateral or involve only a small number of lenders, there is also a much closer relationship between the parties. This often translates into an ability to access much more granular impact data and metrics to track SRI performance.

Furthermore, given the nature of the transactions, structures can be bespoke and agreements may involve any number of specific covenants that the lender must then abide by or risk a default event (and the immediate return of capital). Beyond reporting impact, this could involve the delivery of specific outcomes, not just outputs—outcomes that can only be hoped for and lobbied for within the public debt or public equity markets.

PURE PLAY LEVERAGE

Above all, private debt offers investors pure play exposure to any desired impact theme, alongside financial returns—even more than in private equity. Typically, with private debt, there is very precise use of proceeds and, increasingly, fund strategies are devoted to highly specialized markets.

For instance, in this chapter, you will meet Ben Rick, co-founder of Social and Sustainable Capital, who extends market-rate loans to UK government-contracted charities in the UK. That enables those charities to acquire real estate for the provision of their services, such as sheltering victims of domestic abuse. Another pioneer you will meet is Calvert Impact Capital, where CEO Jennifer Pryce explains their Community Investment Note. That innovative retail product invests in underfunded community ventures overlooked by the traditional asset management industry—all while delivering a 100 percent historic investor repayment rate over more than 20 years.

Private debt may already be part of your diversified portfolio, and these conversations will be of particular relevance to you. But if not, read on and discover how you could leverage loans to positively change and uplift lives, while enjoying commercial rates of return.

"I never cease to be impressed by people who have pursued a life based on the desire to do the right thing and give something back."

SOCIAL IMPACT INVESTING
BEN RICK
SOCIAL AND SUSTAINABLE CAPITAL
SOCIALANDSUSTAINABLE.COM
LI: https://www.linkedin.com/in/ben-rick-0392524a/
TW: @SASCapital_Ben

Ben Rick is the Co-Founder and Chief Executive Officer of Social and Sustainable Capital, a company that provides flexible capital to enable social sector organizations to grow their social impact, tackle society's most pressing challenges and improve the lives of disadvantaged people across the UK.

Ben grew up in London and studied Management Science at the University of Manchester Institute of Science and Technology (now part of Manchester University). Previously he held positions in the Goldman Sachs Treasury Department, at Lehman Brothers and UBS on their corporate bond trading desks, and later was the Managing Director of the EMEA Global Proprietary Trading Group for Bank of America Merrill Lynch after which he began his social investment journey.

Please provide an overview of Social and Sustainable Capital ("SASC").

We manage private credit funds, maybe what used to be called venture debt. We work with small- to medium-size organizations that are actually—in any kind of international sense—micro. Their revenues are typically between half a million pounds a year and maybe 50 million pounds a year, so they're very small businesses on any kind of global scale.

We are lending money to these businesses that are either taking investment for the first time or investment is a small part of what they do, and where making a profit is a hygiene factor for them but not something that drives what they do.

Are they charities?

Yes—but probably not in the way that many people assume. It's easy to think of charities as organizations that raise grants and donations and then in turn give that money away. That's an accurate description of many charities, but not of the ones we work with. Our borrowers are better described as not-for-profit businesses. They are delivering services to local or central government, working with disadvantaged and vulnerable people. They are working under contract and get paid for that service. They may supplement their income to some extent with grants and donations, but our investments are based on their ability to repay any money borrowed by unlocking revenue streams.

Can you give an example of what one of these entities actually does and why they need credit?

They're doing a whole range of stuff. They may be helping victims of domestic violence. They may be working with people who have been released from prison. They may be working with children who've been in foster care and are leaving the system. They may be taking care of adults with learning disabilities. So, in almost all cases they're delivering some aspects of the statutory care that the UK government is required to perform for vulnerable or disadvantaged people. These are services that at some point may have been delivered by government itself. Over the years, government has outsourced that work to people who know it better or can do it more cheaply.

Why they need the money is because, just like any corporate, if you win a new contract to deliver a new service, there's a cost of building the ability to deliver that. Someone has to upfront the cost of that. Then once the service is up and running and you start to receive payment for delivering the service, you can pay down that initial investment. Essentially what it all comes back to is that we're providing capital that puts these not-for-profit businesses into a position where they can deliver a contract and generate a revenue stream.

Now, this is where it goes back to what I said before. That revenue stream is necessary to create a viable, ongoing, sustainable business—but they're not profit-maximizing organizations.

And these are open or closed-ended funds?

They're close-ended and kind of similar in structure to venture or private equity funds. Our flagship housing fund is a 13-year fund with a three-year investment period, of which for two and a half years it's open for investment. We're in the process of having the final close for our first fund, which has gone extremely successfully. There was some anxiety when COVID started, but ultimately the combination of the UK government's focus on housing as a result of COVID and investors' changing attitudes toward impact has been really positive for us. So, we're in the process of putting together the initial stages of the launch of fund number two, which will be later in the year.

Give me an overview of your social housing fund and the impact it is targeted to achieve.

This is very specific and easy to understand I think, if I can explain it. So, working with vulnerable people in the UK typically involves two things. It involves providing them with the advice and support that they need to overcome an issue that they're facing. Maybe they've left a violent partner, come out of the foster system or jail, or they're living with a learning disability. Whatever it might be, part of the role of these organizations is to provide the support that's needed to help them overcome that. But another part of it is to ensure that they're living somewhere suitable and safe.

Charities have been trying to deliver this dual kind of outcome, but they've had one hand slightly tied behind their backs because they've been relying on external parties for the housing element. So, they've maybe been relying on the council or housing associations or private rental sector to ensure that there were suitable properties available for their clients that would hopefully help their recovery or their transition—but certainly not hurt their chances of developing a stable living situation.

What became clear to us is that in this phase, more often than not, housing options were really poor. At one end of the spectrum, they were well-meaning but not suitable. At the other end they were unsuitable and frankly slightly scandalous, in terms of the condition of some properties that exist in the private rental sector. Now, that's disappointing but not completely surprising, because there's no reason why the private rental sector in the UK—where the median number of properties owned by a private city-center landlord is one—could be relied upon for housing disadvantaged and vulnerable people. So the market, for whatever reason—and there's a whole separate discussion about the housing market in the UK—has evolved to quite an unsatisfactory place. But what we were faced with was a situation where these charities could do a great job with disadvantaged people if they could just access appropriate housing.

We, in our travels in trying to understand how we were going to make a positive impact on the world, discovered a group of charities that had taken their fate into their own hands. They had found ways to become their own landlords and either buy or rent properties. They could take control of the housing stock and use those houses that they controlled and owned, or controlled and leased, to ensure that the interventions they were delivering were located in the appropriate living accommodations. What we saw was the huge change in the quality of outcomes that organizations that had access to those properties were able to achieve.

We looked at the space and said, "We need to have a fund that allows residential property to transfer from the commercial profit maximization space into the charitable space, so that it can be offered to clients alongside the support services that charities offer." We were focused on providing that finance.

So that's kind of philosophically and practically what we're doing. If you're a charity, you probably can get a mortgage and some of them do have mortgages. But because of the risk-averse nature of charities, we found that there was a limit to how far they were prepared to extend themselves to purchase this housing and to build these property portfolios. What we understood over time was that the reason was because of the nature of a mortgage. There were some certain factors about mortgages that they found off-putting: the requirement to come up with a deposit; the fact that they were exposed to housing prices; the fact that they were exposed to voids and to government payments; and the fact that they could never really be sure, because of the fixed nature of mortgages, that they'd be able to cover the ongoing costs of these houses.

What we realized, given our experience of working with charities was two things. One, that if we could find a way to share some of those risks or to pass some of those risks from the charities onto the investor base, it would enable them to consider taking on investment. Two, because of the work we did with the investor base, and because we have been investors ourselves, we realized that the risks that the charities wanted to rid themselves of were actually things that, in a great many cases, investors were not worried about. They were, in fact, in some cases positively trying to seek either exposure to government income or to assets that are increasing in value with inflation. We spotted an opportunity to create a very simple structure that de-risked the proposition for the borrower and increased the risk proposition for the investor, but that would still allow the capital to flow.

What exactly is the structure and how does it work?

So essentially, it looks like a mortgage in terms of the legal documentation. Some things that are unique about it are that we provide one hundred percent of the funding to buy the houses, we have security over the houses that are purchased with the money we provide but no claim on the wider activities of the organization, and our return is performance-based. So, we don't have a fixed level of interest. We look at the rental income of the property portfolio, deduct agreed costs with the charity, and then we receive the balance. Every quarter it's a different amount based on the performance of the portfolio of the charity and of the houses themselves.

Then, the final significant difference is at the end of the 10 years, what the charity owes us is a percentage of the value of the properties in the future, as opposed to a fixed amount. So, if they borrow a million pounds from us, in 10 years' time what they owe us is 85 percent of the value of the properties, regardless of whether that's more or less than what they borrowed from us. So, they operate the houses for 10 years and they're guaranteed an equity position in the properties at the end of the 10 years. And at that point, they can use that equity to then go and get a commercial mortgage, refinance our loan, and retain ownership of the properties.

But what is the equity position that they end up with?

They end up with a 15 percent stake in the portfolio, regardless of the valuation of the portfolio. If they buy a million pounds of houses and in 10 years' time those houses are still worth a million pounds, they only have to pay us back 850,000 pounds. So, they can effectively go and basically earn their way into an equity position in the housing. Now, obviously our assumption is—and with UK property it's proven to be the case—that you can't find a 10-year period in history where prices have gone down. The worst performing 10 years in history showed an increase of 1.4 percent a year. So, if the math is right, in 10 years' time these houses will be worth more than what was paid for them. So, in our base case the discount gets the fund back slightly more than was lent at the beginning of the life of the transaction. The fund overall says that on average across the UK we're going to see a continuation of steadily rising house prices. So that on a fund level, the money we get paid back at the end will be more than we lent in the beginning. What it does do for individual charities in each little geography, in each individual transaction, is that they are insulated from being in a negative equity situation, which is what they're really worried about.

How do you select an investment and make your investment decisions?

We look for a couple of key things. The first is we're looking for organizations of a certain size. We're typically looking for organizations with revenue of between one and thirty million pounds, because this is, from an impact perspective, where we think our money can create the most social impact. Like any investor, we look for really high-performing management teams and really great boards. That's really critical to making social investments. We look for organizations that have experience managing housing. We understand they're on a journey and we're part of that journey. But we need to be able to see a track record of how an organization manages housing stock, because that's the bet that we're taking, really.

We really importantly need to understand that they are a partner to their local commissioners, i.e., local government. We reference check with the organization that's ultimately going to be the purchaser of their service. We really need to understand that there's a close, trusting relationship between them and that local commissioner. And we need to really make ourselves comfortable that actually the provision of housing is going to generate better social outcomes for people. So, it's really just evidencing that impact.

Can you give me a real-world example of the type of impact and financial result that can be expected?

The interesting thing about this product is we didn't sit in a room with a white board and a bunch of really smart finance people and come up with this structure. This structure was genuinely co-designed with a charity, without whom we wouldn't have landed on the structure. That organization is called Hull Women's Network, they're in Hull, in the Northeast of England, and we met them quite early-on in our journey and their story was really clear. At the time we met them, they had 99 properties that they managed in the Hull area. They helped women and their children fleeing domestic violence.

The statistic they quoted was that women on average flee and return to a violent perpetrator on seven occasions before they finally break free. What they could demonstrate was that by providing an appropriate, safe house, women left on the first occasion and never returned to the violent perpetrator. They didn't need to describe the social impact any more than that. We were completely blown away. Just providing the right kind of housing meant that women and children could avoid six return visits to a violent perpetrator who may actually ultimately kill the woman. And so, we said, "That's great, why don't you have more housing?" And they said, and I'm paraphrasing, "Because we don't have the financial risk appetite to take on more. Because, ultimately, our goal is to stay in business and if we take on a lot more housing using conventional structures, we run the risk of not being around at all. So, we accept a slower rate of growth because we must endure. We must always be here."

They had 300 women on the waiting list that were trying to flee violent partners. That's how we got into the discussion with them about how there must be a product that would make it possible for them to grow. Now, with our funding since that first time we met that organization in 2017, they have bought approximately 80 houses, which now help women flee domestic abuse on a regular basis. There's a never-ending list of stories of women and children who have been able to rebuild their lives after sometimes many, many years of misery and pain.

What's the total AUM in your housing fund?

This fund is at £75 million. Not only is that large in the social investment world, it's also in line with a lot of commercial funds at the smaller end of the venture market, as well. Obviously, for a green bond fund or a big listed equity fund, that isn't large, but it isn't out of place. There are plenty of asset managers in the UK doing fully commercial business with funds in that zip code. Our next fund in the housing space is going to be £150 million to £200 million. So, for us as an organization, we have a short-term goal of an AUM of £250 million, and a medium-term goal of £500 million.

What are the benefits for your investors?

The real trick with impact investment is the ability to make a fair return doing something that you can be proud of. The truth is, three to five years ago lots of people believed this was the right thing to do, but there was only a small group of people who felt they actually could do that—whether it was because of their mandate or because of the fiduciary responsibility, etc. There was only a small group of people who felt that they could say, "This is the right way to make an appropriate return, so we're going to do it."

What's changed over the last two to three years is that not only do people recognize the importance of putting some of their money to work in a way that generates something other than the pure financial return, but I would say that many investing bodies are actually nervous about not being able to say what it is in their portfolio that is doing that. So, we are finding that people are either pushing themselves to understand what is available in the world of impact investment at our end of the spectrum, or in some cases their stakeholders are pushing them quite hard toward us.

So, for example, I can tell you that there are asset managers in the UK who manage large sums of money for charitable endowments where the charitable endowments are saying to these asset managers, "What exactly are you doing with your AUM that is socially impactful?" And some of those asset managers are losing mandates because they can't describe what it is. When you lose a mandate, you can put a very clear number on what it just cost you by not doing something more impactful. That is definitely helping organizations consider the best way for them to do impact investment in the UK.

I would say that if you look at the journey of SASC, for many years there was an absolute bar that we as an organization needed to get over to be able to attract commercial money. That absolute bar was too high because of the nature of what we did. What's happened now is that's become a relative bar. Organizations are saying, "We need to do something in the impact or social investment space. What's the best fund available?" So we've gone from having to reach some artificially high bar to now just having to be the best product on offer. And not everybody agrees, but there are enough people that believe that our product is the best thing on offer. As a result, we're engaging a far broader range of investors than we would have thought possible three years ago.

This sounds like a win-win situation for the investor. What is their potential downside or the risk?

The downside is we're a small asset manager that got established around 2014. Ultimately, for some people, it's a challenging area because we're funding organizations that are working with vulnerable people. The funds are long dated and there isn't any liquidity. So, you invest in 2021 and you don't get your money back until 2032. Obviously, that's no different from many other private and alternative assets that institutions are increasingly investing in. Pre-COVID, people would have said, "Oh, the risk profile of the housing benefit is kind of tricky because governments cut spending, etc."

Interestingly, during COVID, it was the only area of the property market where you could be confident of receiving rent, because if you invested in commercial property or hotels or shopping centers, I mean obviously you've had a torrid time.

How do you achieve a balance between delivering a financial return to your investors on one side, and deploying capital to these not-for-profits or charities that have real urgent, human needs?

That's the secret sauce—if there is a secret sauce for SASC and any other organization in this space—being credible to both sides of this proposition. So we, I think somewhat uniquely, have two stakeholder groups that are very different. If you're in the venture capital business, you're talking to investors and founders who are both trying to make a lot of money and everyone's on the same page and it's really straightforward. We, as an organization, have to be able to engage with organizations that are motivated almost entirely by purpose and, in some cases, may even find making a profit from investing in these activities quite a challenging concept.

On the other side, we're working with investors who are increasingly interested in purpose but, ultimately, when it comes down to it, there's an underlying financial incentive—and that's tricky. It's quite a hard place to live in that gray area between impact and purpose and profit. It involves constantly reassessing the construction of the products, how we market, who we market to, who we engage with, and who we work with, and it's hard. Sometimes we say, "Who knew how hard it was going to be to try and do a little bit of good?"

To be clear, we aren't delivering the social outcomes. We're in a supporting role, supporting organizations that are doing the hard work. We don't claim the impact of the organizations that we provide finance for. But it's been surprisingly hard to create a sustainable asset manager in this space because it isn't something that, left to its own devices, capitalism probably would have found. It's an interesting clash of cultures.

How has your investor base changed over the years?

Two or three years ago, we'd been going for four or five years and it wasn't clear how we were ever going to make the change away from that small group of highly motivated investors that would allow us to do what we were doing, but ultimately would never provide the scale of capital that would allow us to do things in a meaningful way. And then it just all changed when the investing world discovered impact. But the truth is, two years ago it was very hard to speak to an organization with a billion-pound fund and persuade them to part with 5 million pounds into something like us. Now, the argument is, "Well, I've got a billion pounds, it's just a 5-million-pound investment."

The whole argument has been turned on it's head. It's gone from being too small to be relevant to being very relevant and helpful that, ultimately, it's a small percentage of people's financial exposure. It's been a sea change. I think initially we thought it was a threat because we thought there still is this risk, if people don't understand the difference between green bonds and what we do. Organizations may have a small portfolio of green bonds and say, "Well, that's it, that's my impact investment, done." But actually, I think that initial fear has gone away because I think people really do recognize the difference between an organization issuing a green bond and providing capital to an organization that helps women fleeing violence. I think people do understand that. And it may be that the investor says, "I understand the difference, but I cannot do what you're doing for reasons X, Y, and Z." But that is still positive.

If you could sit down and speak with anyone you wanted to in the responsible investment space, who would it be?

Investment people like me wouldn't make my wish list of people to sit down with and speak to. In a way, the great pleasure of my job is that I don't ever really have to sit down with people like me. The people I love sitting down with are the people who run these charities and operate these services. I never cease to be impressed by people who have pursued a life based on the desire to do the right thing and give something back. I have had people say to me, "Oh, you're so amazing. You walked away from a city career to do this." I mean, frankly, that's sort of a joke.

I've walked away from my city career after I'd made enough money that I could do that in a way that was relatively devoid of fear about my own personal path. The people running charities who, from the outset, dedicate their lives to taking care of vulnerable people, those are the people I like to sit down with. It just never ceases to impress me that people's motivations are what they are, and thank God for people like them.

"Our goal is to make a positive environmental and/or social impact in the world, while at the same time achieving an attractive financial return. That's how we define impact investing."

MICROFINANCE
PHILIPP MUELLER
BLUEORCHARD FINANCE LTD
BLUEORCHARD.COM
LI: https://www.linkedin.com/in/philipp-mueller-3660152a/

Philipp Mueller is Chief Executive Officer of BlueOrchard, a leading global impact investment manager, member of the Schroders Group, that connects millions of entrepreneurs in emerging and frontier markets with investors. As CEO, Mueller leads the executive and extended management team and has oversight of the firm's client and business strategy and resource management.

Prior to assuming the CEO role, Mueller was Head of Investment Solutions, leading the Global Investment Committee as well as overseeing the portfolio management and asset allocation of all funds and mandates. He joined BlueOrchard in 2018 from Partners Group, where he served in a number of capacities in Switzerland and in the UK, most recently as Senior Vice President of Investment Solutions. Mueller holds an MBA from ETH Zurich and a master's degree in Law from the University of Zurich.

How do you describe what you do?

Our goal is to make a positive environmental and/or social impact in the world while at the same time achieving an attractive financial return. That's how we define impact investing.

I'm responsible for achieving the high aspirations and goals that we've set for ourselves, and to maintain our position as one of the pioneering and leading impact investors in the world. I see my role here as comparable to the one of a football coach. To make sure that we have the resources, the team, and the direction and strategy to follow through with our intrinsic motivation to generate a lasting positive impact.

Before you moved to BlueOrchard you spent several years in different roles at Partners Group. What prompted your transition from pure private equity to impact investing?

I had worked on projects related to sustainable investments and decided to work fully in this field. When I was asked to join BlueOrchard, I saw this as a great chance because BlueOrchard is a pioneer, an expert in its field. It's a very dynamic multicultural global company with a great mission which is also aligned with my values. I wanted to, in the end, also align my work with my values and do something with more purpose behind it.

Also, from an intrinsic motivation perspective, I'm a father of three children. I wonder what the world they live in will be like in 20, 30, or 50 years? Impact investing is the most powerful tool to drive lasting change. You can donate something that's a one-off, but with impact investing, you can really change certain things at a scale which you would have previously thought to be impossible. That is really what attracted me to BlueOrchard.

Can you give me an overview of BlueOrchard's mission?

We only do investments which have a positive social and/or environmental impact and at the same time generate market rate returns. BlueOrchard has now been in existence for 20 years—we celebrated our 20-year anniversary this past year. BlueOrchard's formation traces back to the late 1990s and a cooperation between the then Head of the United Nations Conference on Trade and Development's Microfinance Unit in Geneva and the later founding members of BlueOrchard, who in the context of the UN Millennium Development Goals (MDGs) developed the idea of a private investment fund specialized in the funding of microfinance institutions. This idea eventually resulted in the inception of BlueOrchard in 2001.

The MDGs (established in 2000) were the predecessors to the Sustainable Development Goals [established in 2016]. Today we're managing not only the world's first fully private commercial microfinance fund but also the largest with around $2.5 billion under management.

Since then, we have evolved to other asset classes. We manage private equity, liquid instruments like impact bonds, green bonds, and social bonds, and sustainable infrastructure projects.

Can you explain exactly what microfinance is?

Basically, microfinance is a way to advance financial inclusion—financial inclusion means providing access to financial services, such as loans, savings, insurance, or payment services, to people who did not have the chance before. We include people who have been excluded from the financial system, who have a low income or lack sufficient funds for entrepreneurial activities. Microfinance is one of the tools to really make financial services accessible to a population which has not been in that position before.

So, for the smaller entrepreneur at the base of the pyramid, can you share an example of the range of ticket size we're talking about?

This depends on the region, the currency, the sector of the entrepreneurial activity, and the purpose of the loan. It can be about $200 to $3,000, or even to $15,000 in the case of an MSME. There's a big variation in the range of loan amounts. There's also a great diversity in investment partners with whom we work with in the local markets, in terms of their focus and what their priorities are.

Can you describe the process by which you get investors' money into the hands of base-of-the-pyramid borrowers?

This is a long process, in which the whole BlueOrchard team is involved in some way. One part of the team is sourcing, assessing, managing, and maintaining relationships with partner institutions in emerging and frontier markets. We go to the branch, which is the furthest away from the headquarters, to really assess how these institutions operate.

There is another part of that team, which is analyzing these institutions to make sure that the way they are granting loans is sound, and that the terms of these loans are being adequately explained to the borrowers. Then, from an impact perspective, we have a very thorough impact management process, which is developed and applied by a separate team—our impact management team. We are looking at social and governance aspects, and at several aspects of how these institutions operate.

Then, obviously, we also look at the actual numbers. We are performing a very structured analysis which is, I would say, related to what Standard and Poor's or Moody's would do, namely assessing the financial institution. We basically perform a credit rating and also a financial strength rating of that institution to really make sure it is set up soundly—a commercial assessment. Separately, we do a risk assessment on the country's risk, on the regulatory risk, and also the KYC [Know Your Client] risk. So, who owns that microfinance institution, who is involved there, and making sure that from that perspective, the institutions are sound. If we are convinced that this institution is a fit, then there are different types of instruments we can work with to fund the institution. Finally, that institution would pass this funding to its end-borrowers. In a nutshell, we are selecting trusted regional partners in our network based on a thorough due diligence and these institutions then give out the microloans.

And we are also monitoring what's happening during an investment period. So, a) we are monitoring portfolio development and have quite stringent reporting, and b) we are also monitoring it from a social standpoint. Because as an impact investor, we cannot withdraw our money immediately, right? That would have dire consequences for the people who are at the end of that chain. But, obviously, what we can do is influence how these institutions operate and also make them aware of certain

BlueOrchard Field Trip, January 2020. Visiting micro-entrepreneurs in Piura, Peru. © BlueOrchard Finance, 2021.

shortcomings and work with them to improve their operations. Having done that for 20 years, we have a very great network in various countries, and we are also very selective with whom we work together.

Would you be able to give a real-world example of microfinance's impact on the life or livelihood of a bottom-of-the-pyramid borrower?

I once visited an area north of Lima, Peru, where there are a lot of development needs and some areas are very poor. I met with one of the founders of one of our partners, a really well-organized institution. Together, we went to the local markets with some of the loan officers and they knew everyone there, interacting with different people there who sell goods. So, we went to see one of their microentrepreneurs who produces leather works. His first microloan I think was $200 or so, to buy his tools. He is a great craftsman and over time he grew his business. Now, his wife has a shop in one of the more touristic centers and he can feed his family and send his kids to school. He repaid his loan relatively quickly, he then took out another one so they could expand the shop, and so on. And this shows basically what an impact you can

BlueOrchard Field Trip, January 2020. Visiting micro-entrepreneurs in Piura, Peru. © BlueOrchard Finance, 2021.

have by providing such entrepreneurs access to capital. It's about helping people to build an existence. That is at the core of what we are doing.

What are the financial advantages to microfinance investors?

You are investing in a very resilient and stable asset class. Microfinance will not provide investors with double-digit returns, at least not in the current environment, but it will give them a stable and steady return. It's also because it's historically less correlated to other asset classes or markets. That's because in microfinance, typically you are lending to people who are in rural areas, working in agriculture, and who are serving the needs of local communities. They are not directly connected to whatever is happening on Wall Street or the financial markets. It is a resilient business serving local communities.

The return obviously depends on how portfolios are structured, what they're targeting, and so on. We, for example, have set up portfolios for development finance institutions, which are targeting so called "tier three," very small microfinance institutions, for a certain impact outcome and with the aim to building up a market. We also have a Women Empowerment strategy, which targets female entrepreneurs. So, it really depends on the portfolio. The returns are market rate, so that is attractive for investors, and historically less correlated to other asset classes.

What is blended finance, how is it used in microfinance investing, and what are its benefits to private investors?

Blended finance can be described as public-private partnerships for impact investments. The "blended" comes from the capital structure which consists of public and private investors. So, on the public side we have, for example, development finance institutions and multilaterals and on the private side different kinds of institutional investors. Basically, you blend public sector capital with private sector capital. The public sector investors want to leverage and multiply the impact that they can achieve with the funds that they're deploying. So, for every dollar they invest, they want to attract four dollars from the private sector to multiply the effect they can have.

And, typically with these blended finance mandates, they (the public sector investors) have a specific impact goal. They might want to drive a financial inclusion agenda or a climate adaptation agenda, and so on. These are very specifically designed mandates, and the blended finance structure also helps to change the risk return profile of such investments. There are certain areas in which private investors would not invest unless there is a certain enhancement of the risk.

For example, climate change adaptation, where people would not invest in an insurance company in Africa which is aiming at rolling out climate insurance products. You would have to look really hard for private investors, but if you can change the risk return profile of a fund, it's easier to attract them. So, for example, if there will be a first-loss piece in a portfolio protecting private investors to some extent, then some of them would consider making an investment. If, for example, first-loss protection is provided for a quarter of the portfolio, then that means a quarter of the money needs to be lost before I'm hit as a private investor. Then, I'd actually be more inclined to invest in a strategy which is helping climate change and increasing the number of climate insurance beneficiaries and countries, or in a strategy focusing on education finance in Africa.

The microfinance investment space hasn't been without controversies. As a result, have there been lessons learned and any safeguards put in place?

For sure, the industry has matured considerably. BlueOrchard has a 20-year track record and there are others who are close to that.

There have been many lessons for the industry as a whole. Today, we have much more regulation of interest rate caps, we have local credit bureaus, increased central bank control, a certain amount of self-regulation, concrete industry standards, and much more transparency.

So, from that perspective, I think that much of the criticism that has been voiced over time has been addressed by the industry in the last two decades. I don't think that nowadays in this field you can afford to be involved in untransparent practices. Nevertheless, there will always be rotten apples, cases where you have certain institutions which are not following established standards and clearly these are not the right counterparties for us. We have a very strict investment and impact management process, and this is something which we are very much focused on.

I'd like to get your view on opportunities or what you see as the future for leveraging the technology for impact in the microfinance industry.

There are huge opportunities. I think specifically of the markets we are investing in, and how they do not have legacy systems that they need to maintain backward compatibility with. So, on their platforms, they can start from scratch and can basically leapfrog and use the most recent technologies. I think that the development costs are much lower in many of the countries and that the knowledge can be applied universally. You can learn programming wherever you are. And there are exciting new technologies out there from a microfinance and financial inclusion perspective. There are also a lot of advantages of technology because you can reach many more people, people who live in remote areas for example. You can reach communities that you could otherwise only reach through a branch network. There are exciting technologies which will extend the reach and accessibility. But there are also limits to this, because microfinance and impact investing are built on trust and relationships and are about understanding the people and their businesses. So, the personal interaction will never go away completely. But to advance financial inclusion and reduce poverty, I think technology plays an important role.

"A lot of impact investing I see as a bridge to nowhere. And that investment is great, but it's got to be a demonstration to change policy, to bring in private capital, and to show the investment is investible. Otherwise, it's just another investment. That's the whole reason why I do this stuff. It's not for just a moment in time, but to create lasting change."

COMMUNITY INVESTMENT

JENNIFER PRYCE
CALVERT IMPACT CAPITAL
CALVERTIMPACTCAPITAL.ORG
LI: https://www.linkedin.com/in/jennifer-pryce-71456936/
TW: @JennPryce

Jenn Pryce is President and CEO of Calvert Impact Capital, investing in communities, people, and businesses overlooked by traditional finance in the United States and over 100 other countries. She shaped the strategic direction of Calvert Impact Capital to focus on innovation, sustainability, and scale. Pryce has expanded the sectors it works in and developed new products and services to ensure that impact investing is accessible from institutional to small retail investors. Since Calvert Impact Capital's founding, the company has worked with nearly 20,000 individuals, institutions, and advisors to raise nearly $3.5 billion.

Pryce studied engineering at Union College and holds an MBA from Columbia University. She serves as a *Forbes* contributor, a lecturer at Oxford Saïd School of Business, a board member of UNICEF USA Impact Fund for Children, the Advisory Board Chair of Quantified Ventures, and as a member of the Advisory Board of Ecofin and Operating Principles for Impact Management.

Please describe Calvert Impact Capital and your mission.

We've been around for 25 years and are a 501(c)(3) nonprofit financial institution. We recently extended our corporate structure so there's now a holding company called Calvert Impact Capital Charitable, Inc., and we're building new products and services, both for profit and nonprofit under that holding company. Also under that holding company is Calvert Impact Capital, which holds our flagship product, which is the Community Investment Note.

The reason we do our work is to connect private capital to communities. So, providing financial products, education, and access to impact investments is our mission. Right now, we do that through providing financial products. We have a syndication business and work with others to aggregate capital. We are a leader in impact measurement and management.

Provide an overview of the community investing space and where Calvert Impact Capital fits in.

What the community investment space invests in is investible opportunities that traditional banks don't do. So, this is what Bank of America doesn't do, JP Morgan doesn't do: affordable housing projects, microfinance loans, renewable energy that's new and novel, rural communities, Black-owned businesses. There's something about each of these transactions where the perceived risk is higher than the real risk. Because we work close to these communities, we understand these markets and we have increased comfort investing in these businesses or these projects. So, we see a different risk profile.

To move the money into communities, what we have found is there's a whole bunch of private capital over here, and a set of community intermediaries that are working with that. They're offering products and services and education to invest their money in another set of community-facing intermediaries. These are microfinance institutions, affordable housing developers, community developments, and small business lenders. They sit in communities and close to the projects. A whole bunch of us that sit here, like BlueOrchard, like responsAbility, like Calvert Impact Capital. We're raising money from investors and investing it in these intermediaries and impact funds that are sector or geographically specialized—and they are finally lending it to businesses and projects in place. Unlike traditional finance, there's a lot of intermediation to move this capital into the community.

We are creating investment products that bring private capital into impact investments, but we are not making direct business loans. For example, we are not investing directly in affordable housing projects. We are investing in intermediaries that then go on to lend to the business, or to the project, or to the person in place.

Who are the players similar to you, and how do you differ from them?

We sit in a little silo with companies like BlueOrchard and responsAbility, and what we're doing is structuring products that meet investor demands. They have demands around liquidity, around risk diversification. No investor wants to have a direct investment of $5 million in Tanzania. They want liquidity. Most institutional investors want an investment that's five years or shorter. However, many community investments are 10, 20, 30 years in duration, so we're solving for that problem. An institutional investor, they don't want to make an investment less than $10 million, so you need product that has enough size so that they can take a meaningful piece of it. We're solving some of these problems by aggregating and by structuring a product that really meets those investor demands.

And yes, someone like BlueOrchard is doing something similar, and there's us, there's responsAbility, and then the list gets very thin. This is where we don't have a lot of actors and, to me, this is one of the most challenging problems in the impact investing space. We don't have a lot of good ways for the mass affluent, for advised assets, for a CIO that oversees a pension fund, or a financial adviser that oversees a high-net-worth individual's client portfolio to really invest and engage in impact investments. Unless they take the time to underwrite and perform the due diligence on a direct investment themselves, which many people don't have the time or the capacity nor the fiduciary bandwidth to do.

How exactly are you deploying capital?

We have a retail investor base, so our risk tolerance needs to respect a retail investor, so we're quite low risk. We aim to have a diversified portfolio across sectors and across geographies to minimize that risk. We look to intermediaries both because operationally we're all in Washington, DC, and we're not in the field. So, making a direct loan in Tanzania or in South Africa is a riskier proposition and it doesn't align with our risk profiles.

And this is our theory of change: if we can create impact funds, financial institutions in communities where there's not good access to capital, if we can capitalize them, then that's a sustainable, reliable capital source for those businesses in place. So, our goal is to really build out the financial infrastructure across the globe and to allow more businesses to get access to capital.

Give me an example that captures your strategy from both a financial perspective and an impact perspective.

We went into nine impact sectors, so just as a headline we have a different theory of change for each of those sectors: small business, affordable housing, renewable energy, etc. An investor can target their money to any of those sectors or un-target it so they just support the whole portfolio.

We have right now 110 positions in our portfolio across those nine sectors that touch 100 countries. We go out and we have a team of 19 investment professionals. We do all our due diligence, all our risk management in-house and look for investments that meet our social, our impact, and our financial criteria. We have risk methodology that prices our investments in a risk-based pricing model. So, we quantify our risk in all our investments, we price to our risk, and we assess the impact of all our investments.

A very typical investment for us would be in Africa, where there is a group called SunFunder. They are headquartered in Kenya, Nairobi, and they work across the African continent providing businesses that provide pay-as-you-go solar capital to expand and grow. So, they're putting solar home units on individual homes that are not connected to the grid and providing solar power to hundreds of millions of people.

That business model, pay-as-you-go, where an individual leases-to-own a solar panel was a business model that none of the banks in Africa felt comfortable investing in. So SunFunder was a new fund manager that emerged probably about eight to 10 years ago to do that type of lending. We were one of their first investors. We were a debt investor in a blended finance vehicle, so there was equity and there were other investors beneath our investment. Our investment is usually debt only. We do have a few equity investments, but because the profile of our investor is largely retail, we need to keep our risk low. And SunFunder lent that money out and helped grow that renewable energy sector, the pay-as-you-go sector in Africa.

Fast forward to now and there are other SunFunders across Africa, right? Other impact intermediaries, the development finance institutions, have heavily helped grow and scale this field. Now Standard Bank and other banks are starting to lend to these social enterprises, these businesses that are providing the pay-as-you-go. So, what SunFunder did is they demonstrated that these were investible assets. They built a track record, and they went out and were able to share that with more traditional financial capital sources that could scale and grow the sector.

We have about $70 million of exposure to sub-Sahara Africa solar renewable energy. And we probably won't do much more because we've kind of been in there as an early investor and used our capital that demonstrates it is investible. Now the traditional banks are coming in because they're comfortable with that asset. To us, that's victory.

Is your model dependent on working through microfinance institutions or community development financial institutions?

Yes, these intermediaries exist in all the different sectors, so it's hard to say what a typical transaction is because of that intermediary lending. The type of investment we're making is consistent, but the shape, form, and structure varies.

We were the first investor in the Seychelles Blue Bond, which was the first blue bond ever issued. That was issued by the government of the Seychelles, so it's a general obligation to Seychelles, it's sovereign debt. But it couldn't float in the capital markets because it was only $15 million and they had a BB- credit rating. So, this was not going to hit any sovereign desk; it was too small and the yield they wanted for the risk of the rating did not align. And so, we and two other institutional investors took that down. So, we have a sovereign blue bond in our portfolio that doesn't look structurally like SunFunder, but it's doing the same thing.

This was the world's first blue bond. Someone needed to take the risk and demonstrate that it was investible, and we did that.

How do you evaluate risk?

There are a number of strategies: First, we hedge everything. So, if you think about the risk of local currency lending—because we do lend in local currency—if we do any local currency lending in our book, it's hedged so we don't take currency risk. We also have a country risk model where we've looked and created a framework to divide the globe into A, B, C, and D countries. D being the riskiest, A being the strongest. And we've set limits on how much exposure we can have in any of those countries, very much correlated to their country risk score.

When we underwrite an individual credit, two things come into play. Often a fund manager is working across multiple countries so that helps to mitigate the risk and oftentimes with these funds we'll negotiate country or geographic exposures. So, limiting investments in South Africa to 25 percent of the proceeds they raise, etc. with us and other lenders, right? So, this is not just us, this is the LPs collectively. There are negotiations just around country lists and risk limits for these investments we're making. Then, finally, we look at features in our risk scoring model around political stability, ability to get repaid, strength of the rule-of-law, things like this. These are all inputs.

Explain your Community Investment Note and how it works.

That's our center of gravity right now, our flagship product. It's a fixed income product and looks like a corporate bond. We sell it in 1, 3, 5, and 10-year increments. For rates right now, it's 0.4 to 2.5 percent. You can access the community investment note in three ways. One is online, you can buy a note for $20. You can buy it through your brokerage account so you can go on the Schwab or the Fidelity platform and for a thousand dollar minimum buy a note. Or you can just directly write us a check. We have a track record of 100 percent repayment of principal and interest over the 25 years that we've been issuing the note. The growth of the note has been exponential; it's $600 million outstanding balance now, and in 2017, it was $350 million.

Describe your strategy.

Our strategy is to build, grow, and sustain and it's really looking at new, growing or sustaining intermediaries and providing them the capital so that they can grow and scale. Every single transaction has a piece of blended finance in it. We are the private capital that's benefiting from the catalytic capital, so we're getting blended. We don't provide catalytic capital; we don't have that type of resources. What we are is the private capital that's being engaged or brought into transactions because of the catalytic capital that's in them.

How do you perform due diligence in over 100 countries?

It is a rigorous process. We have two credit committees. One is a staff investment committee and the other is a board investment committee, and we bring due diligence memos to these committees. The due diligence memo is extremely thorough. It's looking at impact capacity to repay, the character, the risks and mitigants. There's a pricing model because we do risk-based pricing, and there's a risk analysis that's based on ELR (Expected Loss Rate) probability of default modeling.

Once we make our investment, if it's approved, we also do quarterly monitoring—both impact and financial. We do annual monitoring and we have a very robust process to manage impaired assets, so a classified assets and actively monitored list. We always visit our clients, so we do due diligence site visits when we underwrite them. It's been a little difficult with COVID. And we also travel and meet them at conferences, we talk to them on the phone. With many of our investments, if it makes sense and if it's not a closed-ended fund, we renew and grow our relationship over time. There are some partners we've had in our book for 20 years and we have grown our investment as they have grown, so we do evergreen lending as well.

Is "greenwashing" an issue in community investing?

Where there's greenwashing, I think, in community investing, is not having an impact measurement and management process and infrastructure. So, there are some community investing actors that just collect data from their borrowers and pass that back to their investor.

But we're a founding signatory on the Operating Principles of Impact Management—as are about 150 other impact asset owners or managers. We're advocating for people to have an impact measurement and management process. So how you make your investment, how you conduct due diligence, how you collect data over time, how you assess expected impact, and looking at when you leave an investment, are you leaving with the impact in a positive place, what they call "impact at exit." It's a whole process of impact measurement and management and having it support your theory of change, your vision, and your mission is what the Operating Principles for Impact Management has been advocating for over the last two and a half years.

That authenticity, that integrity of how you measure impact, I think is what differentiates authentic and deep impact from more of the reporting and window dressing. If you're not doing that, then you are simply passing back data you get to your investor and not questioning if you're having negative impacts as well as positive impacts. You're not questioning the ESG of the actual intermediary, the fund you're investing in. All of that is missing.

So how do you measure, verify, and report impact?

The foundational piece is we have an impact scorecard we put every transaction through. It has a section on community impact, so looking at the Five Dimensions of Impact that the Impact Measurement Project put out, which is best practices and what the field has coalesced around as well as the ESG of that fund itself. So, what their own environmental, social, and governance policies and procedures, etc. are. So, is that fund itself doing positive things in the world? That's half of our impact scorecard.

The other half is looking at the impact that our portfolio is having. So, our investment in these intermediaries—the build, grow, sustain strategy I talked about earlier. We're assessing if our capital is providing additionality, if it's helping scale and grow, if it's tied to our vision and our mission. We take that scorecard, which is a set of questions, and we embed that in every due diligence memo. And it's a point of discussion as is the ability for that entity to repay our investment.

Once the investment is made, we collect annual impact data and manage the impact risk of our investment. If we see deterioration in the impact, we monitor it like we would monitor credit deterioration. When we exit an investment, and there are three of these on our website right now, we do success stories. So, we assess our role in advancing the impact of that investment, that intermediary. This is all codified. We have an impact and ESG policy, like we have a compliance policy, like we have lending policies. Everything I shared with you and more is codified in that policy.

What do you know now about social impact investing that you wish you knew in 2009 when you showed up at Calvert?

The investments we're making are solving very complex problems. They're not just an investment. It's not just about financial return. The impact piece is much more than just collecting data. It's about a market that's broken and it's a complex problem that we're trying to solve and finance is only one piece of the solution. So, you need to work with government; you need to work with business. It needs to be a multi-stakeholder solution at the end of the day. We can't just be an investment shop. We also have to think about how does policy help resolve the systemic issue. How can business work to help this issue and show and demonstrate what we've been doing as an opportunity for people to come along?

Describe an investment you were skeptical of that turned out better than you thought, and the lessons learned.

I'm actually living through one again, and it's this role we've played in raising capital for the small business recovery funds that we set up in states across the United States. When we started doing this, I just questioned what we were doing. To me, it felt like a bridge to nowhere. We set up these funds, we give small business and other loans and then what? We've kicked the can down the road. Why? What are we doing here?

And what's exciting to see now is the federal government is coming out with money for each individual state to dedicate to small business lending, to use it to leverage private capital. What we're creating now is a public bond offering, and we're actually working in partnership with a large commercial bank to do this. To create a public bond where investors can buy the bond, the public money is being leveraged, and the proceeds are going to continue to capitalize the small business funds that we've set up across the nation.

Now that they can get ongoing capital and recycle capital, they can be an ongoing, reliable, sustainable source for the next five years. If they can do that, they've sized the credit need in the market that we're addressing as a $60 billion gap that exists. Then we can begin to really address what is the ongoing structural lack of access to capital for these small businesses because there aren't enough community banks to support it.

But what if we can find a way to continue to clean off the balance sheets of those banks and give them more money, sell those loans out to the market, get more on, and we're getting the rating agencies in to rate those assets? Then I think we've got a way to really access the capital markets into the small business market, where there has never been piping before. And once we open those pipes, then we've got it.

A lot of impact investing I see as a bridge to nowhere. And that investment is great, but it's got to be a demonstration to change policy, to bring in private capital, and to show the investment is investible. Otherwise, it's just another investment. That's the whole reason why I do this stuff. It's not for just a moment in time, but to create lasting change.

Chapter Eight

Alternatives: Venture Capital

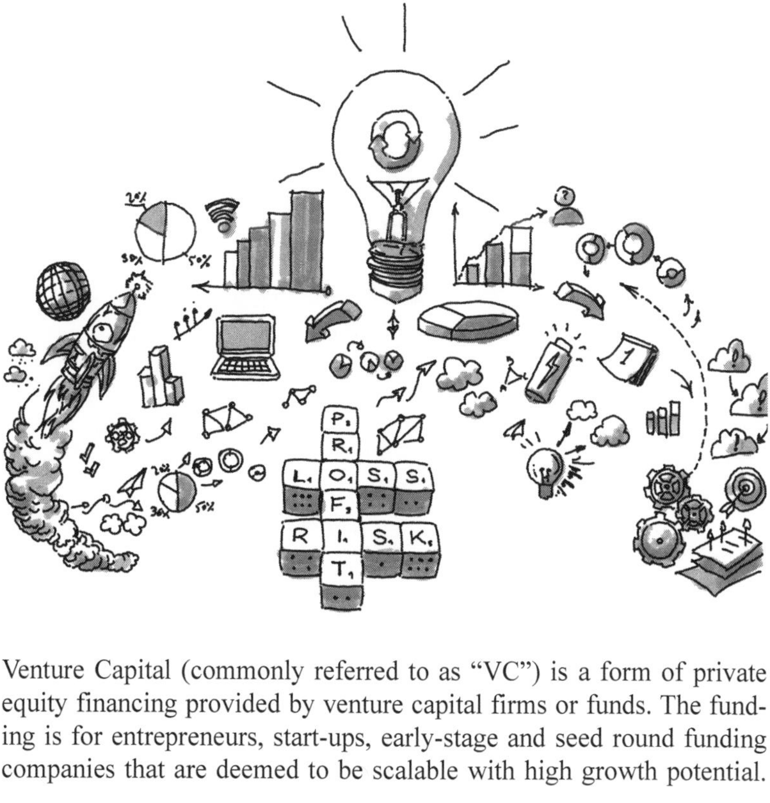

Venture Capital (commonly referred to as "VC") is a form of private equity financing provided by venture capital firms or funds. The funding is for entrepreneurs, start-ups, early-stage and seed round funding companies that are deemed to be scalable with high growth potential.

Venture capital funds manage pooled investments from well-heeled investors, investment banks, and institutional investors, and these funds are only open to accredited investors. Sovereign funds and notable private equity firms have more recently joined the crush of investors searching for high-return multiples in a near-zero to negative interest rate environment and have participated in large ticket deals.

We've already covered Private Equity in chapter 6 and Venture Capital is technically a subset of the Private Equity asset class in terms of strategy. However, its risk/return profile is so different from Private Equity that it is considered a totally separate asset class. Also, the VC general investment philosophy and process is different. In addition to capital, VCs are expected to bring substantial managerial and technical expertise to their portfolio investments.

HIGH RISKS, HIGH REWARDS

Like Private Equity, Venture Capital investing involves the purchase of equity stakes in private, unlisted companies. Unlike Private Equity, however, it typically involves investing in startup, early-stage, and emerging companies that investors believe have high-growth potential or have demonstrated high growth at the very earliest stages of their evolution when many of the corporate structures and functions expected of a more mature company (e.g., sales, marketing, operations, governance, etc.) have not yet been developed.

Accordingly, because startups face high uncertainty, VC investments have high rates of failure compared to the other asset classes presented here. Indeed, many investors are quite frank in admitting that they back businesses that have not even identified a profitable business model to pursue. In those cases they are, however, confident in the idea (in terms of product-market fit) and the high quality of the management team that is committed to it.

Some Venture Capital firms go even further, inviting entrepreneurs to participate in associated accelerators that encourage budding entrepreneurs who don't yet have an idea. The investor's logic is that great ideas without execution most often fail. But great teams have the creativity to pivot until the right idea or business model is found, and they have the resilience to face the inevitable challenges.

The risks are high. A 10-year VC fund typically targets to return three times the fund's money in order to deliver a 12 percent IRR to their investors, while the majority of their portfolio start-up companies fail. However, the rewards for catching a "unicorn" (a start-up valued over $1 billion) can be exponential. Sequoia Capital invested $8 million into WhatsApp in 2011, and a further $52 million in a subsequent round. They exited for $3 billion when WhatsApp was acquired by Facebook in 2014 for $22 billion.[1]

But for every WhatsApp "Cinderella story" out there, there are far more Romeo and Juliet-style tales ending in tragedy. A classic example is Quibi, the mobile streaming site. Founded by Jeffrey Katzenberg, the former chairman of the Walt Disney Studios and Co-founder of Dreamworks SKG, and led by the former Hewlett Packard CEO Meg Whitman, it raised $1.75 billion of venture capital before shutting down six months after its 2020 launch.[2] In fact, it is estimated that three out of four venture fund-backed start-ups fail.[3]

SETTING PRIORITIES: SOCIAL IMPACT, ECONOMICS, OR BOTH?

While the Venture Capital industry emerged after World War II and, in earnest, in Silicon Valley in the 1960s and 1970s, the impact-oriented venture landscape evolved from venture philanthropy. The term "venture philanthropy" was first coined by John D. Rockefeller in 1969 and, appropriately enough, "impact investing" was coined nearly 40 years later in 2007 by the Rockefeller Foundation. But only a minority of VCs self-identify as impact investment funds, despite the significant social and environmental impact their investments and portfolio companies have.

In this chapter, for example, we hear from Amy Novogratz, Co-Founder of Aqua-Spark, a global investment fund in the Netherlands dedicated to investing in sustainable aquaculture. For Aqua-Spark, impact is the mission and the driver. "Virtually all of the experts agree that our oceans are already overfished," Novogratz explains. "Some areas are really depleted. Aquaculture can actually be a really great solution, but we have to do it right—and showing how is our reason for being."

At the same time, we will also hear from Sharon Vosmeck who leads Astia—a venture investor that backs women-led, high-growth businesses. While Astia obviously has huge social impact (women-led start-ups only receive approximately 2.3 percent of venture capital funding [Crunchbase, 2020]), she emphasizes the economic-first principles of their strategy rather than the social dimension:

"I know from abundant research that if you do nothing other than include women in your solutions, you achieve two things that really matter. One is that you get a higher return. So just with my investor lens on, I want inclusive teams because the returns are higher. On the economic side, it's estimated that if women have the same access to capital as men—I don't mean broadly in the economy, just in the venture economy—we'd have a six percent increase in GDP. No other single factor could increase growth of our economy in that way."

THE NEW NORTH STAR

Barry Eggers, Chairman of the National Venture Capital Association and a founding partner of Silicon Valley's Lightspeed Venture Partners, predicted in a blog post in December 2019 that, "Social impact will become a new North Star for our industry." Meanwhile, TechCrunch—the leading commentator for the industry—reported that Impact Tech (understood as technology solutions targeting any one of the 17 UN SDGs) have increased 280 percent between 2015 and 2020.

But, as in traditional VC, the successful delivery of impact will likely all come down to people in the arena, like Dutch entrepreneur Peter Arensman, founder of Future Food Fund. "There were a lot of people in the world who had less beneficial circumstances in their lives than I had," he explains in this chapter. So, he decided to invest 100 percent of his business's gross profits to create economic progress in countries with extremely low living standards. "I created a commercial investment vehicle, but the money only goes to companies improving the world. That means, in general, the financial return is a bit lower—but you also measure a return on people and a return on the planet."

TRUE COMMITMENT, POST-COMMITMENT?

A company may be pursuing an impactful business model today, but if it discovered a more lucrative niche, would the founders continue to prioritize impact above profit? After all, every experienced VC investor will acknowledge that initial long-term financial projections—given the rapid pace of change of start-ups—are pretty much hit and miss, and mostly miss. Therefore, "pivoting" is often lauded in early-stage investing. But in responsible and sustainable investing, could it lead to mission-drift?

In this chapter you will find a common theme among VC investors who self-identify as impact investment funds, that may offer an answer. Not only do they evaluate early-stage teams for creativity, intelligence, and resilience, but also for their underlying values, character, and emotional commitment to their greater mission.

"I want inclusive teams because the returns are higher. It's been estimated that if women had the same access to venture capital as men, GDP alone would increase by six percent. No other single factor could increase growth of our economy in that way."

WOMEN-LED VENTURE CAPITAL

SHARON VOSMEK
ASTIA
ASTIA.ORG
LI: https://www.linkedin.com/in/sharonvosmek/
TW: @Vosmek

Sharon Vosmek is CEO of Astia, a global organization that works to level the investment playing field for startups that include women in leadership roles. Among her many accomplishments, she developed Astia's proven approach to investment that eliminates bias in the investment screening process and contributes to the success of female entrepreneurs and their ventures. Sharon has spoken at the United Nations and at a number of universities on the topic of building inclusive innovation ecosystems. Sharon is a member of Astia Angels and Managing Director of the Astia Fund, a $100 million venture fund.

How do you describe what you do?

I'm CEO of Astia and one of the managing directors of the Astia fund. At Astia, what we do and what my life's work has become is ensuring access to capital for companies that include women leaders. I've been doing this since 2005.

Can you give me an overview of Astia, your mission, and your theory of change?

Let's start with the "why" this matters. I don't see this as a social *raison d'être.* Don't get me wrong. I think there is one, there is absolutely a social case to be made, but I actually see this as a real economic challenge. . . . I'm an economist by background.

First, all net new jobs in the last 30 years were created by companies that were venture-backed. Companies like Amazon, Walmart . . . they actually shed jobs, ultimately, right? Once you've hit that level of success, they're job killers rather than job growers. Job growth happens out of the innovation economy.

Number two, life's full of great challenges, but it's more so now than ever. We have a pandemic, an economic crisis, a climate crisis, and are feeding a growing population. These are real-world, really difficult challenges that will be addressed through innovation. The solutions for them might not even exist yet, but they'll be addressed through innovation. Well, if we leave this space of innovation to white men only—and white men of a specific pedigree, i.e., Wharton, Harvard, or Stanford—we're not going to get as robust a set of solutions, because the problem set will be mis-defined. Their own experiences won't allow them to push the boundaries of the problem set.

My favorite research on this is MIT's professor Malone's, on inclusive teams and their ability to innovate and how they out-innovate even top-performing, super-intelligent homogeneous teams.[4] They are always outperformed by heterogeneous teams, regardless of intellect. And as an economist this matters, because we need real solutions, not tinkering at the edges. This is an all-hands-on-deck moment to get to real solutions. So, I actually don't see this as a social problem.

Equally, I know from abundant research that if you do nothing other than include women in your solutions, you achieve two things that really matter. One is that as an investor, you get a higher return. So just with my investor lens I want inclusive teams because the returns are higher. On the economy side, it's actually estimated that if women have the same access to capital as men, just in this space—I don't mean broadly in the economy, I just mean in the venture economy—we'd have a 6 percent increase in GDP. There is no other single factor that could increase growth of our economy in that way.

Can you expand a little on that GDP increase statistic and where it comes from?

I used to be on Hillary Clinton's advisory body for entrepreneurship when she was Secretary of State. They did a phenomenal job of measuring the opportunity and impact to GDP and the potential of women. That statistic was right out of their commission and their work and a recent McKinsey report has nearly doubled that estimate.[5] Babson College expanded on that research.[6]

For me, it's about efficiencies in markets. It's about return on capital. When you overlay gender, especially on this part of the economy, because women are so profoundly underrepresented, the trick is it's actually really easy. If you did nothing other than gender, you'd impact all of these other things.

The other interesting thing is the UN found that as it relates to Sustainable Development Goals (SDGs), if you do nothing other than gender you actually end up addressing all of the other goals. Goal number five is gender inclusion. Even with no other goal, if you just do that one, you'll hit your economic targets—and you'll hit your environmental, your health, your food, you hit all of the other goals. So, the context of Astia for me is not the social one, it's the economic one. Don't get me wrong, I'm a woman. I care deeply about that, but that's different.

My motivations as CEO of Astia are actually as it relates to the opportunity as an investor. I've been investing for 20 years and I'll put my performance up against anyone's in Silicon Valley. And I've been called arrogant for saying that, but I say that with all humility. I don't create the results, the entrepreneurs do. I'm just stating the obvious. The economic impact is massive; what could be done if we simply trigger or unleash more venture capital into companies that include women.

What are the key statistics and metrics you cite?

A key statistic in venture capital to understand is it's a driver of the economy disproportionate to the amount of capital it deploys. So, because you're more comfortable with capital market or private equity numbers, venture numbers may look really small, but they punch well above their weight in impacting the economy. For the 20 years that Astia has existed, only between 2 and 3 percent of venture capital each year got invested into teams with women CEOs. Equally deplorable is that between 5 and 7 percent got invested into teams that have women anywhere. The rest, 95 percent of venture capital, is invested into all-male, predominantly white teams.

How does investing in companies with women as leaders or founders deliver better results to investors?

I'll give you some examples. One of the current fads in Silicon Valley is the unicorn, right? And if you think about the companies that have come out of that fad, I'd struggle to find their business model until very late [in their funding journey]—you know Uber, LinkedIn, even Amazon—all required more venture investment to be sustainable. I think about the hundreds of millions of dollars that went into these unicorns so that they could go public. That's an interesting business model. I'm investing in companies that don't have access to that same amount of capital. So where do they find capital? Customers. That's going to always deliver a higher return to investors than growing through venture investment.

What's interesting about companies that include women and people of color and diverse perspectives is they tend to have a stronger grounding in customer traction. I don't know the cause and effect, I'm an economist, but I will say correlationally that when you put women in the executive suite, along with men because I'm a believer in inclusion, when you bring all and diverse parties to the table, you get a more robust solution. One that tends to be more grounded in the market, because that's the market. The market is men, women, and people of color. If you can bring that market understanding into the team, it only makes sense that you would see a stronger resonance with customers.

I'll give you some examples of what that means. We tend to see seed and Series A investments that already have revenue, pretty substantial revenue. I have a portfolio of 64 companies right now. Within it we've only had four failures. So, we can tolerate 2x and 3x multiples out of a company, because we have fewer failures in the portfolio. Absolute failures are just very rare because our companies that we invest in tend to already have customer traction.

What is the typical failure rate that you benchmark against?

Most venture firms talk about a 10 and one. Ten failures and one successful company will make up the whole fund. That's the venture benchmark.

Do other VC's recognize that you get a better return with the investments you're doing?

We've deployed just over $30 million. We've been able to pull in and syndicate over $550 million. We leverage [i.e., crowd-in capital] very nicely. For us, the two measures in the marketplace about how we changed the market are, number one, that syndicate numbers matter as much as how much we'd deployed. Number two, if you now look in the market, you're seeing a conversation emerging from men and women about how to ensure that their deal flow has women and people of color in it. You see funds focused on ensuring that they do that, and funds being raised in order to address that.

How many deals do you screen per year?

In 2020 we looked at 1,200 deals, and it was just over USD1 billion of investment opportunities and in just Q1 2021, we've looked at over USD 1.7 billion of investment opportunities.

How many of those deals did you invest in?

We deployed just over $4 million last year, and we tend to do about 20 investments a year.

I understand you've developed a trademarked method of screening investments to eliminate gender, race, age, and geographic bias, the Astia Expert Sift™.

What we've developed over our 20-year journey is not only a methodology, but we've also built our own platform where community members, 5,000 of them around the globe, can weigh-in on their assessment of a business. They do it based upon their own backgrounds and they do it with tools that remove exposure to gender, race, and age. They're given documents, because there's great research that shows when you read a business plan versus have a business presented to you that you assess it differently. Also, when you read versus have it presented to you, you can't know the gender of the team nor the race of the team and you're not required to assess the individuals. Instead, you assess the business. So those are some of the tweaks to the process that we do.

Equally, we don't ever change the questions. The exact same questions are asked of every company. What this helps prevent is questions that have bias embedded in them, like, "Can you really do this?" Well, that's a weird question to ask, but it's a very common question in the venture industry.

The other types of questions are, "Who else has invested in this deal?" We're never allowed to ask that question because it may be that no one else has invested in this deal. And the reason may be because she's a Black woman. It may have nothing to do with the business.

So, we have a fixed set of questions that we've been asking for 20 years. We bring in, on average, 30 individuals for any individual company. It's not four people around a table. It's 30 individuals and I highlight individuals. They don't know each other's opinion of the business until after they've done their own assessment. So, no group think, no lemmings following each other. Instead, it's individual assessment. The beautiful thing is that for 20 years we've been running this Sift™ and it continues to perform well for us as investors.

So, by the time we hit intimate space [actually meeting in person with someone], we know we can trust the community because the Astia experts have weighed in. We can trust the data we've seen, and we can trust the Sift™ because it continues to perform. So, we move into intimate space with a different set of trust in place so we can invest across race and gender and age.

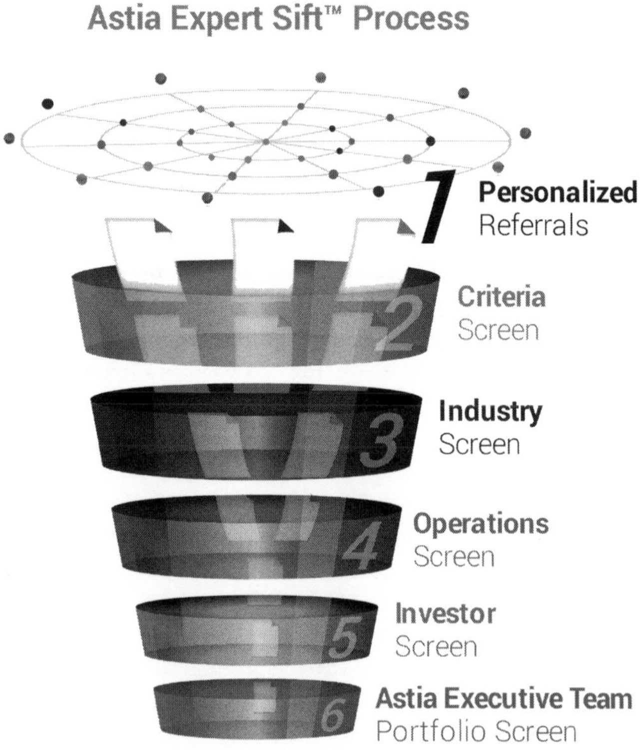

Astia Expert Sift™ Process. *Source:* Astia

What's the typical VC process?

Number one, most business transactions occur in what I'll call fairly intimate business settings, boardrooms. C-suites, that's equally intimate. Then you move it out into a social context. Golf courses. Increasingly intimate. The reason I call them intimate is because you're really only invited into those rooms. You can't self-nominate into those spaces. You're invited in. Historically men ran businesses, so they occupied those intimate spaces. To get women into those intimate spaces is quite difficult.

Venture capital was founded by some great men and a few women. Those men conducted business in these intimate spaces around board rooms or out for a drink. It was just more comfortable to invite other men in because socially, how do you explain to your wife that you and I are going out for a martini to talk about a deal? It's really difficult, but that's where the deal happens. I'm not advocating that's where a deal should happen. I'm highlighting that's where it happens.

So, with a typical VC process, the first thing they do is they require an introduction. Right away they've put bias in their sourcing, because they've said they don't accept anything over the transom. You must have an introduction. You've got to know someone who knows somebody at the VC firm. Number two, then they do a first meeting. I can tell you having sat in many of the first meetings, the first meeting goes like this: "Do I like you? Are you attractive? Do I feel good when we talk to each other? Do you listen to me?" It's all very bias laden assessment in that first meeting. If you make it past that—according to John Doerr, if you're a White male dropout from Stanford or Harvard, then you're going to make it past that[7]—the next is the partner meeting, when you're not even present. This is that other intimate space I was mentioning. You don't get invited into that room, ever. Right? That's the room where it happens as they say in [the theatrical play] Hamilton and you're not there. That's when they talk about you, when you're not there. And that is the most laden with bias because you, even if you met with that entrepreneur and you liked that entrepreneur, now you've convinced a bunch of people who haven't met that entrepreneur to do the deal. And that is so laden with racial and gender bias, because your partners will say, "Well, where did he go to school and what else has he done? And who else has he worked with that we know?" And you'll notice I'm using the word "he" because that's the operative word here. Ninety-eight percent of venture partners are men.

I mean, that's the real problem here. It's not about where the dollars are going. It's that general partners are all men and there is a preponderance of White men from Stanford, Wharton, or Harvard.

Do your investors typically invest in Astia because of your mission, or because you bring great deal flow?

I think most of our LPs come to us originally because they like the idea of what we do, and then they stay for the returns.

Can you give me some examples of the type of investors that typically invest in Astia?

Within the venture fund, for me it's notable that we have Jim O'Neill, who's the former chief economist at Goldman Sachs. I just love Jim. He's like, "I want to see the returns. I like the returns. I'm going to invest all day long in women, because I see the returns."

Priya Mathur, the former board president at CalPERS, the largest pension fund globally, is an investor. Equally, we have some impact investors. So, that's been curious. For the last 15 years that I've been at Astia, impact investors have told me that women or gender is not impact. And now suddenly something's changed, because we have Portola Creek Capital, an impact advisory group here in San Francisco, who has a number of their clients who have invested because they measure gender as impact. Tides Foundation, their investment team invested, and so did Toniic members. I'm pleased to see it because, as an economist, I always believed that gender was impact.

How else is Astia disrupting the traditional VC model?

One of the really big things we've done is change words. We used to use the word "mentor" for our community. I think it was 2006, when I was working with Professor Tom Kosnik at Stanford on our fourth or third business case, we surveyed how VC's invest. They invest in companies that they advise. I was like, "What does that mean?" We were calling them "mentors" and many of them were VC's, so we changed the word from Astia "mentor" to Astia "adviser." Overnight, with that one word change, we doubled our funding success rate. At that time, we were not investing ourselves, we were just taking deals up to the venture community. We went from a 30 percent funding success rate to 60 percent, with one word change, by telling the VC's in our network that they were advising our company rather than mentoring.

Why do you think so many investors still leave so much money on the table . . . 50 percent of the opportunities and the growth [i.e., women-led high growth ventures], especially in a community that likes to fancy itself as progressive and disruptive?

First and foremost, we should never underestimate the power of that body of research that shows that when we are presented with facts that challenge our assumptions, we don't learn from those facts. We become further entrenched in our assumptions. And that's just human nature. Stanford's done great research on it. We see it time and again in politics; people vote against their self-interest. We see time and time again, people making personal decisions that are against their interests. There's just something about when you are presented facts that challenge your assumptions, instead of being open to what is the truth, we bet on our assumptions.

I see that very present in venture capital. I've been CEO of Astia long enough to know I am dismissed as an executive and I'm dismissed as an investor by most VCs and by many in Silicon Valley. The more research I show about not just our performance but broadly the performance of women-led companies in the market, the more I see venture capitalists believe more in their own systems and processes.

What do you see as the most important challenge in the VC space at this time?

I think venture's greatest challenge—if it wants to be relevant to this next set of problems that we have to address—climate crisis, pandemics, health, feeding the planet, a growing population—is that it needs to professionalize itself and grow up.

"Over one third of the world currently depend on fish as their major source of protein, and as population and demand for protein grows, we know we can't get more from the ocean than we currently do. We're investing in a vision of a future where we have seafood and fish protein on our plate in a way that doesn't harm our environment."

SUSTAINABLE ACQUACULTURE VENTURE CAPITAL
AMY NOVOGRATZ
AQUA-SPARK
AQUA-SPARK.NL
LI: https://www.linkedin.com/in/amy-novogratz-1184b12/
TW: @AQUASPARKIMPACT
FB: @AQUASPARK.NL

Amy Novogratz is Co-Founder of Aqua-Spark, a global investment fund based in Utrecht, the Netherlands. Aqua-Spark invests in companies developing a sustainable, optimal food system all along the aquaculture value chain. She brings almost two decades of experience in fostering collaborative solutions to some of the world's big challenges. Novogratz helped start the Social Policy Action Network; developed and produced Chat the Planet, a web and television entity that bridged young people globally; and served as director of the TED Conference's annual TED Prize for almost a decade. She has led more than 20 global collaborations across a broad spectrum of sectors, including healthcare, education, science, technology, conservation, art, and activism. She currently serves on the boards of eFishery, Energaia, and Xpert Sea.

Can you give me an overview of Aqua-Spark and your mission there?

Aqua-Spark is an investment fund dedicated to moving aquaculture into an industry that's more sustainable, more assessable, and healthier. The demand for fish and protein is going up at a pretty steep curve. We can't get more from the oceans than we currently do, and current wild take amounts are questionable. Some areas of the ocean are really depleted. Aquaculture can be a great solution, but we have to do it right—and showing how to do so is our reason for being.

What percentage of the world's food protein is fish compared to meat?

Over one-third of the world depend on fish as their major source of protein. Aquaculture is bigger than wild caught fish for human consumption and it is bigger than beef, as well.

You apply an ecosystem approach to portfolio management. Who are you investing in and how are you executing this strategy?

We invest all along the aquaculture value chain. We invest in farming operations. We invest in technology to make them more efficient, more transparent. We invest in disease battling, we invest in feed ingredients. We've also invested in cell-based aquaculture. We invest all the way to the market, in consumer facing products. We invest all over the world, because every part of our vision is around a globally connected aquaculture industry. I think that out of our 22 companies, we're in 16 countries. We're really investing in this vision that we will have a future where we have seafood and fish protein on our plate in a way without harming our environment.

Could you describe how you select an investment, make investment decisions, and your due-diligence process?

We believe very much in the power of a network. We have 60 aquaculture experts as a wider part of our team. We have about 1,500 companies that we keep in our pipeline at all times to track. We form relationships with a lot of those companies and when we find that they're investible and they're at the right stage for us, we start those conversations.

The first thing we look at is what is this company solving? Is it one of the big challenges in aquaculture? Does it fit into our ecosystem? Is it something we're missing now, something that nobody else is addressing on that same turf? Is it something that will benefit or add to the ecosystem and something that the companies inside the portfolio will benefit from as well? So those are the absolute checkpoints, and we get to know the team quite well.

We have a pretty stringent due diligence process here with a really lengthy sustainability checklist. We always send at least one or two of our relevant experts to do due diligence on-site. Before going on-site, we do a couple of different stages of getting to know the company—interviews, references—and then we sign a term sheet. Where many groups sign term sheets all the time, we want to know that if it all turns out to be true, that we're going to make this investment. So, we always sign a term sheet with the real intention to invest, and at that point we do on-site due diligence with experts.

Tell me about Aqua-Spark's "Shared Values Manifesto.'"

So, it has a couple of purposes behind it, but one is basically to put all your cards out on the table and ask them to do the same thing by signing it or not signing it. Like, this is why we exist, this is what we care about, this is what we want to work on and this is how we plan to work on it. So, it lays out the vision of what we think aquaculture can be. It lays out ideas around collaboration, sharing knowledge, agreeing to kind of promote ideas together.

It has some more practical things in it, like what it means to be a part of an ecosystem portfolio and the idea that if a colleague portfolio company is selling something that you'll look there first and if they offer the best price, you should probably go with your portfolio company. With a number of our companies, we have most favored nations agreements as well. That means that their colleague portfolio companies have a special deal to the product that they have in the market, the best price that they have in the market. In general, it's really signing up for a way to build together. We also have a number of "social musts" in there as well. Every employee must be paid a living wage. We have things around gender and diversity and your commitment to what your company stands for.

How do you return capital to your investors? You talked about this patient capital approach, but how does this work in terms of returns?

It's a dividend-based model. We had told investors that when we signed them up that by next year, we'll start to pay out dividends and we are on track to start to pay off dividends. It'll start small, but it'll gain each year. Investors can also—even though we're long-term investors—redeem their shares in us at whatever the valuation of those shares is at the time. We have a redemption mechanism where we can raise new monies to buy them out or they can find somebody to sell their shares to directly. Our fund model is a co-operative where our investors will help decide its future.

Could you describe a profile of your fund's typical investors? Do they invest with Aqua-Spark out of passion or because of the returns, or both?

We have 250 investors from, I think, 30 countries, with mixed profiles. We didn't have official cornerstone investors, but if you look who we launched this with, they were more leaning toward conservation investors. For sure they cared about the ocean. But as we've grown, investors that care about the food space, more and more have come into the folds that are from the industry or are connected. In general investors are starting to get this opportunity. I think many of them have an impact lens. Others see that it's a no-brainer that we need to produce more protein and we need to find better ways to produce protein and it's going to have a financial advantage at one point. And so, it's really a mix.

It is mostly family offices and high net worth individuals, a couple of institutions. Some institutionals like Louis Dreyfus Company and a German pension fund. But it's mostly individuals. And I think the reason our investor network is expanding so rapidly at this point is because it's also become a real community of doers and pioneers in this space.

We do a lot to engage our investors. We're really on this road together and they know it and it's a fun experience. I think that gets lost a lot when we talk about impact and ESG investing. This is a moment in history and we're all doing something different together, we're making change, we're building, we're using creativity. It's bonding, it brings meaning. I think if you ask our investors, most would tell you they really just enjoy being a part of what we're building.

What do you benchmark your returns against?

Initially we looked at what the listed aquaculture space was, where they were, and we ended up somewhere above 20 percent. To us, if it were above 24 percent, that would be a commercial return in the aquaculture space, which is what we think we need to prove the business case for sustainable aquaculture and make these practices the new commercial norm. The last couple of years we've been at about 20 percent and that's net of fees.

What would be the risks, if any, to your investors that would be distinct from any general risks that investors would have to non-sustainable aquaculture investments?

It seems like a no-brainer that the future is going to be sustainable aquaculture because it has to be, but a lot of it hasn't been proven yet. If you look at what people are willing to pay for fish, we're not yet at a place where people are willing to pay a premium across the board for more sustainable practices. We have a lot to prove, a long way to go. I mean, if you look at RES systems, some of those land-based RES systems got a lot of hype and a lot of investment recently, but we see they're still having major technology risk. It's just that a lot of the real promise around sustainability is unproven because it is not yet at scale. There's really no other way than cleaner, greener, more traceable, sustainable feed ingredients, etc. as we continue to grow this industry.

What do you know now about sustainable investing that you wish you knew when you launched Aqua-Spark?

I'm glad I didn't know a lot back then, to be honest. I think our kind of naive way of looking at what was possible really helped us think ambitiously and put something together that, had we understood this space as well, might've been different at the beginning. I don't think I realized how nascent it was back then, how little real focused activity there was, and the amount people were really putting behind pure sustainability. Like when we try to get co-investors to sign up for sustainability before a profit, there is really an uncomfortable moment.

The world's not in great shape, and we need to figure out how to move into a future that can support us. That needs to be first and foremost. It's great that we have this whole movement toward impact, but there are lots of different definitions of impact. I think we all need to really step up a bit and do what it takes to get real solutions to help them take off.

If someone wants to get into the sustainable VC investing space, how would you advise them to do so?

There are so many great pitching events and conferences focused on this space right now, and a number of dedicated funds. I would either invest in a fund or create a network and connection to it. There are also a number of accelerators now, which is a great opportunity. We have an aquaculture accelerator in our portfolio, Hatch Blue, helping early-stage companies become investable. They're usually looking for mentorship and other ways of helping beyond just capital. It's a great way to get into the space and be a part of it.

"We're talking sustainable agriculture, we're talking rural areas, we're talking working with local communities. It takes a long time, it's not a short-term investment. It's a long-term perspective. It requires digging in, digging deep, and driving it."

LATIN AMERICAN NATURE-POSITIVE BIODIVERSITY FUND

TAMMY NEWMARK
ECOENTERPRISES FUND
ECOENTERPRISES.COM
LI: https://www.linkedin.com/in/tammy-e-newmark-6974aa1a/

Tammy E. Newmark has been a leader in impact investing for 30 years. She serves as CEO and Managing Partner of EcoEnterprises Fund, a pioneer in investing growth capital in nature-positive companies that drive social justice and protect the Earth's biodiversity. She has led EcoEnterprises Fund from its launch under The Nature Conservancy in 1998 to spinning off a women-owned investment manager in 2010. With the third fund under management, EcoEnterprises Fund has invested in nearly 50 unique emerging companies in 11 countries in Latin America.

Prior to EcoEnterprises Fund, she was a founder of the first venture fund that specialized in renewable energy, clean technology, and green investments in developing markets. She has worked for the International Finance Corporation and JPMorgan Chase. Newmark is co-author of *Portfolio for the Planet: Lessons from 10 years of Impact Investing* (Earthscan/Routledge Press, 2011) and holds an MBA from the Wharton School of the University of Pennsylvania.

What is the EcoEnterprises Fund and describe your role there as CEO?

EcoEnterprises Fund is a venture fund for nature. That's been our investment strategy for over 20 years. We're a small, nimble "boutiquey" group that focuses on investing growth capital in nature-positive and social impact ventures in Latin America. I oversee the team as CEO and Managing Partner. I'm the majority owner of the GP and the Fund Manager.

How many funds do you have?

Since we launched our first fund in 2000, we have managed three funds. Fund II is in wind-down mode now and Fund III is in its investment period.

On the genesis of the EcoEnterprises Fund, what was the original premise of The Nature Conservancy?

The Nature Conservancy is one of the largest global environmental organizations. It's extremely innovative. It creates different tools to preserve and conserve critical ecosystems and landscapes. EcoEnterprises Fund is one such example. When we launched, The Nature Conservancy realized that it must work with communities on sustainable livelihoods to ensure long-term management of local natural resources.

One of the main principles underlying EcoEnterprises Fund's strategy is to work with community groups in-country to demonstrate ways to use investment and entrepreneurial ingenuity as a tool for conservation in the region.

Why is your focus solely on Latin America?

We began in Latin America given the tie to The Nature Conservancy's programs and the focus on biodiversity businesses. When you look at rural economic activity in Latin America, most of it is related to agriculture. So, our portfolio allocations began agri-based across the whole value chain. We invest in forestry, agroforestry, aquaculture, regenerative and organic agriculture. We include ecotourism and emerging opportunities as well.

Why should investors be interested in natural capital?

Natural resource management is critical globally, of course, and there is now a recognition of the link between climate, biodiversity, and planetary health. There has been a mainstreaming of thinking in terms of valuing the planet's natural assets and investing for long term sustainability. This has been our underlying investment thesis for all these years.

Explain why the economic needs of rural communities are inextricably linked to the kind of investments you make.

Most of the companies that we work with either grow or sell products that rely on strong natural ecosystems and local community involvement. We have a company that replanted deforested degraded cattle lands with organic lime trees, for instance—in such case, the company has a vested interest in employees' well-being as well as small producers who sell product to the company from their lands. The community is incentivized to protect the integrity of the natural resource base to create a sustainable model rather than continue with slash and burn agriculture or over-harvesting of a particular crop.

How do you ensure due diligence when the worldwide supply chain is notoriously complex and opaque?

I think that transparency, tracking, and traceability are increasingly important in the marketplace. In Europe, there are enhanced regulations and protocols to ensure that companies know where all their ingredients are from. In Fund III, we've partnered with a group Union for Ethical BioTrade in the Netherlands. It has been a very strong proponent of supply chain traceability. Retailers now require certifications which offer more transparency such as BAP[8] or GlobalG.A.P.[9] We encourage our portfolio companies to obtain such certifications.

What is your preferred investment structure?

Quasi-equity in which we could get upside but retain the ability to obtain current income alongside a kicker. We need structured exits to get our money out. We've learned that straight equity in Latin America in our niche of deals, because of the stage, the type of businesses, and the exit opportunities is a less optimal instrument. Distributing returns and capital back to our investors is the priority.

Describe your investment process, how you screen, your due diligence and how you make an investment?

We've been investing in the region for over 20 years, so we know the lead companies in the space and have an active pipeline. From Fund I, we created the pipeline and the deals that weren't ready, we pushed to Fund II. There were a handful of deals that we financed in Fund II that we actually saw six to seven years earlier in Fund I, and the same is the case for Fund II and Fund III.

In Fund III, thus far, we've seen over 400 deals. The reason being is that we're one of the only players in our niche. We generate our pipeline from companies we've worked with in the past or co-financiers that we've done deals with, or our investors, or just general solicitations when we're out and about. We know the industry, we know who the movers and shakers of the region are, we are increasingly seeing the children of some of the traditional business leaders in the region getting into more sustainable businesses.

We have a conventional investment process just with a unique investment mandate. We undertake due diligence that a traditional venture fund would do, but also focusing on environmental and social impacts, such as visiting suppliers and the local community. We also rely on local experts, our network and lawyers that are in-country to do further scrubbing of the deal.

We have an Investment Committee that has been working with us for many years. Our investors are part of that committee as observers. We have an Impact Committee that provides insight into the environmental and social attributes of our deal, and we have our environmental and social management system, which is very much integrated into the investment process.

We have a risk rating system whether it's on the environmental and social side or on the business side. It is part of our due diligence across the board—the type of analysis, evaluation, and managing for impact and risk for every single transaction. The team has been working together for close to 20 years and has seen similar transactions in our specific industries. So, our experience enables us to create solid portfolios.

Provide a couple of examples of investments that you've made and how they meet your criteria.

All companies need to have growth potential, make returns, generate cash for repayment, have a vision pertaining to its social and environmental mandate and execute on that strategy. Increasingly, becoming "B" certified[10] has been a positive trend in Latin America. Some of our companies are already "B" certified or are moving toward that goal.

Sambazon is in our portfolio, an acai company which sells sustainably harvested product from communities in the Brazilian Amazon. We have a really fascinating company Ecoflora, a member of the Union for Ethical BioTrade. Ecoflora uses the biodiversity in Colombia to produce a natural blue colorant for food and beverages. The company works with local communities and created an agreement, the first of its kind in Colombia, under the UN Convention for Biodiversity on Access for Benefit Sharing (ABS) protocols with local communities. We look for companies that are really pioneering unique ways of either working with local communities or adding value to local biodiversity.

We have also recently invested in a next generation business. In each fund we like to invest in emerging opportunities, and this alternative insect protein company uses waste as base food. That's a very interesting circular economy company.

Acai market in Brazil. ***Source:*** **Sambazon**

We also have an aquaculture company that utilizes re-introduced native species for its operation. Insect protein, in turn, is increasingly used as feed in aquaculture. We look for those complementary activities in the portfolio as well as ensure the portfolio is well-rounded in terms of country, stage of development, sector, and instrument.

What is your target investment size?

We look for deals that have the minimum sales level of $1 million. We want to see some operating history, although we've invested in a few new ventures that have emerged from existing companies. Our ticket size ranges from about $1.5 million to $10 million. We'd like to keep it about $3.5 million. For instance, some of the companies on the eco-tourism side are smaller ventures because of the limited footprint. Small is beautiful, and you really can't deploy more capital into those type of ventures.

Part of the investment strategy is putting some money on the table and then doing follow-on financing—tranching our commitment based on milestones. We aim to pile into the winners to help them scale further and expand beyond regionally, or into other products and innovations.

Does your increased AUM reflect an increase in the supply of capital available from investors or an increase in demand for capital from entrepreneurs?

It's a combination that goes together. I've always said from the beginning that we will stay in business if there is a need and if we can provide that leadership to help create the market. Once the local capital markets in Latin America take this on, then that's great—we work ourselves out of a job. But right now, financiers are not focused on these transactions, are not providing our type of capital nor our high-touch engagement. We're seeing the bubbling of it which is encouraging. There's an increasing need for more capital because of the growing deepness of sustainable business opportunities in the region.

Why is mainstream capital overlooking these transactions?

Markets go where they can make returns and mitigate downside risk. In Latin America, for instance, there is much more of a vibrancy associated with tech deals, with education deals, with health deals, with renewable energy. It'll get there sooner or later, but it's not there yet [for natural capital].

What is the high-touch technical assistance that you provide to your portfolio companies?

We make sure that the company has all of the elements to succeed. Some companies are very strong on financial management, whereas other companies are not. With the business advisory support that we provide, we try to identify where we could add value—whether it's forecasting, cash flow, pricing, marketing or governance.

A lot of times small companies don't have a functioning board of directors or shareholder communication. All of those sorts of base elements of internal capability which are missing, we support with our team, or we bring in consultants or specialists. This also includes improvement to environmental and social outcomes.

Describe the profile of your fund's typical investor and why they invest with EcoEnterprises.

Investors are interested in EcoEnterprises Fund for all of the reasons given above related to our impact investing mandate and because we have a track record, we have experience, we've been here for some time. What they see is what they get, we're extremely transparent. If investors want to participate at the Investment Committee level, at the Impact Committee level, or come down and visit our companies, they're most welcome to do that. So, we have a very engaged investor base and many of the investors from Fund I have come into Fund II and from Fund II to Fund III. That continuity has always been one of our secret sauces.

How have your investor profiles changed over time?

We have seen more consideration from European and U.S. private investors, family offices and institutional investors who are interested not only in learning and investing in the space, but in co-investment opportunities. I think that's where we see more traction. We have many of the same investors over time, like development finance institutions or larger foundations.

Are these specialized private equity investors big or small players?

One of the things that we have always found important is that if there is a U.S. or European investor who wants to come in for a small amount, we are open to that. We see it as our effort to be a change agent, to provide that communication, that education, that learning about the space, to show that investing in our niche is a good investment strategy. Consequently, we do have some investors who came in with small bite sizes in an earlier fund, and then upped their commitment in a later fund.

What downsides are your investors exposed to that are different from macro investors in this space?

Obviously, we do have a whole strategy of risk mitigation. We also have a very comprehensive environmental and social monitoring program. We're very mindful about the environmental and social benefits that accrue from our companies. Our concentration on how to manage those risks and enhance positive environmental and social impact outcomes is all part of our strategy.

Getting back to risks on the investor side, we have a track record and frameworks in place which provide comfort. We have analytical and monitoring systems; we know what we're doing in our particular niche of business.

An example is we invested in a pioneering organic spice company in the first fund. And at one time in the marketplace, the cardamom prices went through the roof. The local community that the spice company was working with decided to cut down trees to plant more cardamom. What did the company do? It worked with the small producers in the community to reforest, work on sustainable supply and demand dynamics, and improve oversight and certification schemes.

What's the necessary interplay for nature restoration between private capital and government regulation?

What I'm encouraged to see, especially over the last 10 years, is that there has been a push across all of those different leverage points to better address conservation and climate solutions. Our value-add is working on a company-by-company basis to use entrepreneurship and private sector investment at the local level as that positive change agent. And to find those folks that make a difference on the ground to serve as sustainable models.

I've always been a bottom-up versus a top-down girl. That's been the way we work. You've got to prove and demonstrate results. Using regulatory incentive systems will also bring about significant change. But we roll up our sleeves and get to work to invest in long-term fundamental shifts in thinking and doing as it relates to natural capital and sustainable business.

What are the implications of new entrants raising significant amounts of capital in the sector for Latin America? Is there a risk of increased impact washing?

I think that this is how markets evolve and how business transforms. There are large scale infrastructure deals, renewable energy deals, and sustainable companies that are beyond our bite-size and are more applicable for these other players. Our niche is quite different.

I find the complexity, integrity, and dynamics of our deals, and what is needed at our level of investment will not change anytime soon. Perhaps by Fund V, but certainly for Fund IV we're not seeing it.

If you had to name the one most important challenge in the sustainable VC space at this time, what would it be?

VC sustainable investing is a huge field. And it depends on how you define VC and sustainable investing. Moreover, there's a lot going on in ESG. Even when you use the term natural capital, there are different ways to come at it.

This is a similar challenge we experienced. In our book, *Portfolio for the Planet*, the first chapter is all about definitions because right before we went to press, the term impact investing emerged. I was like, "oh, this is perfect as it enables various players in the wide sustainable investing field to coalesce and gain an understanding of what we are about."

In our particular niche, I have to say, the overall challenges have remained constant. Generally, as in the venture investing business, you're dealing with entrepreneurs, small business and growth.

You are a woman-run fund. Although that's not how you market it, do you view it as a competitive advantage?

I think investors are increasingly interested in social equity, having women more involved in leadership at the investment as well as at the company level. We've made this commitment part of our operating philosophy from the get-go.

Gender smart investing now is an active strategy. For Fund III, we committed to the 2X Challenge.[11] For us, it continues to be a vital consideration with our focus on community and Indigenous peoples. Over the years, we observed that a lot of the small producers are women, a lot of the company's employees are women, and a lot of the executive teams are women. We have always encouraged women involvement. We're just now collecting more data on gender, gleaning lessons-learned, making it part of our communications to raise awareness and looking for more ways to elevate women in our portfolio.

"I would say it's harder to find companies now, startups and scale-ups, that are not contributing to sustainability than the other way around. Eighty percent of startups have a strong sustainability chapter in their business plan."

SUSTAINABLE AGRICULTURE VENTURE CAPITAL

PETER ARENSMAN
FUTURE FOOD FUND
FUTUREFOODFUND.COM
LI: https://www.linkedin.com/in/peterarensman/

An experienced entrepreneur and investor in sustainable agriculture and food chains, Peter Arensman is a strong business development professional with over 30 years' experience. He founded the BAS Consultancy in 1998, is also a Founding Partner of the investment company People, Planet, Profit, and the venture capital Future Food Fund. He sits on the boards of several companies, is a Guest Lecturer at Wageningen University, and holds Masters Degrees in Business Economics, Financial Law, and Agricultural Engineering.

Around 2009, you founded PPP—People, Planet Profit. What led to that?

When I started BAS Consulting (a consultancy supporting Chief Financial Officers), I came to the conclusion that there were a lot of people in the world who had, let's say, less beneficial circumstances in their lives than I had. I decided at that time with my business partner that if one day we made money with BAS Consulting, we were going to give away 10 percent of our gross profits to charity. We created a foundation called BAS Gives. Over the years we spent well over a million dollars of our personal money, which we gave to all kinds of smaller foundations specialized in education projects in Africa.

But the more I visited these projects, the more disappointed I got about the result because there was always a short-term result with hardly ever a long-term result. So, I decided to change the whole strategy and invest 100 percent of our gross profits in world-improving companies, to create economic progress in countries which have very low living standards. I created a commercial investment vehicle People

Planet Profit, but the money only goes to companies improving the world. That means, in general, the financial return is a bit lower—but you also measure a return on people and a return on the planet.

That was about 13 years ago, when the term "impact investing" didn't exist. I was motivated by a Dutch guy, Eckhardt Wintzen, who was already "Mr. Sustainability" starting somewhere in the 2000s. He was really the founder of sustainability thinking in the Netherlands and introduced me to the "triple P" bottom line [concept] of People, Planet, Profit—which made me so enthusiastic. I thought if you combine these three words in everything you do in your life, and if everybody would do this, the world will be a great place to live.

Was People, Planet, Profit Eckhardt Wintzen's term?

Well, when you look it up on Wikipedia, it's an American thing. So it's not his, but he introduced it to me and I could still get the URL: peopleplanetprofit.com.

When we started, we focused on two areas: sustainable food and sustainable energy, specifically hydro power. We invested in a fair-trade fruit company sourcing their fruits in developing countries, and in a fair-trade coffee company in Ethiopia. But now we are actively investing in a pipeline all geared toward a sustainable food chain, and our goal is to make a more fair food value chain. The things we invest in are coffee, cacao, chocolates, nuts, tea, and tropical fruits.

Why did you found the Future Food Fund as a separate company from People, Planet, Profit?

People, Planet, Profit was my own thing and was more or less my private thing to get my money from BAS Consulting into sustainable investments. By that time, I had had some negative experiences with direct investments. [Independently], I had invested some money as an LP myself into small IT funds and I really liked that structure. They were all small funds and there were like 15 or 20 LPs and they were all entrepreneurs like myself.

In 2015, I thought "I'm going to do this myself. I'm going to set up a fund just like the ones I'm an LP in, but I'm not going to do it in IT. I'm going back to my roots which is in the agriculture arena, Ag Tech and Food Tech." This seems quite normal now but in 2015, nobody was doing that.

Also, I did not put any impact targets in the fund plan at that time because I already had my own impact vehicle which was People, Planet, Profit. So, I thought this is something new, geared toward innovation in agriculture and foods. And if people want to make impact, they can put money in People, Planet, Profit.

What is Future Food Fund's mission?

It's a relatively small fund, a total of €14.5 million. The biggest part is being generated by 20 LP's, all entrepreneurs from my personal network, and about six million euros has been invested by the Government of the State of the Netherlands, the Ministry of Economic Affairs. Which means that with this fund we can only invest in companies with headquarters here in the Netherlands, because the State of the Netherlands is not giving me the money to promote economies in other countries. We promised our investors we would do 10 investments of between half a million and a million and a half or more. Let's say the minimum investment is a half million and the maximum investment is three and a half million. And we do not invest in companies that don't have a very clear innovative element.

How much capital have you deployed to date?

We did six of 10 investments so we've deployed about 50 percent of the money. I founded the fund in 2015, our [investment] activities started a year later, and now we have a very hot pipeline. I expect we will have our 10 investments before April 1st of 2022 and then we have six more years to exit all of our investments.

How do you see the Ag Tech sector, and what issues are you trying to address?

Let's start with saying that there is no shortage of food in the world. People always talk about food waste and nine out of 10 discussions about food waste are emotional. Some people like to combine, of course, starving children in Africa with throwing food in your bin in the Netherlands or in Switzerland. That's not a good comparison because the food is here, it's not there. It's very easy to produce food for everybody; it's not very easy to distribute it in an honest way. That's a complex thing, and it's even more complex to produce food in a sustainable way. Food production now has a lot of negative elements and that's something which really drives the sector. So, I would say all funds investing in foods look at improving the system, but not so much improving efficiency.

Making it more sustainable and also more efficient is, of course, fantastic. Take, for example the weeding robot. If you spray Roundup,[12] you don't need a weeding robot because there are no weeds. So, 10 years ago everybody was spraying Roundup. Now we've come to the conclusion that maybe Roundup is not very healthy for people and it's definitely not very healthy for the soil and everything in the first 30 centimeters of the soil is dying all over the world. That means that 30 years from now we won't be able to grow anything, because the soil can no longer support the plants. But if you don't spray Roundup, then your wheat is overgrown by weeds so the harvest results plummet. You get a whole new demand for new products, for example, the weeding robot.

If you look at drone technology, for example, it is being used more and more in agriculture. Every square meter, every square foot in a field of corn, for example, has different characteristics. Some parts have a lot of weeds, some parts don't have many weeds. Some parts are dry. So, you can optimize the revenue of big fields of corn, etc., by using drones when the crops are valuable enough to deploy all these extra techniques and technologies

In Australia, they're used to flying helicopters to see where their assets are, but this is not necessary anymore. Sensor technology is a big part in the whole Ag Tech world. For example, it makes it easier for the farmer to keep track of his cows. There are many companies developing sensor technology for all kinds of different purposes.

By investing in tech as a VC, aren't you competing head-on against big mainstream Silicon Valley funds with much larger size and clout?

I think that we are a bit more in the early stages, so we invest when there's revenue, but the revenue can be very low. For example, when we invested in an inventor and manufacturer of asparagus harvesting robots, he sold two of his prototypes to a farmer and then he asked us to invest. So, these bigger Silicon Valley Ag Tech investment companies are a typical exit candidate for us.

You say that you invest in companies that disrupt food value chains. What does this mean and how does it affect your portfolio?

An example is when the big fast-food chains changed completely from real meat to meat alternatives, like Beyond Burger. That's a very successful company, with a huge valuation. That's what will disrupt the whole husbandry chain, these huge farms all over the world with thousands of cows, tens of thousands of pigs, millions of chickens. That will be disrupted if we start consuming plant-based "meat" products.

Can you explain your portfolio approach and how you identify and screen your investment targets?

I wouldn't say it's rocket science; it's just disciplined work. It all starts with getting a healthy pipeline, of course, which means that we visit a lot of seminars and trade shows. We try to make ourselves known in everything that has to do with the food chain or with agriculture, and we try to attract startups and we get into contact with them. Then we have to pick the best deal. I think one in every 50 or 100 companies in our pipeline eventually becomes a deal we invest in.

Basically, there are three things we look at. First of all, the business model itself, how a company makes money. Second, it has to be very scalable. The third thing we are selecting right now is the team. We have a very clear vision of what a team should look like, and when the team is not complete, we don't invest.

Future Food Fund does not have a sustainability component in its fund plan, but I would say it's harder to find companies now, startups and scale-ups that are not contributing to sustainability than the other way around. So, 80 percent of startups have a strong sustainability chapter in their business plan.

Could you give me an example of the type of investment transaction that you prefer?

I think one of my two favorite investments we have in our portfolio right now is Pieter Pot, the packaging free grocery delivery company. Pieter Pot is the first online supermarket to deliver "packaging-free" groceries by filling products in reusable jars and delivering them to consumers. The jars contain food and non-food products from both the Pieter Pot private label and well-known A brands, from rice to sweets, from olive oil to shampoo. Empty pots are taken back to be

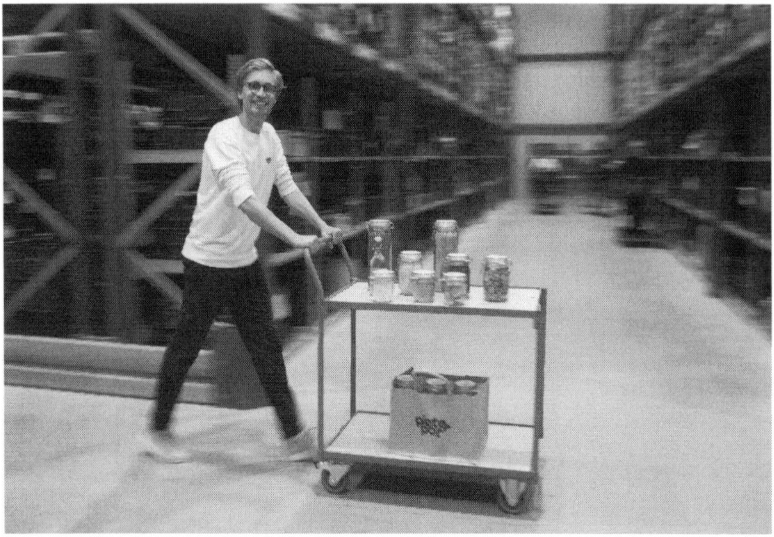

Pieter Pot greatly reduces packaging waste. *Source:* Used with permission of Pieter Pot

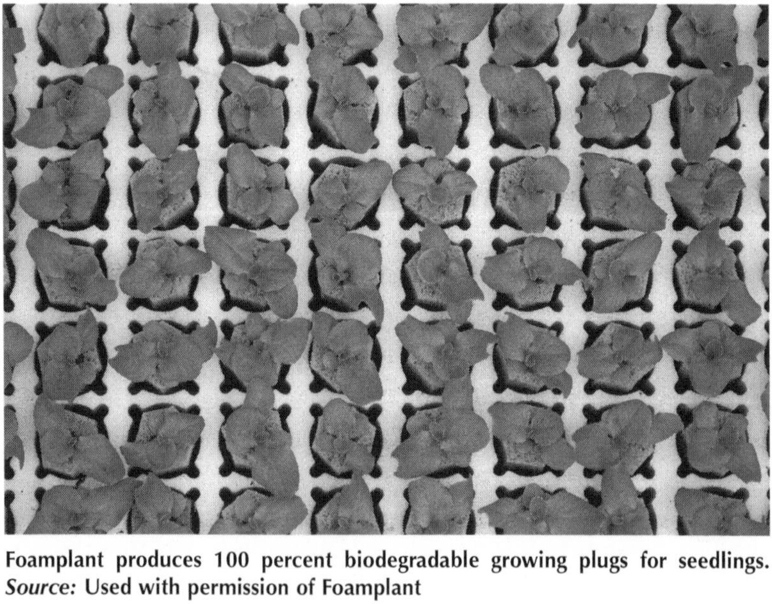

Foamplant produces 100 percent biodegradable growing plugs for seedlings. *Source:* Used with permission of Foamplant

washed and refilled; a circular process which greatly reduces the quantity of plastic packaging.

The other one is called Foamplant which produces biodegradable growing plugs and soils (GROWFOAM®) and it's a large and profitable business worldwide. Growers used to grow their seeds and seedlings on peat or stone wool, but both of those growing substrates have their limits. Stone wool substrates are nowhere near biodegradable and peat excavations destroy valuable moors and peatlands.

So, with Foamplant we've developed a growing plug and substrate that is made from biopolymers and therefore 100 percent biodegradable. GROWFOAM® is also certified for home and industrial composting, is pathogen free, automation ready and easy to implement in all major growing systems. Leading vertical and hydroponic farms worldwide are already using the GROWFOAM® substrates in their farms.

Is your fund open or closed-ended, and what are your targeted returns?

It's closed-ended and we need to sell off all our portfolio companies within the next seven years. But we haven't had any exits yet. Our target is a money multiple of two and a half. That means for the money you invested, you will get two and a half times as much back. That will be between, let's say, 15 and 20 percent IRR.

So that's two and a half in seven years?

It's a bit complex because, for example, when you are an LP and you invest one million euros in our funds, you don't have to give me the one million right away. You commit to it and you fund every time we do a capital call. In general, it will be five, six, or seven years, more or less.

I know you started with 20 or 25 entrepreneurs. Was that by design or by default?

First of all, 90 percent of my personal network are entrepreneurs, but secondly—and this is very relevant for the fund—we have the [personal] knowledge of the entrepreneurs.

Each of our LPs of course has a big network. So, we encourage our portfolio companies to ask all the questions they have about how to grow their companies fast and we just e-mail them to our LPs. And we're all very experienced. Together, we have made every single mistake you can make in growing a company. So, we are of huge added value to the portfolio companies.

The LPs love to be engaged and invest their time when they can help. They invest to make money, but they also invest because they think the market space is very interesting. They also invest because the entrepreneurs, the people who started these companies are nice people.

What impact are you trying to achieve with your second fund, Future Food Fund II?

People who step into the Future Food Fund II will have the benefit of the fact that Future Food Fund has already built up the present pipeline, but we will rule out companies who have a negative impact—because there are some of those companies in the pipeline—the ticket size will be a bit bigger in the new fund. We will also have the possibility to go abroad. Of course, investing abroad always presents additional challenges, because it's very hard to manage a portfolio company which is not close to you.

If you had to name the one most important challenge in the VC sustainable investment space at this time, what would you say it is?

I think in this particular market, scaling up is the challenge. I'm talking about sustainable investments in the Ag Tech and Food Tech world, because everything goes much slower than for example, in IT. If you invest in IT, everything goes very quickly. I've given this a lot of thought, and it also has to do with the fact, of course, that we are talking about seasons, so when you invest for example, in the asparagus harvest, there are only two months a year you can test your products. It's a slower market which means also scaling up goes slower. That's the biggest challenge I would say.

What do you know now about sustainable investing or impact investing that you wish you knew in 2015 when you launched the Future Food Fund?

I think what I know now is that the all scale-ups have a very separate Impact chapter in their business plan. I wasn't aware of that five years ago. I'm also a lecturer at the Wageningen University right now, I'm lecturing Masters students who want to become an entrepreneur in this area. They're being taught by the university about the Triple P canvas model, while I was taught the normal canvas model, "just go for profit." All the students now are being taught Triple P canvas model. This gives a new insight that ignoring impact would be a very dumb thing to do these days because all entrepreneurs are very passionate about impact.

Have you passed on an investment that turned out to be way better than you thought and what did you learn from that?

Well, I think we passed on one investment which in the end we regretted. We passed on it not because we didn't believe in the business model, but it's always a combination, of course, of the valuation. So, we thought the valuation was too high. My lesson was, don't walk away when there's a valuation discussion which comes down to less than 10 percent. When there's less than a 10 percent difference in valuation, you should reconsider.

If someone wants to get into the VC Ag Tech or Food Tech investing space, what would you suggest to them?

I would subscribe to "AgFunder," that's a California newsletter which kind of comprises all investments in this area worldwide.

Chapter Nine

Real Assets

What we have covered thus far are financial assets—including stocks, bonds, cash deposits, and anything else that derives value from a contractual right or ownership claim (e.g., a claim on shareholder dividends).

Intangible assets are not physical in nature but can, nevertheless, be of huge economic value. They may include patents, trademarks, and copyrights—or often simply represent the market value of brand recognition. According to *Forbes*, the Apple brand alone in 2020 (excluding all other financial and intangible assets owned by the company) was worth over $240 billion.[1]

Finally, there are real assets, a separate asset class. These are physical assets that have an intrinsic worth due to their substance and properties.

WHAT'S REAL AND WHAT'S NOT?

These assets, unlike others that we have been discussing, are physical—you can touch them, they are tangible, and they have intrinsic worth. They can be natural—like mined precious metals—or physical, like the machinery needed to process them. They also include real estate (housing, offices, data centers, logistics warehouses) and forestry and agriculture, which include both the underlying landscapes themselves and the processing assets (like sawmills and milking sheds) that sit alongside to monetize them.

Today, approximately 20 percent of real asset AUM is invested in infrastructure, 57 percent in natural resources, and 23 percent in real estate. Within infrastructure, investments can include rail, airports, roads, telecoms—all of which will need to navigate toward a Net Zero new normal.

Within natural resources this still includes oil and gas, of course, but is increasingly weighted toward solar, wind, and battery storage as investors attempt to decarbonize the energy sector. It also includes an ever-higher allocation toward sustainable forestry, as those who can't reduce their carbon footprint any further look to natural climate solutions to offset carbon where urgently required.

REAL ASSETS, REAL ADVANTAGES, REAL DISADVANTAGES

Real assets are traditionally included in an investor's portfolio for a number of reasons related to risk and return. On the one hand, they often provide current and long-term stable income. Because their cash flows are linked to inflation (operators can often simply increase their prices) they can act as inflation hedges within a portfolio, while other financial assets underperform in inflationary environments.

Furthermore, in low interest rate environments (or at moments in the economic cycle where public equities are reducing their dividend payouts), real assets usually maintain high, sometimes contracted, yields. Lastly, they have a historically low correlation to equity markets and bonds, which can reduce the overall volatility of a well-constructed portfolio. Depending on the real assets involved, there can be the additional advantages of asset appreciation and favorable tax treatments in certain jurisdictions.

That said, airports, forests, and windfarms are big ticket items that are a lot harder to sell than single stocks traded on the public equity markets, so the advantages of real assets must be weighed against the much lower liquidity of the investments. There may also be other logistical disadvantages. It's relatively simple to store or transport $1 million of share certificates. Housing or moving $1 million of physical gold is a whole different matter.

REAL(LY) SUSTAINABLE ASSETS

Real assets have played a critical role in creating the unsustainable world in which we live. Examples include deforestation resulting from extractive mining, nonstop hydrocarbon drilling, and the use of carbon-intensive steel and cement in real estate.

Nonetheless, there is now an increased realization that real assets must play one of the most critical roles in delivering a sustainable future. The need for renewable energy capacity is clear. But mining also has a critical role to play. Electric vehicles, wind turbines, and solar panels will all remain dependent on mined metals. Furthermore, the biodiversity crisis is more recently being recognized as perhaps an even greater, albeit interrelated, threat to humanity than climate. Therefore, sustainable forestry is coming to the forefront with strategies that move away from damaging non-native monocultures toward those that support ecosystem recovery and rural livelihoods (all while absorbing atmospheric carbon).

In this chapter, New Forest's Radha Kuppalli speaks to the increased demand for sustainable forestry investments over the past 24 months—particularly urgent given recent research conducted by the World Economic Forum that estimates that $44 trillion of economic value generation—more than half of the world's total GDP—is dependent on nature and is therefore exposed to nature loss.[2] Forestry has a role to play.

"Forestry is increasingly being considered by institutional investors, particularly members of the Net Zero Asset Owners Alliance, or those taking on decarbonization targets. They're now looking for investments in climate solutions and forestry as one sleeve of that. They are looking at how do I invest in forestry to decarbonize my portfolio? How do you have to manage a forest to be climate positive? That could be everything from the kinds of strategies and the way you're managing assets, to the inclusion of carbon finance and carbon credits in the underlying product and the strategy for that forest. Also, the whole bioeconomy piece: how can forests contribute to new industries around mass timber and replacing fossil fuel-based products?"

What could be next? The interviews that follow are from innovative investors who provide keen insights into where the current momentum will lead. There is the emergent theme of Natural Capital as a potential new asset class in itself; the transformational impact of technology (from LIDAR on drones for forestry to the relentless application of Moore's Law in battery technology); and perhaps even the convergence of carbon-absorbing trees and real estate with the development of cross-laminated timber high-rises.

"We saw the heart of sustainability as the effective and productive use of resources. If you cracked it, sustainability was a competitive advantage."

SUSTAINABILITY DRIVEN REAL ASSET INVESTING
DAVE CHEN
EQUILIBRIUM
EQ-CAP.COM
LI: https://www.linkedin.com/in/dypchen1/
TW: @EquilibriumCap

Dave Chen is CEO and Head of Product Development and Research at Equilibrium, where he is responsible for strategy, executive leadership, and developing the firm's investment products and asset strategies. Formerly, he was a General Partner at OVP Venture Partners (2000–2007); CEO/Co-Founder of GeoTrust (acquired by VeriSign in 2006); Founder of The Ascent Group; and served on the San Francisco Federal Reserve Bank Board. Chen is an Adjunct Professor of Finance at the Kellogg School of Management at Northwestern University (2009–present) and has taught sustainable finance and impact investing at Stanford GSB from 2011 to 2013.

What was the genesis behind the formation of Equilibrium Capital?

We formed Equilibrium about 12 or 13 years ago and we had a very simple premise, which was that sustainability was not couched in the word "advocacy" or "responsibility." Sustainability was couched in the word "competitive advantage." We saw it as sustainable trends, sustainable services, and sustainable products. We saw the heart of sustainability as the effective and productive use of resources. If you cracked it, sustainability was a competitive advantage.

And the reason that we were so compelled by that is that we are effectively students and we go to school on people. We got to know dozens of folks that had built these multi-billion-dollar enterprises, or very significant enterprises, that were attacking sustainability not at the high level, but at the substantive minutia.

Can you give an example?

We had the benefit at the time that we formed the company of going to school on people like Ray Anderson [Founder and Chairman of

Interface, Inc., one of the world's largest manufacturers of modular carpet for commercial and residential applications]. Ray was a marketeer enough to know that he needed to put a face on sustainability, in his case the product focus on biomimicry. But the substance of what he did in sustainability was all about productive reuse of waste streams, recycling, closed loop, stretching, etc. These are all boring and mundane things, but he was a balance of sustainability being substantive expense and competitive advantage and, at the same time, showman enough to be able to talk about the snap and sizzle of sustainability.

Ultimately, we developed the investment thesis that sustainability was a competitive advantage. It was about an economic shift, mispriced assets, and market inefficiency at the information level. And we came to the conclusion that if that were the case and we could uncover this, then we would see an alpha opportunity.

Why did you choose to focus on real assets?

At the time that we created our company, most of the [sustainability] conversation at the time was around impact investing, which was centered around social enterprise. The other stream was the tapering down of the life cycle of legacy SRI, which is all about exclusion and "being responsible." We saw the opportunity for what is effectively an alpha play. We thought that we could best express that advantage in an asset category that was very large, generally not professionally managed, and where institutional capital had not really made a presence. And that was in the area of real assets.

So, the first thing we did, we avoided seeing sustainability as an asset class—and, 10, 12, or 14 years ago, there was this big conversation about this being an asset class—but we didn't see it that way. We saw it as a strategy that cut across all asset classes. But we chose to penetrate the area of real assets and then, specifically, we saw that the big real assets categories—real estate, forestry, agriculture, energy—these were all massive. And we chose ways that we could use what we perceived as our competitive advantage, to build portfolios within those categories.

So, the second part of this company is that, at the heart of our DNA, we're value chain analysts. Because we're a small player, we have to look for value chains where a significant shift is taking place driven by sustainability, where it allows a new player to create a new position by taking advantage of a shift in the value chain.

The third thing is that we made the hard decision that we were going to go counter to the trend at the time and go back to what most of my team knows, which is institutional investors. This was a decision that we made about 2010, and if you remember around that time, the center of this conversation, whether it was SRI, sustainability, or impact investing, was around ultra-high net worth investors. We made the decision that the ultra-high net worth market that was interested in this category was very much about advocacy and not about putting a lot of money to work.

So, beginning about 2010 or 2012, we went out and focused our company on building these strategies for pension funds and sovereign wealth funds. And we believed our message and our strategy would resonate with them because we talked about sustainability using the vocabulary of risk and the vocabulary of opportunity and competitive advantage.

So, the company has been built on these three central points: One, sustainability is about competitive advantage and shifts in value. Number two, it's expressed in real assets. Number three, we focus on serving institutional clients.

Who are your investors and have they changed over time?

Today we've got about $2 billion plus on the platform. I would say that about 90 percent of our clients are pension funds and sovereign funds. At best, we have 3 or 4 percent "impact investors," and 3 or 4 percent of our investors that are endowments or foundations.

When we started in 2010 or 2012 to really go out to the market, I would say the vast majority of our capital was not mandate-driven capital. It was plain vanilla asset allocation out of the real assets buckets. The funny thing is that as the world has evolved in the last three or four years, many of the institutional investors have evolved with sustainability or climate or climate adaptation overlays across their entire portfolios. And that's accelerated over the last two years. I would say that for most people now that we are investing with, we fit a mandate, in many cases retrospectively.

Can you describe your proprietary funds?

Our two proprietary platforms are our Waste, Water Energy Products, now re-badged carbon transition infrastructure, that is approximately

$300 million in funds, and then our Controlled Environment Foods fund platform—which today has approximately $1.8 billion.

Are these open or closed-ended funds?

Closed-ended. You might ask the question, if these are long-term real assets, income bearing products, shouldn't they be open-ended? And shouldn't they be long-lived? The answer is, they should be. Ten years ago, for investors and more specifically some of the consultants, something that everyone talked about but very few actually accepted to sign-off on was an open-ended fund or an open-ended investment vehicle. It's only now that folks are starting to ask the question and want to allocate to open-ended vehicles, whether they're REIT-like structures or not. Or open-ended fund vehicles as the logical receptacle to long-lived assets and which are income bearing and playing in the right set of growth-oriented sectors.

Describe your Controlled Environment Foods fund.

The Controlled Environment Foods fund platform is exclusively invested in high-tech controlled environment greenhouses. These are $50 million to $100 million assets. In the greenhouse space, we are now among the largest owners of greenhouses in North America.

There are three broad categories of crops that are currently contemplated or already exist in our greenhouses. One is known as vine crops. These are generally tomatoes, cucumbers, and peppers—but they include other vegetables like eggplants. This is the most mature category of greenhouse grown crops and traces its history back to the Dutch.

The second category, and it's much more nascent, is what is broadly called leafy greens. Those would include lettuces, spinaches, and the incredibly nascent field of Asian vegetables. Asian vegetables are very important. Because we're Western-centric, we forget that there are four billion people on the other side of the planet that actually have a high vegetable diet and they eat different vegetables than we do. And they eat more of them. So, we're constantly monitoring the evolution of greenhouse applications for the broad set of leafy greens.

The third category are the soft fruits which would include strawberries, blackberries, blueberries, and raspberries. The strawberries in Northern Europe, centered in a handful of producers in the UK and then across both Holland and France, have been grown indoors for many years but in the United States, they have not. That's because when God decided to grow strawberries, he created the coast of California, perhaps one of the most beautiful climates and soil types for growing strawberries.

You know that America has the benefit of wide-open spaces and availability of land, so for many years there's been no reason to think about indoor strawberries. But the times have changed. And you're going to see the growth of indoor strawberries for a multitude of reasons. And you should not be surprised that high-value crops—like the year-round availability of beautifully grown cantaloupes and other types of fruits like that—will also see their way into the greenhouse over the course of the next decade.

Do you see crop production broadening beyond those three categories?

I think it's going to be a long time before we start talking about grains and other things. But the idea of controlled environment agriculture is, in many ways, the use of fermentation sciences to produce proteins and fats. Ultimately, to manufacture the fats that are in dairy products and bring the health of dairy products, but without as much use of cows. And we're on the precipice of that.

So, you're going to see the rethinking of agriculture taking place on multiple dimensions. The reason that we called it the Controlled Environment Foods fund and not the Greenhouse fund, and the reason that the S curve is so important to us, is that we see a successive series of S-curves that we will be attaching ourselves to.

What do you see as the most likely targets?

We haven't even begun to touch the fruits or the families of leafy greens yet. Most people talk in hyperbole about feeding the world and about the next generation of agriculture. But if you just do the math, you begin to realize the scale of change and execution that's going to have to take place.

In the world of climate and climate adaptation and climate change, it will be infrastructure development, as much as technology development, that will actually be the lever that we use to change the world. There might only be a dozen technology firms in solar and in wind that make the windmills and make the solar cells. But it's the ubiquity of the solar fields everywhere you drive and everywhere you look there is a windmill farm. So as important as it is for us to talk about the companies that create the solar cells, it's also important to look at the infrastructure investor and developer who has made those cells ubiquitous across rooftops and countrysides. The same thing will happen with the food system.

Do you take technology risks in your controlled environment greenhouses?

Part of our insight was that we did not need to take technology risks. But we're exposed to technology obsolescence in the same way that a data center owner is. The landlord has to maintain a constant evolution of the underlying infrastructure of the data center. Otherwise, they might suffer from the fact that they have an inefficient or non-cost-competitive data center. So those assets need to be kept up to speed, up to technology life cycles.

Similarly, if you look at the way you underwrite solar and large-scale wind fleets, you build into it that every seven or 10 years you're upgrading this system or that system. The windmill blade may have a useful life of 20 or 25 years, but the gearbox is changing. The software management system is changing. Any of these technologically dependent, long-lived assets have to be maintained and upgraded, so we do the same thing in our underwriting and the management of our assets.

What is the long-term impact of unlinking geography and climate from where things can be grown?

The easy agricultural strategy for years has been to find great Mediterranean climates. We all want to live in Mediterranean climates, right? We all want to grow crops in Mediterranean climates, and that's all beautiful when the climate is stable.

If you actually believe that climate is changing, what makes you think that the geographies with Mediterranean climate aren't going to be affected, like that hunk of land in sweet-spot Provence, that is a gorgeous Mediterranean climate? Climate change can be for the better and worse. It can be dryer; it can be wetter. It can be sunnier; it can be cloudier. People don't really think about climate change. They talk about it a lot, but they really don't think about it a lot. The climate is changing, and agriculture is ground zero for climate change.

Let me take a couple of absurd examples to illustrate this. Let's say that you picked Provence because it has 330 days of sunshine a year and you sited your beautiful wind farm and your beautiful solar field in Provence because it's so damn gorgeous. And you underwrote it for 330 days of sunshine for your solar. And because every day is very stable and predictable you know that the morning starts off with mild breezes—beautiful for having a cup of coffee. And by the afternoon, because the earth heats up in Provence at a very predictable rate, you get these beautiful, gentle winds that come whipping through and cool the day but also generate wind. Very predictable. Beautiful. All of a sudden, Provence's climate changes so that it's cloudier and the temperature gradient starts to change. It's still beautiful, but with a 10 to 15 percent change in the weather pattern your underwriting based on the number of photons that strike your solar field is off. The wind now is not as predictable because the ground heats up differently and all of a sudden your wind is volatile. This disrupts your underwriting. You underwrote it with the assumption that what is historically true in the past will be historically true in the future, right?

So, how long until this beautiful piece of dirt that you bought, which is not movable, that you bought because it was a beautiful Mediterranean climate, is no longer a beautiful Mediterranean climate? And you know that the greatest predictor of quality and quantity in agriculture is the weather, right? It's why in all the movies you hear guys in the trading pit screaming about "My God, did you read the weather report? Brazil is going to go into a drought, orange juice prices are going to go nuts."

And we're hearing more of those conversations in real life, right?

You get three farmers together anytime over a cup of coffee or tea, anywhere in the world, and within a minute or two the topic will always turn to weather.

So, when I talk about distributed abundance, it's the same reason that Saudi Arabia is a country with a border that happens to sit over a massive pool of dead dinosaurs. They won the country lottery. The reason the United States became a superpower in the 1800s and 1900s is because we had the Mississippi Valley that had a river that was huge and had access to a transportation network across one of the most fertile places in the world. So, we won the climate and geography lottery, right? It wasn't anything we did.

Now climate change starts taking place, and weather is the number one predictor of quality and quantity. So, the lottery ticket changed. The second thing is resiliency. Resiliency was a fun word to say on panels because it made you look smart. COVID gave it a face and actually made it visceral.

Now we have DIY climate-controlled environment agriculture, I can distribute away from the land and away from the climate. It's really hard to grow a tomato when most of your year is cold and dark. So, one of the largest buildouts of glass greenhouse infrastructure in the last decade was Russia. So that's the ultimate in DIY and BYO—bring your own and do it yourself.

What will be the drivers of this trend going forward?

Any number of reasons will drive this trend. Challenges we have to face in the next few decades include water stress, climate volatility, climate shifts, and the need for resilient food systems. There's the need to reduce volatility, potentially, in times where the natural systems are going to become more volatile, and the desire for regionalism and the need for food safety. And we saw that and were willing to bet on it. When we started the fund five years ago, we used the wording that this was a complement to field agriculture. Increasingly, it's becoming a replacement for field agriculture.

"If you miss out on big systemic changes, this can be punitive in terms of returns—if you picked the best tobacco company in the '70s, it didn't matter, you would always have been trumped by any tech company. It's going to be a prerequisite for success in the future to have a purposeful approach to investing. The secular shift toward thoughtful, purposeful, responsible investment trends grounded in climate is so powerful, that if you're not in the boat, you're drowning."

SUSTAINABLE REAL ESTATE INVESTING

BASIL DEMEROUTIS
FORE PARTNERSHIP
FOREPARTNERSHIP.COM
LI: https://www.linkedin.com/in/basildemeroutis/
TW: @Basil_FORE

Basil Demeroutis is Managing Partner of FORE Partnership, a purpose-driven real estate investment firm active in the UK and Western Europe. Its mission is to prove that driving environmental sustainability and positive social outcomes is good for investors' financial returns.

Prior to setting up FORE Partnership in 2012, Demeroutis was a Partner at Capricorn Investment Group and, earlier, he was Managing Partner of Jargonannt Partners in Germany. He is passionate about sustainable property and has aligned FORE Partnership's investment strategy with his, and the company's investors' core values. He earned a BS in Aerospace Engineering from Cornell University.

Introduce us to FORE Partnership and its novel fund structure.

We believe in a low carbon future in which property is a force for social good. I think there is a duality of both the E and the S of ESG, in our mission. We've been doing this now for nine years, have raised a couple of hundred million of capital, and around seven hundred million euros of property value. We've purchased about 1.1 million square feet of real estate across 13 assets. I'd say we're at the big end of the small end of the mid-size firms, where we've carved out a niche for ourselves in that domain. We have one office in London, with seven or eight employees.

Our assets tend to be focused in two areas. Offices are about two thirds of our portfolio, and secondly a bucket I would call "living."

Within living there are three separate sleeves: "Co-living" is micro apartments—small, urban, city-center flats, primarily bringing affordability to key workers and young professionals. The other two are senior living and affordable housing which is bottom of the pyramid housing for people who are really on the cusp of homelessness and marginalized populations within urban city centers.

If you think about oriented, values-aligned investing, you would not necessarily come up with the typical private equity fund model where it pits GPs against LPs. There are plenty of examples of LPs suing GPs, GPs suing LPs, classic examples involving Carlyle and other perpetrators who have accelerated transaction fee expenses and were sued by the SEC. Those are case studies of basically bad behavior pitting the financial titans against the poor, understaffed, and under-resourced SEC and LPs—who are both trying to follow the marbles in this shell game of private finance.

That's why we came up with this structure we call a club model which we've used up until now. We give investors back some discretion and allow them to allocate capital as they see fit, on a deal-by-deal basis, while at the same time forcing them to effectively invest in our transactions.

In our version of the club model, we have asked investors to "soft" commit. If I asked, "Do you want to see all of our deal flow and pick and choose which ones you invest in?" I think 99 percent of people would say, "Sure, why not—free lunch." So, we get people to commit to a program of investing, and then they have to invest in every deal. But as a group they can veto it, and in addition they can decide how much to invest in each deal.

What are your target returns to your investors?

We try to hit a 12 to 15 percent net IRR. I think IRRs can be a bit deceiving in real estate. We are moving more toward a three-part return profile, so 12 to 15 percent IRR, a 1.6 equity multiple, and double-digit cash-on-cash. I think if we were to hit two of those, we would be happy.

It probably speaks as much to the holding period as anything, the fact that maybe we were to find something that has an 8, 9, or 10 percent IRR., but if it gets to a 1.6 multiple, and at the end of the stabilization period we're delivering double-digit cash-on-cash, why not? I don't think we should hold a gun to our own head with IRR.

Describe the impact of the built environment both in terms of human well-being and environmental and social impact.

This is part of the urgency in our mission that we feel. I certainly think the climate crisis is, we can all agree, real and getting worse. Equally, I think real estate is probably one of the greatest untapped opportunities that exists with incredible amounts of work to be done.

Probably something like 2, 3, or 4 percent of the buildings out there are actually "green." We've all committed as countries to be net carbon zero by 2050—or in some cases, 2045, like Manchester and others in the UK. But we are incredibly behind. Every building that's not currently achieving carbon neutrality is going to need to be refurbished, renovated, repositioned, or rebuilt in that period of time.

What's shocking when you think of it is that buildings roughly have a 30-year refurbishment lifecycle. If you've got a building that's got air conditioning and a mechanical electrical kit, that gear usually lasts for about 30 years. Building fabric lasts longer, but we're now within that refurbishment cycle, 2020 to 2050. So, every building that's effectively being refurbished now needs to be net zero carbon—today.

Another interesting statistic is that something like 80 percent of the buildings that will exist in 2050 have already been built. So, we've a huge task ahead of us in terms of the industry. Real estate is responsible for about 40 percent of the global CO_2 greenhouse gas emissions. I think that's the statistic that's widely touted. Seventeen percent is residential, 11 percent is non-residential, 11 percent comes from the construction industry. It's roughly about the same for energy consumption—buildings use about 36 percent of global energy consumption. It's huge; it's the largest single sector in terms of environmental impact.

If we want to tackle greenhouse gas emissions and CO_2 emissions, we have to tackle real estate, which for all intents and purposes has not yet been touched in terms of getting to zero. In terms of its culpability, it's huge.

Something like 70 percent of global energy consumption and CO_2 emissions come from cities. It doesn't come from cows and fields and all this fun stuff that we like to talk about; it comes from cities. So, it's our built environment, and it's getting worse. We've made great strides but we're also building more and more square feet which is eroding the gains we're making. Between 2010 and 2019, total final energy demand has been up 7 percent, although energy intensity on a per building basis is down.

So, we're actually moving in the wrong direction. Cities and buildings are producing or consuming more energy today than they were a decade ago.

Do you focus on the environmental impact then, over social impact?

I think we would say that the E and S [of ESG] are deeply interconnected. We also recognize that buildings are a potential delivery vector for social change. If you think of it, we spend 80 or 90 percent of our time inside buildings. Buildings have huge negative impact on communities but could also have a positive impact.

If you're trying to tackle food poverty, or jobs and skills training, where will you do that? No matter what kind of program or the activity, that activity needs to happen somewhere, and it needs to happen within the built environment. When you think of our urban systems in an interconnected way, you start to realize that buildings are actually at the center of change. That system comprises government, social organizations, retailers, transportation, and infrastructure. At the center core of all of that is buildings.

We look at our buildings as a way to deliver social outcomes as much as environmental outcomes. I'll give you an example to try and bring it home. Let's take our building in Scotland called Cadworks. In that particular case, we wanted to make a big push around cycling and micro mobility. We took out the parking garage entirely, and instead we put in state-of-the-art cycling facilities with showering and changing and stretching facilities, with lots of different options for people in the building to hire a bike, or ride a scooter, or their own bike. People with disabilities have equal access, and we made it fun—we put a cycle-in ramp and you get to the cycling facilities by riding in on this really cool glass ramp that runs through the reception area of the building. It encourages people to cycle because we take a lot of the barriers away.

Then on the social side of things, we say, let's not just put in a bike rack and think that we're somehow changing the world. How are we changing social outcomes? Let's make that bike rack work a lot harder.

We found a number of social enterprises in Glasgow who are using cycling as a way to solve some key social issues. There's one called Soul Riders that takes used, disused bicycles—that you may have in your garage or your garden shed—and repairs them in their workshop. They employ people at the fringes of society to do the bike repairs, and train them up, giving them a job and new skills. They teach them how to be bike mechanics, which gives them a sense of purpose and worth. They fix the bikes and then they give the bikes back out into society to people who may not be able to get to work because they can't afford the transportation, or who may have health issues and want to cycle, or they can't afford a bike for the kids. So, they use cycling as a way to address these social outcomes within Glasgow.

We partnered with them, and we're going to give them a small workshop space in our building. Even when the building was being refurbished, we ran a big bike donation drive from around the property industry. We've brought in 60 or 70 bicycles in terms of donations for Soul Riders. We've also partnered them up with other social enterprises that we're working with. There's one called Social Bites, which is a small food shop that, again, has a social purpose. They feed the homeless and address food poverty and food insecurity. We gave them a bicycle, maintained and repaired and operated by Soul Riders, which is now doing food deliveries.

There's a kind of connective tissue between what we're doing on the for-profit commercial side—fantastic infrastructure that will attract tenants—and then the social side. It's all around the theme of cycling.

Just to put a bow around it and why we do this, we think its brand reinforcing for the building. It's authentic. We can involve tenants, too, by putting in place programs where they can bring their bicycle in to be repaired by the Soul Riders folks in the building and get some exposure to the great work that the charity is doing. Maybe they'll go on a cycle ride with young, impoverished people, and we'll bring occupiers together with the social enterprise. It creates this interconnectedness between the tenants of the building, the building itself, and purpose. Ultimately, I believe this is a key factor influencing how people make decisions: purpose and values. And for us, this hopefully creates stickiness so tenants stay longer, the building rents faster, and ultimately drives rental values higher.

Our vision for the future is quite clearly this deeply interconnected system where buildings are agents of change to some of society's greatest problems. Be that climate or social issues around jobs and skills.

How do you select your investments?

We are constantly thinking about, "Is this a canvas on which we can paint our vision?" Typically, we like buildings in the 20- to 30-year-old range—1980s, 1990s buildings, concrete frame, good structures, where we can add a floor or two on top, fundamentally sound. They are going to be there for the next 50 to 100 years. We like those kinds of buildings, and they have to be renovated anyway. So, we're not taking something that's just been done five years ago and then ripping out all the kit. I think that's wasteful.

We like them in relatively prominent locations and think we should do it in a way that's highly visible, so it could be exemplar for others.

How do you integrate ESG?

We try to drill ESG into every aspect of the building from design to operation. I'll give you a quick example, which is a 100,000 square foot building called Tower Bridge Court in London. We're putting in a three and a half thousand square foot "urban village hall," which is a multifunction space that tenants in the building can rent out for a fee and use for events. But equally, we're also programming activities in there with social enterprises and community groups. It might be a school that needs a space to run an art exhibition for their kids for a week. It might be a social enterprise that needs to have a fundraiser or skills workshop around technology and computer coding.

By putting that inside the building, we are trying to deeply integrate the occupants of the building into that activity. If it's a training course on computer programming, for example, every company has an IT department, why can't their IT people come down and spend an hour to teach someone about how to build a computer network? Again, I think that integration of community, both within the building and without the building, is really essential. That's what we mean in terms of integrating the E and the S and creating opportunities like that for impact at multiple levels, across multiple problems.

Give me an example of an investment you made, how you selected it and the result.

So, Windmill Green was an empty building for seven years on a big square in Manchester, three or four buildings away from what you would think of as being the center of Manchester, St. Peter's Square. It had been empty and long overlooked for seven years and there had been a variety of planning applications that had been brought forward to knock it down, all of which had failed.

When we bought it, it had planning approval for a 17-story office building which had been opposed by many, including Historic England at the time. Although it had planning permission, it was unfinanceable because the business plan required an assumption that you would hit rents that had never before been achieved in Manchester. When we looked at it, it was basically a dead deal, but we said why are we knocking this building down? It's a perfectly good building. It was only built 30 or 35 years ago; it's perfectly usable. Maybe we can come up with a business plan that doesn't require such high rents.

So, we bought it. We had an architect come up with a plan that would take it from roughly 50,000 thousand to 80,000 square feet. We took off the facade, went up two floors, did a little bit of infill in places to improve the floor plates, and then implemented a wide variety of social impact and environmental sustainability pieces. We reduced the operational carbon footprint of the building by around 85 percent. We put solar panels, a huge green wall, and attractive staircases to help health and wellbeing by encouraging people to use the stairs as opposed to taking the lifts. We put in cycling infrastructure, and during the construction we hired homeless people who were literally sleeping right around the corner. We did skills training workshops for ex-military service personnel who were jobless. We went to juvenile groups that were helping kids who had lost their way and tried to get them into the construction sector. We got them skilled-up and gave them jobs and apprenticeships on the site.

We also did things on the social side around marketing and branding. Every one of our brochures has photographs and images. Rather than hire professional photographers and illustrators, we went to the local community colleges and gave them to their students as projects. For the construction hoardings around the building, we went to Shillington College where we worked with art and design students. We had them briefed by our marketing teams like a professional project and got them to design posters that we ultimately used on the building. We gave them real world experience that they could put in their CVs. They were incredibly proud, for two years, their artwork was adorned on the outside of the building. Hopefully it helped them get jobs. We did lots of things on the social side; we put art exhibitions in the reception area for local upcoming artists.

The building received recognition for its environmental sustainability in particular and was, ultimately, the first multi-let office in Manchester to get BREEAM Outstanding (an international building standard rating) recognition. It won a number of social impact awards for delivering impact within the context of a commercial office building.

Did the impact that you built into that affect the financial returns?

At Windmill Green, our business plan was at £28 a square foot in rent, and now post-refurbishment, we've hit £36 a foot. The highest rent now being achieved in Manchester is £37.50 for new construction, so it's within a hair's breadth of new builds.

I think the reason why it's been so successful, is that people buy your *why*, and Windmill Green has a powerful, very self-evident *why*. You walk into it and see it and it's deeply integrated and authentic. From the materials, it has this "makery" type materiality to it. The staircase is folded sheet metal that you can imagine someone bending—the hand-rails carved of wood, the stone on the floor. There's a gigantic living, 6,000-plant green wall, the largest in Manchester. It has this authenticity and materiality around it that I think resonates with people when you combine it with the social agenda.

What role does concrete and steel play in climate change?

We've been thinking about concrete and steel for quite some time as many others have. There's a staggering statistic, that if concrete was a country, it would be the third worst emitter behind China and the United States. If steel was a country, it would be number four, they're awful. These are hard to abate sectors, with complex challenges that are very difficult to address. But when you think about it, we've been building buildings the same way today as we have for the best part of a hundred years. There's been almost no innovation in building construction since we built the first skyscrapers in New York. At FORE, we're spending time with people who are doing innovative things in concrete, steel, and other materials. For example, we're using cement-free concrete wherever we can, which reduces the carbon footprint of concrete by something like 80 to 85 percent.

I think this level of detail that we get into is a competitive advantage of ours because we understand how things like concrete and steel are made. The difference between steel made in a basic oxygen furnace and steel made in an electric arc furnace, for example, one can have as much as 40 percent recycled content steel, and the other can have as much as 85 percent. We're doing things on a building-by-building level, very hands-on, because you've got to really understand where your ingredients are coming from.

Is there greenwashing in the real estate market as a result of ratings and certification confusions?

I think there's definitely a perception of greenwashing because when things are not clear, unambiguous, and measurable, it's up to you to tell me what you think good looks like. Who's to say you're right, and I'm wrong or vice versa? Or that one building's better than the other? It's like net zero carbon, there's no agreed definition of what net zero carbon is, it's the most complicated, convoluted measurement you ever come across.

When we talk about carbon in buildings, we don't actually talk about carbon, we talk in terms of kilowatt hours per meter squared per year. Tell me, what does a kilowatt hour per meter squared per year look like? Describe it physically to me. I have no idea. I can tell you what a ton of carbon looks like. It's a ball of CO_2 roughly 10 meters in diameter. I understand that. So why are we measuring buildings in kilowatt hours per meter squared per year?

And we know an average office building uses up to two hundred kilowatt hours per meter squared per year, and a good building uses seventy-five. I mean, how do we visualize these things? How do you measure those things and how do you validate and verify them? And what do you include and what do you not include? You've got landlord space; you've got tenant space. Some standards include some amount of energy use and tenant space, but not others, some exclude tenant space altogether. It's a mess.

"The land use transition that needs to happen . . . is a couple of things: One is stopping tropical deforestation, which is roughly 10 percent of total global emissions. And the other big thing we need is something like six hundred million hectares of reforestation, most of that in emerging markets, over the next 10 to 15 years. It's just a matter of getting the capital flowing there."

SUSTAINABLE FORESTRY INVESTING

RADHA KUPPALLI
NEW FORESTS
NEWFORESTS.COM.AU
LI: https://au.linkedin.com/in/radha-kuppalli

Radha Kuppalli leads New Forests' Impact and Advocacy group and has been with the company since 2006. She has primary responsibility for positioning New Forests as the world's leading asset manager providing forestry and land-based investment solutions through New Forests' impact strategy, reputation, and brand. She has oversight of the sustainability, communications, and markets research functions at New Forests and heads the company's advocacy and thought leadership strategy. Kuppalli is a director of the Board of New Forests Pty Ltd, member of the company's Executive Committee, and a member of all Investment Committees. She is also a Non-Executive Director for Timberlink Australia and Greening Australia and chairs Greening Australia's investment committee.

Her 20-year career has been focused on driving capital markets toward investing in climate change solutions and sustainable development. She earned an MBA and a Masters in Environmental Management from Yale, serves on the university's Advisory Board at the Center for Business and Environment, and is an associate of the Yale World Fellows Program.

How did you end up in forestry, land management, and conservation?

Following my studies, I had a one-year fellowship at the Carnegie Endowment for International Peace, and as that year was coming to a close, it occurred to me that it's always been about the environment for me. That's what I care about.

At 22, I decided that the most important environmental issue facing us was climate change. At the time I thought that the only way that we're going to address climate is through business and getting capital and business focused on climate solutions and investing in a different kind of future.

Describe your current role at New Forests from an investment perspective.

From an investment perspective, I help shape product development and investment strategy. I work closely with our investment teams on what the market wants, what clients are looking for from an asset allocation and impact perspective, and how we provide that.

Provide an overview of New Forests, your investment strategy, and your investors.

New Forests was founded in 2005. We have approximately $5 billion under management, covering about 1 million hectares, or about 2 million acres, of sustainably managed plantation forests, conservation areas and natural forests, timber processing, agriculture, and carbon projects across that global portfolio. We're an institutional funds management business, we have very large, blue chip institutional clients, including public pension funds, private pension funds, insurance companies, and sovereign wealth funds.

Most of that capital is coming out of a few places like Northern Europe, including the Netherlands, Sweden, Denmark, the UK, and Germany. We also have some very large Canadian clients. We have a bit out of the United States and some other European countries and a little bit out of Australia.

The bulk of our clients are large investors, who are writing 50- to 250-million-dollar checks as they invest in our funds. These are investors looking for exposure into real assets, and they're fundamentally looking for low volatility of returns and steady income.

Forestry in particular is quite interesting because you've got a biological asset that grows, and as it gets bigger, it actually gets more valuable. So, it's unique as an appreciating asset. And typically, because you've got that biological growth, there tends to be a bit lower volatility of returns. When you have forestry assets planted 20, 30, or

"Penola Plantations in South Australia, an asset in New Forests Australia New Zealand Forest Fund." *Source:* New Forests

40 years ago they're now mature. They're like a tree farm providing steady income.

We have a series of funds that are investing in sustainable plantation forestry in Australia and New Zealand. You've got domestic demand, but also strong export economies into North Asia.

We're the only institutional fund manager with a dedicated forestry strategy to investing in Southeast Asia. The history of forestry in Asia has been unsustainable logging of natural forests. So, if we're going to meet the rising timber demand and meet our economic objectives, but also environmental and social objectives, you need to see the industry really move into responsibly managed, certified, sustainable plantation forestry—so that we've stopped deforestation of our remaining tropical forests and concentrated on investing in sustainable landscapes where we're balancing sustainable production and conservation. That's what we've been doing in Asia for well over a decade.

I think we've really been a leader in our approach to sustainability. People in New Forests have been involved for more than 20 years in environmental markets and have viewed for a long time that we need to develop investment strategies where we can monetize the carbon value or the biodiversity value of forests in order to protect nature.

Explain the traditional role of forestry in investor portfolios and the attraction of the asset class.

Forestry has tended to have a low volatility of returns, which is attributable to the underlying biological growth. Forestry is an appreciating asset class. As forests get bigger through biological growth, the asset actually grows in value. Forestry tends to be positively correlated with inflation. That's tied to the fact that timber demand is correlated with GDP growth. So, those have been the underlying characteristics.

It's a good diversifier and a truly international, globalized asset class, and there's not one timber market; you can get exposure to pulp and paper markets, construction markets, or housing.

For most of our institutional investors, timber is sitting in their real assets or natural resources portfolio. But if you'd asked our clients 10 years ago, why they were investing in timber, it was low volatility of returns and correlation with inflation. But the third reason, even then, was sustainability. Investors saw that you could manage forestry assets with good stewardship. You could invest in assets that had third-party sustainability certification. There's this view that well-managed forestry assets were kind of a nice thing from a sustainability perspective, and for our European clients that was particularly important, given the interest of their stakeholders and their pensioners and members.

The thing that has really accelerated in the past 24 months has been the sustainability imperative. Forestry, I think, is increasingly being considered by institutional investors, particularly members of the Net Zero Asset Owners Alliance, or those taking on decarbonization targets. They're now looking for investments in climate solutions, and forestry is one sleeve of that. They are asking: How do I invest in forestry to decarbonize my portfolio? How do you have to manage a forest to be climate positive? That could be everything from the kinds of strategies and the way you're managing assets, to the inclusion of carbon finance and carbon credits in the underlying product and the strategy for that forest. There is also the bioeconomy opportunity. How can forests contribute to new industries around mass timber and replacing fossil fuel-based products?

Has investor demand increased because of increased global interest in growing trees, or increased demand from new emerging income streams in the marketplace?

I think it's both. The underlying fundamentals of timber and the forestry asset class are very sound. Good returns tend to come down to whether you bought the asset for the right price at the right time. I think there have been some U.S. institutional investors who got turned off by the asset class because of some of the poor returns following the global financial crisis.

But I think for those investors who like forestry, those market fundamentals are always there, and that's a core source of comfort. I think now there's this view that there's a new value here. There's carbon. How do we monetize that? How do we think about that? What does it mean for my own climate balance sheet as well as a new source of income?

Explain your investment selection and due diligence process.

If we take Australia and New Zealand, which is where the bulk of our assets under management are, we will raise a fund that has a hurdle rate. Historically that's been 6 to 7 percent real rate of return or 8 to 9 percent nominal. That's something that we set with the investors at the time of raising the fund. We're essentially trying to get a series of market exposures that will support achievement of that hurdle rate.

For example, in Australia and New Zealand, you've got three key markets. You've got, in Australia, softwood markets, or growing pine trees, which are pretty much all consumed by the Australian domestic construction industry. We're growing eucalyptus trees sold as hardwood chip into the pulp and paper industry in China and Japan.

And, in New Zealand, you've got again softwood logs, the bulk of which are exported into China, India, and Korea. We are trying to get a balanced portfolio of market exposures across those three markets.

Our due diligence process assesses the quality of the forests. We're conducting forest inventory. We're forecasting log prices. We execute discounted cashflow analysis. These are complex biological assets, where you are looking at biological growth as well as the underlying financials.

The environmental screen comes into play in different ways in our different regions. We have a social and environmental management system that governs our whole global portfolio, including, for example, setting criteria around third-party certifications we get across every single asset we own. We have a preference for what's called the Forest Stewardship Council, or FSC, certification.

New Forests has an ESG and impact performance framework that we call our Sustainable Landscape Investment Framework. We measure the performance of our assets against six themes: productivity, land use planning, ecosystem services, shared prosperity, governance, and risk management.

In our million hectares of assets that we manage globally, about a quarter is actually natural forest and conservation areas that are integrated into the management of our landscapes. We're working closely with NGOs to ensure that we're meeting local biodiversity and conservation objectives. But we're also looking at shared prosperity with communities, measuring employment benefits, gender diversity and employment, safety issues, as well as governance and risk management. These areas form the overall picture of how we manage assets through the entire life cycle, from acquisition to exit.

A deep dive into environmental and social due diligence at the beginning of the investment is critical and shapes the management activities over the life of those assets.

Explain what carbon finance is in the U.S. context.

In the United States, we have a carbon forestry strategy where we're underwriting assets looking at the timber value as well as the ability to manage assets for carbon and sell it into the regulated California carbon market. That's a unique proposition, where we're having to do complex geospatial analytics, carbon modeling, and biological modeling, to really look at the full value of that asset from a timber as well as a climate perspective.

Our investments are centered around the California carbon market, which is a cap-and-trade market. It also includes a forest carbon protocol, which enables forests across the United States to sell carbon credits to regulated emitters in California who are required to reduce their emissions over time.

U.S. forests that have historically been managed with a light touch, that haven't been harvested very aggressively, and that have carbon stocks that are higher on average than other forests in the region in which they're located, can monetize that high carbon stocking above the average carbon stocking baseline. If the forest is allowed to grow even further beyond that baseline, enhancing the carbon stocks in the forest, that growth in carbon sequestration can also be monetized. Depending on the forest, the California protocol creates this incentive to maintain existing high carbon stocks, protecting them for 100 years, potentially increasing the carbon stock of these forests. You're actually able to continue harvesting the forest, as long as you maintain a certain level of carbon stocking. We've estimated that this strategy can not only create these climate mitigation outcomes but could also add two to four hundred basis points above a timber-only management approach.

What are U.S. conservation easements?

Conservation easements are a particular kind of U.S. legal instrument, where you can basically forego the development rights on a particular property, or forego certain kinds of timber harvesting, and get paid for that opportunity cost. So, we look for opportunities to sell conservation easements where possible.

We just completed a conservation easement transaction with an Indigenous group, the Yurok Tribe of Northern California. We've had a long relationship with the Yurok. In 2014 New Forests registered the very first California carbon project with the Yurok on their land.

In this recent easement transaction with the Yurok, we identified a particular parcel of land, currently under ownership of one of our European clients as part of a forestry asset, that was under ancestral ownership of the Yurok Tribe and has particular cultural value for the Yurok. We worked with the Trust for Public Land, who were able to secure financing for the conservation easement for the Yurok. We were able to rematriate the land back to the Yurok. It created a great economic outcome for our client as well as meeting the economic and cultural objectives of the Yurok. So, we're really proud of that transaction.

Do you always consider social impact and measure social outputs?

Absolutely. The engagement that we have with communities is incredibly important. We purchased a large forest estate in the North Island of New Zealand a couple of years ago. It had been owned by a company that had not really paid attention to its forest management. Forestry in New Zealand is basically done on these extremely steep slopes, so you have high susceptibility to erosion. There was this massive storm event a couple of years ago. All of this timber debris washed into the local river, damaging people's homes. It was just terrible.

And so, when we bought the asset, we really undertook an extensive process of engagement with the local community. We had to change those forest management practices and reduce the susceptibility to erosion, and we partly did that by giving some land back to conservation and just saying, we're not going to harvest in those areas. Also, we had a conversation with the local communities to say, look, this is what we're doing, and this is how we're going to manage these issues and make sure that you're not in danger. In fact, when we had another storm event about a year after we bought it, the impact was less, but people also knew how we were going to manage any cleanup.

Sustainable forestry is 30 percent of the climate change mitigation solution, but only 3 percent of capital is being invested in it. Why so little?

I think that from an institutional investor perspective, forestry is still a pretty niche asset class due its relatively small size compared to other real asset classes, like real estate and infrastructure, and most of the capital in forestry has been invested in mature markets. But if you look at the land use transition that needs to happen in order to get to our Paris Agreement climate targets, the outlook for forestry investment shifts considerably. First, to achieve our Paris Agreement targets, we need to stop deforestation, particularly tropical deforestation, which is roughly 10 percent of total global emissions. How do you make that investible? There are emerging markets for reduced emissions from deforestation and forest degradation (REDD[3]), although REDD has been fraught in terms of international climate policy discussion over the past decade. So, it just hasn't been made investible yet.

The other big thing that needs to happen is significant reforestation. We need something like six hundred million hectares of reforestation, most of that in emerging markets, over the next 10 to 15 years. That's a very complex proposition, because we're going to be dealing with hundreds of millions of family farmers. We're going to be dealing with emerging markets. We're dealing with land tenure issues. Even in a place like Australia, you're going to be dealing with land use competition, where we're going to be trying to figure out, do we use this land for conservation? Do we use this land for production forestry? Do we use this land for agriculture?

We know what needs to happen in the energy transition. It's just a matter of getting the capital flowing there. The transition that's required in land use is much more complex. I think, increasingly, the investment appetite is there, but now we need investible solutions. That's really the crux of the problem that we need to solve.

What New Forests tries to do is demonstrate how things can work successfully and try and attract more capital into the sector.

But there's a really important role to be played by government. We need robust climate policies and strong carbon pricing mechanisms and price signals, because a lot of the carbon markets right now are just tinkering on the margins.

How do you balance the need to deliver financial returns to investors using commercial forestry with biodiversity and ecosystem recovery?

Ultimately, we need more financing mechanisms to draw capital into biodiversity enhancement. In the fund that we're raising right now for Asia, we've introduced this blended finance concept. About 85 or 90 percent of the capital is just going to be mainstream commercial rate of return capital.

But we're also bringing in impact investors who will take a concessional rate of return. It ends up augmenting the cost of capital of the fund by 50 to 100 basis points. By virtue of the fact that we've got some of this concessional equity coming into the fund, in exchange for that, the fund will invest a portion of its committed capital into non-revenue generating impact activities—ecosystem restoration, habitat restoration, habitat connectivity, forest conservation and also community programs like outgrower schemes and developing agroforestry programs.

This concept has had a really positive response from mainstream institutional investors. They want to invest in the fund because of this blended finance, because they view it as a way to balance their commercial and impact objectives.

Who are these impact investors?

We co-created that blended finance structure with the [David and Lucile] Packard Foundation. So, interest is coming from the Packard Foundation but also a corporate investor and some government capi-

Mekong Timber Plantations in Laos, an asset in the New Forests Tropical Asia Forest Fund portfolio. ***Source:*** **New Forests**

tal. It's been really fascinating to see the mix of investors interested in going into the concessional equity tranche.

Are they invested *pari-passu* or are they first-loss capital?

We decided not to do first-loss. The way that we've structured it, without getting too technical, is that the waterfall of distributions is predominantly going to the mainstream investors. They would be expecting a 12 to 14 percent return. For the impact investors it would be more like 4 to 6 percent.

What future role will technology evolution have on sustainable forestry and nature-based investments?

I think there's a whole range of technologies that are going to be really impactful. Geospatial analytics has a real opportunity to drive down the cost of forest measurement and forest monitoring. If we think about how we want to scale up carbon markets, being able to utilize remote sensing and remote sensing driven protocols around stopping deforestation, there's a huge role for geospatial analytics to play in terms of assessing, measuring, and monitoring outcomes on the ground.

The whole area of FinTech will be impactful. We've had lots of conversations with people recently about how you tokenize biodiversity and enable people to support projects on the ground through blockchain and tokenization. And some of that work is now floating its way into new carbon trading platforms.

There's interesting drone technology now where people are shooting seedlings out of drones, to try to do large scale reforestation and some of that technology is getting better and better.

Certainly, the whole area of bioeconomy and plant-based materials, wood-based materials substituting for different kinds of bioplastics, making new materials for cars and buildings. There's an interesting company out of Finland, Stora Enso, that has extraordinary research and development around these new kinds of products, and we're really excited about that.

If you had to name the most important challenge in the sustainable real assets space at this time, what would it be?

For us, the central challenge is driving more capital into emerging markets.

What do you know now about sustainable investing and impact investing that you wish you knew when you showed up at New Forests in 2006?

Asset allocation is everything. I'm constantly trying to think through and work through how we can come up with new ways to help our clients and investors understand the value of the asset class and in an asset allocation framework. I think that's a central challenge and we've tried to raise capital for products before where it didn't fit neatly into [investors' portfolios], such as a mitigation banking fund for wetland and stream mitigation in the United States. Although the strategy was sound, no one knew where to put it and we had to shelve it.

Did you ever make an investment that you thought ticked all the boxes, but in the end didn't turn out? What lesson did you learn?

We had an investment called the Malua Biobank in Sabah, Malaysia. Essentially, we were trying to monetize the biodiversity value of this incredible rainforest in Sabah through the sale of biodiversity conservation certificates. It was a voluntary biobank and we wanted to sell the biodiversity value into the palm oil supply chain. It was very well structured as an investment, but the demand was completely untested.

We spent years and a lot of social capital with the government of Sabah, but ultimately it wasn't successful as an investment.

We learned so much about taking a risk, the challenge of voluntary demand for biodiversity products, and how to structure an innovative investment. Frankly, in some ways we were just 10 years ahead of our time, because now there are plenty of people who are trying to do that, looking at new ways of financing these biodiversity conservation projects. The structure was fundamentally sound. If we were doing that now, with the FinTech technology that we were just talking about and recognizing what people are valuing now in terms of nature, maybe it would have been a successful investment. I guess the lesson learned is that timing is everything.

"In 1973 our founder, Dick Dusseldorf, said: 'Companies must start justifying their worth to society with greater emphasis placed on environmental and social impact rather than straight economics.' He was so far ahead of his time in recognizing that. So that is part of our DNA, which really does pervade the way we think."

CONNECTED COMMUNITY REAL ESTATE INVESTING

MICAH SCHULZ
LENDLEASE GROUP
LENDLEASE.COM
LI: https://www.linkedin.com/in/micah-schulz-b5612191/

Micah Schulz, Head of Office for Lendlease's Investment Management business, is responsible for driving strategy, innovation, and performance across the team and managing 27 Australian office assets totaling over A$18 billion in value. Schultz leads the team of office fund managers, investment managers, valuation managers, leasing managers, and analysts.

Previously, he was a Fund Manager for Lendlease's A$6 billion Australian Prime Property Fund Commercial. Prior to Lendlease, he was Assistant Fund Manager for Investa Property Group's flagship wholesale office fund, ICPF, and was a Fund Manager at Centuria Capital.

Schulz holds a Bachelor of Business Management (majoring in real estate and development) from the University of Queensland, and a Graduate Diploma in Applied Finance from Kaplan Professional (formerly FINSIA).

How did you come to sustainability real estate investing?

Australia has been a global leader in the sustainability space for real estate. I suppose I had the benefit of that existing in the background earlier in my career. It probably became something that I started to think about more tangibly when I was at Investa, working as Assistant Fund Manager on their flagship fund. Investa was quite involved and an early leader in the sustainability space, as well. Through the course of looking at our assets, you just naturally talk about NABERS[4] ratings, you talk about capital initiatives that you're rolling out, and you look at that from a sustainability perspective as well as an operating efficiency and return perspective.

One of the things I was aware of was that the Lendlease funds kept winning the Global Real Estate Sustainability Benchmark (GRESB) real estate assessments.

And more generally, I was very aware that Lendlease was a very prominent sustainability leader in the Australian market and, indeed, globally. But it wasn't just a dramatic moment. I would say that it was something that built up gradually.

Another influential element was that there is an investor in the market here called the Clean Energy Finance Corporation. It is a government

Lendlease International Towers Sydney Trust won World's Most Sustainable Fund in GRESB 2021, scoring a world-first 100 out of 100. *Source:* GRESB

sponsored entity and they have a mandate to invest in an impactful way where they can affect change. I engage with them because they're an investor in one of our office funds at Lendlease, and I also worked with them prior to joining Lendlease. That actually urged me to lift my knowledge capability, just in the way that I had to interact with them, in terms of having some proficiency in sustainability and also how that fed into more general investment considerations.

Please provide me an overview of Lendlease.

Lendlease is a globally integrated real estate company, with operations around the world. At our core, we're a leader in shaping cities. We've been recognized as an award-winning organization in creating urban precincts, new communities, leading workplaces, and also civic infrastructure. Through all of that we have built up recognition as having exceptionally high sustainability standards. Lendlease has about A$40 billion in funds globally. Of that, about A$28 billion worth of funds under management is in Australia.

One of the other key elements in terms of Lendlease's focus—it's really our purpose statement—is that we're creating value through places where communities thrive. I think that's a really powerful underpinning that sits behind the organization's behaviors and includes the focus on sustainability and social benefits. To create places where communities thrive and where individuals thrive, by definition they need to be sustainable. They need to make a positive contribution that goes well beyond just the commerce or the economics.

Your founder, Dick Dusseldorf, is quoted on your website saying "Companies must start justifying their worth to society with greater emphasis placed on environmental and social impact rather than straight economics." Why is sustainability so important to Lendlease?

I think we were so fortunate to have Dick Dusseldorf as the founder of the organization. When you pause and reflect on that quote of his from 1973, it's quite remarkable. You'd expect to hear that kind of language from all sorts of CEOs these days. It's just so far ahead of his time in saying that or recognizing that almost 50 years ago. So, that is part of our DNA and at its core, I think it's just a recognition of a win-win philosophy in business, which really does pervade the way we think about it.

If you align yourself with positive environmental and community and social outcomes, that should not cut against delivering a commercial outcome for your investors. If you have your values and long-term objectives in the right place and you look at a win-win outcome, I think you can have confidence that you will be vindicated. It will ultimately reward you in a financial sense, as well as in a reputational sense. You'll have an engaged and passionate staff, and investors' backing and other stakeholders' support.

Can you tell me about the Sustainability Framework and how it is used?

Our Sustainability Framework is really a powerful guide of our focus. It aligns with us being one of the first property organizations to be a PRI signatory, which I think was back in 2007. Essentially, we maintain a responsible property investment policy, which is regularly updated. In our policy refresh in 2019 we had three key imperatives, which each have a related environmental and social focus area. So, sustainable economic growth, vibrant and resilient communities and cities, and a healthy planet and people. Those were the three key imperatives.

In 2020, we added some more acute measurable sustainability targets. Those include being a one and a half degree aligned company and creating A$250 million of social value by 2025. We use that as a really strong guide or criteria to assess our investment decisions.

We have our own responsible property investment strategy for our funds, as well. We use that to measure investment opportunities and how we're performing across our existing portfolio. So, we're continually challenging ourselves and making sure that we're staying ahead of the market, in terms of the way we view sustainability, social opportunities, and benefits for our investors.

Prior to 2014, Lendlease's sustainability actions were specific to individual developments, but it seemed to be company-wide after that. Why?

A strong part of the organization has been development. I think Lendlease saw individual development opportunities as being the most effective ways to push the boundaries on sustainability performance and really lift the market.

I will add that the best opportunity to make a material impact is at the start, during design and construction. That is an appropriate area of focus because it's very difficult to retrofit, compared to the outcomes you can achieve if you get it right from the beginning. So, that focus on individual projects was a really powerful way to move the market forward.

As we've evolved, however, we've recognized that we have a significant portfolio of existing assets, and there are a whole host of opportunities to lift their performance.

Are commercial tenants willing to pay more for buildings with higher sustainability ratings, resulting in a premium offering that drives increased risk-adjusted returns?

It's a complicated answer because, unfortunately, it's difficult to isolate that as a sole driver of value because it's typically highly correlated with asset quality in general.

Earlier on, I would say that correlation was particularly acute. It was often brand-new premium grade developments that clearly had leading sustainability credentials, and it's hard to isolate what the driver of value is there. Is it the sustainability credentials or the other features of the asset? In the space in which we play, which is very high-quality real estate, it is more or less "table stakes." It's a ticket to play.

One of the ways to look at why it's important from a marketability, leasing, and performance perspective is that it's almost like reverse screening. This is gradually changing, but you have a lot of tenants or tenant representatives, and indeed investors on the capital side too, who aren't necessarily overtly applying a premium for sustainability. But they're certainly going to take an unfavorable view on an asset if it is below expectation.

What we are definitely seeing is increasing momentum year-on-year, in terms of an emphasis on sustainability. As you've probably seen in the broader conversation globally at the moment, it's accelerating dramatically. Politically, it's accelerating dramatically. In terms of interventions that are being made by various governments around the world, it's accelerated dramatically. I think that's happening in real estate, as well.

In aggregate, if you could look at the broader trends, there's clearly more and more emphasis on sustainability credentials in terms of the buildings that tenants will occupy. We're seeing more and more organizations overtly having their own ESG criteria, and their own level of accountability to their investors or even to their staff, which they are applying to their office choices.

The other thing to add on the value of sustainability is how we see that value manifesting on a risk-adjusted basis, and indeed on an absolute basis for our investors. We want to be sustainable, and we see it as a win-win. But we are also highly accountable for the raw financial performance that we can deliver for our stakeholders, so the contribution of sustainability to this is critical to understand.

You've got the overt value metrics that are very common in the market around cap rate or initial total return expectations. But then you've got a lot of factors that play through at different points in an asset life cycle, including operating efficiency and other qualitative sustainability factors that can heavily impact rents and tenant retention.

Probably the final piece, which is commonly at the back end, is risk. That's risk associated with resilience against climate impacts that might emerge in the long-term, but also risk of obsolescence. There we're seeing the pace of change and the minimum expectations for how an asset performs shifting so dramatically that if you don't act proactively and make sure that you're doing what you can to position yourself for those future shifts, then your obsolescence risk is heightened. That has a significant financial cost at the end of the day, even if it's not something that can be clearly identified and quantified right now.

What is the impact of the built environment in terms of human well-being and social and environmental impact?

The impact of carbon or embodied carbon in the built environment is a very significant contributor to the world's carbon emissions. In fact, transporting and manufacturing building materials accounts for approximately 10 percent of the world's carbon emissions. Clearly, there's an amazing opportunity there to make a big difference. In our sector it is essentially cement, steel, and aluminum which are the key products that contribute to embodied carbon. Those are products that we're working really hard to decarbonize in our business, but we've got to recognize that we've got a long way to go.

One of the first steps for us is actually putting that flag on the hill in terms of absolute zero carbon neutrality and using that very ambitious target—which we openly haven't fully solved for yet—as something

Lendlease constructed Daramu House from engineered timber. *Source:* Lendlease

that can drive change in the real estate supply chain. On a related note, engineered timber is a really interesting opportunity.

We've used engineered timber for several commercial projects now around the country and in fact the world, and it's a really exciting area to shift the dial on embodied carbon.

That's because there's the carbon capture in the timber, which represents about a 24 percent reduction in upfront embodied carbon, relative to a comparable asset that's built in a conventional sense. If you include sequestered carbon, that actually shifts to a reduction of about 48 percent, so it is quite a dramatic impact.

Are you a big fan of mass timber because you see that as the only real pathway to net zero?

Net zero is a journey and we don't yet know what our pathway exactly looks like. I think the first step is clear purpose and intent to find a way. And I'm also an optimist in terms of what technological innovation can achieve.

I think we've seen profound changes when you look back over a relatively short period of time. And that historical trajectory, I think, actually means we have the ability to be cautiously optimistic in terms of achieving absolute carbon zero outcomes over the kind of horizon that everyone's talking about. We have a commitment to be absolutely carbon neutral by 2040. We will have to really seriously look at what that pathway is over time, but I am confident we'll find a way to get there.

Describe your investment strategy.

At a high level, our funds tend to be flow-through trusts managed on behalf of our investors. They range from pooled funds, which tend to have many investors, to more concentrated club vehicles. Or, in some cases, direct mandates for a single large investor. Generally, these tend to be Australian superannuation funds or global pension or sovereign wealth funds. For the kind of profile that we deal with, they're all very focused on high quality real estate, long-term returns, and a return profile that plugs into broader diversified investment allocations.

We have clear criteria tied to our strategy, and we assess all of our opportunities against those criteria. Focusing on the office sector, which is the area I'm responsible for, there are more conventional measures around the grade, the location, risk around tenant concentration, the expiry profile, etc. We look at these measures too. But our point of difference is how we emphasize what can be summarized under two distinct categories: the locational and physical attributes, and then the asset management, operational, or people layer over the top.

On the physical side, we focus on major gateway CBD markets that have strong economic dynamism and diversity and therefore a virtuous cycle of growth and resilience in terms of depth of market, deep pools of capital, and lower volatility. These major gateway CBD markets also have clear agglomeration benefits, which we think are a really powerful force that drives the growth of cities over the long term and will continue to drive ongoing success. That's due to the way that those agglomeration benefits translate into economic advantage and also experiential outcomes for users.

Then, within these markets, our strategy is heavily focused on highly sustainable, healthy, technologically enabled assets in connected precincts. I describe these as assets that are embedded into a broader precinct "place-identity" that our customers can connect with, in the sense that it offers a significant ground plane that they can see and experience. These assets have vibrancy and amenity that really adds richness. In the case of an office, it's the place where our customers go to work and where they're trying to juggle a whole bunch of things in their lives, in terms of being productive and employed. But they are also satisfying other needs, whether its amenities like childcare and health services, or in the social sense, such things as restaurants and other exciting events.

We look for precincts that have exceptional public transport connectivity, diverse service offerings, and access to green space or nature. Those are the physical attributes.

Then there is the asset management, or the operational layer over the top, where our focus is on curating a leading experience offer for our customers which leverages the physical attributes I've described and then uses technology to communicate and facilitate different levels of service and experience.

The last key pillar of our strategy is authentically demonstrating a positive social impact. This social impact element is really important and builds on our longstanding success in traditional sustainability leadership, to which we made a conscious choice in 2019 to go much broader in the health, wellbeing, social purpose, and community areas. We've tried to build that out into a broader social impact that focuses on ways we can really connect with our end customer on a personal level.

So probably a key overlay for us is thinking about some of the longer-term characteristics that might not be immediately in focus for the broader market.

One of those areas is sustainability, as I've said. Another is this belief we have in the importance of creating really positive customer outcomes. We believe that if you get it right for the end user, they will have high loyalty and advocacy toward the product. They will lobby the decision makers in their organizations to stay in that location and maintain access to all of those really valued services and experiences.

In terms of the way we do our due diligence on an opportunity, we go through the whole gamut of financial analysis and sensitivity analysis. Articulating our strategy is a really important element in all of that. Obviously, you have to review your market dynamics and form a view on what the outlook is for the market and where this particular opportunity sits within that context as well.

How do you measure your investment's impact?

There's a conventional approach where you look at the market, you benchmark where you think rents and other key assumptions should sit, and then you overlay what I would call tilts based on qualitative factors that you believe in, to establish a view on how you think an investment should perform over typically a 10-year horizon. There are typically some distinctive reasons why you think an opportunity is compelling or attributes of that opportunity should be compelling, based on your strategic view. Our challenge is to find a way to convert that into assumptions that actually flow through to demonstrate why we believe there will be return outperformance, therefore being a worthwhile place to allocate our capital.

As it relates to ESG, we have a whole series of criteria and we have functional experts in health, safety, and sustainability, who review and provide sign-off with our latest targets or minimum standards. That includes pathway to net zero and pathway to absolute zero. We need to have an understanding of what the impact is going to be on our broader portfolio. On our broader mix of NABERS ratings, for example. To the extent we might believe that asset could be deficient on these ratings, that isn't necessarily a reason not to buy it. It actually could be an opportunity, so long as we have identified that there will be ways to lift that asset so it is complementary to our broader portfolio and will take us where we need to get to in terms of our longer-term aspirations.

Describe an example of an investment you've made that demonstrates the impact of your strategy.

An asset that we just recently reviewed against our original acquisition assumptions is Two Melbourne Quarter, part of the Melbourne Quarter Precinct in Melbourne's CBD.

When we first started to negotiate that acquisition, there was a five-star NABERS rating target on it. We negotiated that we would be targeting lifting this to a five and a half star NABERS rating.

What we had to do was go through a review process to work out what the pathways would be to lift the NABERS rating. Solar panels on the roof and automatic blinds on the facades, for example. Then, in the review, we looked back and said, "We made a commitment to spend capital, to investigate a pathway to get ourselves to a five and a half star NABERS rating. How did we do?" And we've demonstrated that we've achieved above a five and a half star NABERS rating within the budget that we set ourselves. Similarly, we demonstrated that we achieved leasing and valuation performance ahead of our original underwrite assumptions.

Two Melbourne Quarter. Source: Lendlease

Is there confusion caused by the plethora of different ratings and labels for energy use and building sustainability across different dimensions in the real estate industry?

I think the terminology is well understood and valuable at the sophisticated end of the market for real estate and sustainability experts. But there can be a lot of confusion for underlying customers who just see a lot of jargon and acronyms.

I think it is incumbent upon us to find ways to articulate in layperson's terms what we're trying to achieve and what matters. That is something that we're really focused on. In fact, it's actually a key part of one of our overarching strategic priorities, which is to find ways to truly connect with customers, to share information with them in a way that resonates for them and makes sense to them. I think everybody can relate to ESG if you just cut it down to the bare bones of healthy outcomes for you, your friends and family, your community, and your planet. You just need to find a way to translate the jargon into what it actually means in practical, relatable terms.

Does this result in "greenwashing?"

I don't see greenwashing as a big issue, at least in our space, because our sector is hyper-competitive on ESG. There can be the risk of focusing on the label and the marketing benefits instead of actual benefits. But because of that competitiveness in our marketplace and also the rigor of our ratings and the increasing sophistication of tenants and investors, what everyone is pushing for from a marketing perspective is actually resulting in real tangible benefits or genuine bottom line, impactful outcomes.

The other thing to add is that the industry is not just hyper-competitive, it's also actually hyper-collaborative, as well. Most major real estate organizations have a team of sustainability experts, and those experts have their own forums where they regularly connect. There's a phenomenal sharing of information and participation in working groups and forums—all with a shared desire to advance ESG and sustainability measurement and verification efforts, such as ratings and certifications. That's all serving to support the integrity of the certifications, which ultimately means that greenwashing is minimized.

What does the built environment need to do to address the nearly 30 percent of biodiversity loss it is responsible for globally?

I think the industry needs to commit to sustainably sourced materials. We need third party credible credentials so that we can make sure that we're actually confidently doing that. I think that's probably the key way to achieve that. You need that verification and credibility across the supply chain. So, it's no easy task, and I very openly admit that's the challenge. But I think we've already seen a significant demonstration of a will to make that happen over time.

The other area closer to home is we need to keep pushing to find opportunities to incorporate habitat into building design. Examples of that in our portfolio include green roofs and walls in our assets.

What role do you see technology playing in furthering the real estate industry's sustainability objectives and driving social and environmental impact?

Probably one of the most significant areas is data. It's such a fundamental building block to understanding how things work and how changes can result in beneficial outcomes.

We have a digital business at Lendlease called Podium. A big focus for Podium is understanding data and ultimately looking at how we can get into the space of autonomous buildings. That includes technologies like digital twin modeling. With it you can use insights to design well from

Daramu House green roof and solar panels. *Source:* Lendlease

the outset, because you've been able to digitally game-out scenarios and find errors before you've actually physically constructed something. That ultimately reduces waste and optimizes performance efficiency.

In a similar vein, there are smart management systems that you can use for built assets that allow you to process data, interpret impacts, and integrate into other technology around, for example, weather forecasting. In real time you can adapt in a way that dramatically improves operating efficiency, and therefore has a big impact on emissions and waste. I think this is a really exciting space and the rate of change is phenomenal.

What is the most important challenge in the sustainable real assets space at this time?

It's tackling embodied carbon in materials. That's the most important challenge for real estate.

What do you know now about sustainable real estate investing that you wish you knew when you started at Lendlease in 2016?

The importance of fighting as hard as you can on a new project, to get in there early when a building is being designed and developed and push those boundaries as far as you can.

It can be so tempting to value-engineer initiatives out for a whole host of reasons, but retrofitting is just so much more expensive than getting it right up front. The market is moving so quickly that you're amazed to look back and say, "I thought we were moving so ahead of the market, but now it just feels like it was almost essential that we did that."

That's an important lesson that I've learned over time through experience.

How would you advise someone who wants to get into the sustainable real estate investment space?

My perspective is you don't need to be an expert to have a big impact. You can have a big impact without being schooled in sustainability, but by having an open mind and a curiosity and willingness to learn about things like environmental impacts, technological changes, and shifting social trends.

The other thing is being open to and hungry to find really high-quality expert advice. I think if you do this, you can bring insightful knowledge into day-to-day investment business and customer decision-making and really make a massive difference.

I would suggest focusing on a way to package sustainability expertise with very practical building operation or investment expertise. Then you can commit your skills to what I call the pointy end of the investment decision-making process. So, you're not sitting on the side as somebody who just understands everything about sustainability but doesn't actually get the real-world process where change will be effected.

Chapter Ten

Some Closing Thoughts

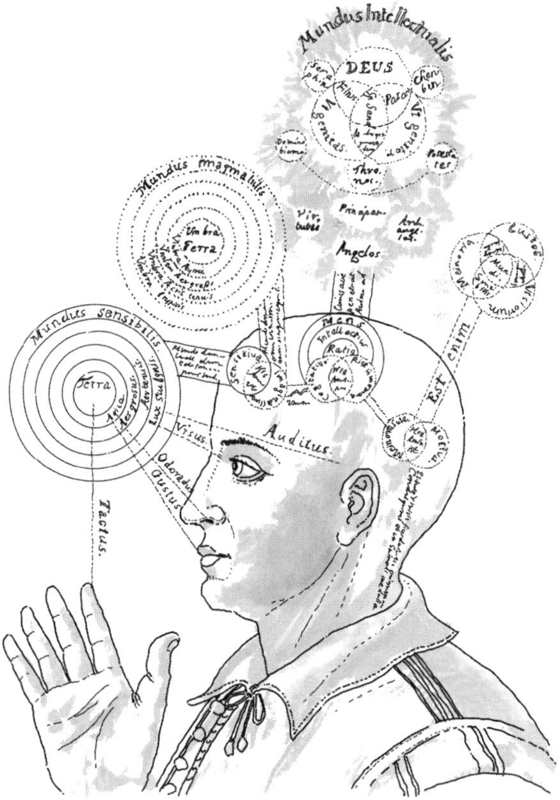

> "The more you know, the more you know you don't know."
>
> —ARISTOTLE

> "There are known knowns. These are things we know that we know. There are known unknowns. That is to say, there are things that we know we don't know. But there are also unknown unknowns. There are things we don't know we don't know."
>
> —DONALD RUMSFELD

> "A good plan violently executed now is better than a perfect plan executed next week."
>
> —GEORGE S. PATTON

I have a confession to make. I was dragged into this project, proverbially kicking and screaming, by someone I originally knew professionally, but with whom I have developed respect for, and become friends with, over the years. He is a strong believer in SRI and was persistent with me over a number of years—eventually pushing me to seriously contemplate the writing of this book.

I was resistant, because most people who set out to write a book about the complex world of finance and asset management approach it armed with lots of well-researched answers and groundbreaking insights. As Aristotle asserted, I'm quite familiar with how much I know and how much I know that I don't know . . . and the latter is much larger than the former. Indeed, with more years of experience, this seems to be expanding at, what economists refer to as, an increasing rate.

After dragging my feet a while, I finally contacted a few professional investors that I know in the space, and asked them what kind of book on sustainable and responsible investment they would be interested in reading. Surprisingly, their answers were fairly consistent. Nobody wanted to read yet another book by an "expert." In fact, they all said that they have several sitting on their bookshelves, most picked up or given out at some SRI conference. All of them still unread.

But then they all went on to say in similar fashion, "What I really would like to know is, what are *other* people doing." What they said they wanted is some "on the ground reports from the trenches" on what other professional investors are trying "out there." They wanted to know more from people "doing the doing" in the arena and whose faces are, metaphorically at least, "marred by dust and sweat and blood,"—in the words of Theodore Roosevelt.

In one way or another, they all likened themselves to a gourmet restaurant owner completely consumed with running their business. Focused on the quality of the plates coming out of their kitchen, trying to ensure a comfortable dining experience for their clients and, in the end, never having enough time or opportunity to dine out at other venues to meaningfully understand what other chefs were doing.

These investors' responses really shouldn't have come as a surprise. Quite apart from the constantly changing dynamics of the financial markets, the responsible investment industry is evolving at a rapid pace. It is experiencing substantial AUM growth and the challenges and hard questions that we all should be asking ourselves seem to grow and accumulate day by day.

A line of dialog from the 1970 film *On a Clear Day You Can See Forever* comes to my mind: "Answers make you wise. But questions make you human."

Since I am human, my confidence and inspiration to attempt this endeavor came from knowing that I have some level of access to people who are spending every day out there pushing their particular Theory of Change, in an attempt to deliver positive impact outcomes. So, I thought, what if I asked a number of notable professional investment pioneers in the SRI space exactly what they are doing? What if I try to pull the curtain back on how they are approaching the different issues that we all face and expose investors who might only be familiar in one asset class to the possibilities in others.

With this idea in mind, I then sent out a survey to several thousand professional investors across the major asset classes from my company's CRM system, asking them who they would be interested in hearing from. From those responses, I developed a list of interviewees across six major asset classes and developed a varied set of ideal investors to interview. I wanted it to be a cross-section from the most successful, largest, and well-known asset managers on the planet down to people who are out there flying far more under the radar—trying to make a difference from wherever they're at.

Nearly everyone I contacted is crazy-busy, and I expected that I would be lucky if I got any of them to sit down with me for half an hour. My good fortune was that they generously and graciously offered me the opportunity to ask away, like a curious child. Their diverse viewpoints and experienced perspectives provided meaningful contributions—and prompted more curiosity and related follow-up questions than I could pose. The conversations, without exception, were all very thoughtful, and the shortest discussion I had was just over an hour. Some went on for well over two hours, and a couple of interviewees asked if we could continue the conversation on another day when we ran out of time.

Having been disillusioned with the sound bite culture of business interviews in the financial press, I wanted to take the time to understand the context and the personal journey that each of these individuals took in their lives to end up being accomplished investors focused on SRI. The interviews presented here represent a fraction of the content of our conversations, because of space limitations of the print format. But the complete interviews of most of the interviewees are available to listen to in a podcast format, referenced at the end of the book for readers who are interested to know more.

Along the way, I personally found what I hope you will find—that the sum of the interviewees' individual parts became somehow greater than the whole. It was the American philosopher and psychologist William James who first said, "No decision is, in itself, a decision." Whether or not we act purposefully, every investment we make has impact—in some way or another. Therefore, each of us is already an impact investor—positive or negative.

Likewise, each of us is the author of our own life, and it's never too late to change directions. As Jed Emerson deduced, "we have to, on the one hand, have the courage of our convictions, but the confidence to evolve and shift and grow."

It's never too late to begin a new chapter and decide to act purposefully and do our part to impact the world, as the people presented here are doing.

SOME LESSONS LEARNED FROM WORLD CLASS INVESTORS

If you find value in this book it comes wholly from the answers of the people interviewed. This book has been entirely approached with questions. Simon Bond told me, "I always say I got where I am today by asking stupid questions. I still reserve the right to ask stupid questions." Questioning is a uniquely powerful tool and is often the only thing that stands between us and learning something new.

Here are some observations on a few key recurring themes that bubbled to the surface during the course of these interviews:

THE SRI TRAIN HAS LEFT THE STATION

It is an exciting time to be an SRI investor who wants to generate impact. As all of the interviewees emphasized, SRI has evolved rapidly within the last several years, and continues to do so, moving far beyond mere negative-screen avoidance strategies to become an increasingly proactive impact approach across multiple asset classes.

No longer relegated to the financial fringes, SRI is becoming mainstream and recognized as not just the right thing to do, but also a smarter, more holistic and impactful way to invest. Daniel Klier made it clear that Arabesque's mission is to mainstream sustainable finance and is providing investors with sophisticated data, analytics, and AI to customize any investor's strategy.

Increasingly elevated media attention on ESG financial performance and funds flows has moved investors from what Mitch Reznick called, "ESG aware, to ESG focused, to almost ESG determined." Along with this mainstreaming, in many cases SRI is competitively profitable, too—something that not too long ago may have been difficult to predict, let alone prove, even by the smartest people in the room.

Even diehard traditionalists and former naysayers are now forced to acknowledge the writing on the wall as Bram Bos indicated: "It's pretty clear that over the last couple of years if you compare a green bond portfolio to a normal fixed income portfolio, the green bonds have been doing better and not worse."

CULTURAL TRANSFORMATION

We are more aware of the significant, inherent risks in continuing to ignore important issues such as global warming, the growing wealth disparity, and the harsh fact that billions of people lack basics such as adequate healthcare, clean water, and food security. With the largest wealth transfer in history underway, the Millennials are changing the way the asset management industry operates—and any investment management firm that doesn't adapt will soon be out of business.

As Jean-Philippe de Schrevel said, "It takes forever to convince the gatekeeper of a family office when you're doing the right thing . . . but it takes me 20 minutes to convince the younger Gen X and Y generations. They were born in a world that is having these problems and they know that they need to do something about it."

Marisa Drew underscored that the Millennials think differently, saying that she "finds the receptivity of the younger generation to the concept of impact investing, the concept of sustainable finance as being just natural to them," while at the same time institutional investors are "coming in earnest" with a "whole wave of big walls of capital that want to follow ESG principles."

For asset managers, the call to action has passed. Now is the time for action.

SRI IS VALUE-ADD

More and more, SRI is increasingly becoming part of the standard risk analysis and evaluation conducted by asset managers in all asset classes. While firms used to have a separate department apart from the traditional financial analysis to analyze sustainability, the main trend now is for these activities to be one and the same.

Mark Dowding stipulates that his team does a full ESG analysis and audit on all of their alpha sources. Matt Patsky spoke to this in his powerful statement about how including environmental, social, and governance in the investment process is, in his mind, a fiduciary obligation and professional responsibility. His experience has showed him that "if you are just simply buying broad benchmark products, you're losing value, and you're also firmly separating any concept of having responsibility for the impact of money." To put it in unequivocal terms, he said, "You've thrown that out the window."

Dave Chen concurs by explaining that he and his team consider sustainability—and the effective, productive use of resources—as a competitive advantage. "ESG allows us to become more informed investors," adds Mitch Reznick. "Being a more informed investor allows you to, with as much precision as possible, allocate risk or allocate volatility contribution that is aligned with that view. More than likely, it makes you a better and more informed investor."

In fact, predicts Basil Demeroutis, "It's going to be a prerequisite for success in the future, to have a purposeful approach to investing." Then he issues something of a warning worth heeding. "The secular shift towards thoughtful, purposeful, responsible investment trends grounded in climate is so powerful that if you're not in the boat, you're drowning."

MEASURING IMPACT

At the end of the day, every single one of these discussions comes down to allocating investments to achieve desired returns, impacts, and outcomes. As Peter Drucker famously said, "If you can't measure it, you can't manage it."

Of course, objectivity is often easier said than done. In the world of SRI—where standardization, metrics, tracking, transparency, and a clear and common language and terminology are still works in progress—there is a plethora of terms, acronyms, and jargon that is used and sometimes misused, daily. People define sustainable and responsible investing in different ways, and apply different metrics, acumen, and principles to measure SRI performance and sustainability.

Bram Bos spoke to this, describing the challenge that arises when there's no one way to quantify impact measurements while there is still lots of debate around the subject. But he also emphasized that quantitative proof is not the only thing that you want as an investor. Daniel Klier added that you need better data, and you need a technology platform to manage the data, because the human brain can no longer handle the amount of financial and nonfinancial information that needs to be considered.

There's no doubt that technology has played a huge role over the last 10 to 15 years, both in terms of understanding more comprehensively the issues at hand—but also by providing the tools to manage and assess impact. But, as Jed Emerson wisely observed, "I think technology has enabled a whole host of issues to be surfaced that we traditionally have not adequately paid attention to . . . all of these metrics are just telling stories about what happens in community, what happens in companies, what happens in ecosystems. The technology hasn't done anything new; it's simply showed a reality that we have ignored."

While all of us yearn to have certainty in the outcomes we are achieving, in the end, SRI investment analysis by definition blends non-quantitative criteria with quantitative financial data that necessarily incorporates a myriad of judgement calls. Jean-Philippe de Schrevel displays unusual intellectual honesty when he says, "if I invest in a chain of hospitals in India, I can tell you how many poor people I have helped in these hospitals, how many hospitalizations I've had and what is the income level of those people that have been served. But have I changed the healthcare system in India? Well, I don't know. I think I have positively contributed to it, but there is an intellectual honesty limit in attributing the causality to my sole action and investment. We are contributing to it. We can count the outputs. We can report on the outputs. We have a suspicion that those outputs are contributing to the outcomes. Now, are we the only ones realizing this outcome? Certainly not."

ASK QUESTIONS: ACTIVE ENGAGEMENT

The majority of SRI investors interviewed count on active engagement with the management of their portfolio companies as a means to effect impact and outcomes. SRI investors can play an active role as they analyze, scrutinize, and advocate. What are the company's business practices? How do they treat their employees? And in what ways do they interact with and impact the communities where they operate? What kind of governance do they adhere to—both internally and externally? How does management respond to these questions?

When mistakes or controversies come to light, how are they resolved and what protocols are followed to ensure they are not repeated? These cultural components are increasingly important, because investing for the greater good is also about ensuring that verifiable social responsibility is behind all investment decisions and products.

Mark Dowding reminds us that it's not a one-size-fits-all approach. Investors have a voice and can take a public position, and if you speak out on issues "that you feel matter, you can punch above your weight. And you'll get a bit of a hearing which will get you access and give you the opportunity to be part of the dialogue."

Alina Donets is convinced that capital allocation and effective communication with management can eventually translate into more effective decision-making at the corporate level. She has witnessed first-hand how companies start appreciating the interest of their investors and increase their focus on the businesses that the majority of investors are interested in. "We think that capital allocation and active engagement eventually helps to increase exposure to the right business activities," she says.

But this takes effort and requires dedicated resources in the organization, as Mitch Reznick underscores: "You need frameworks in place, skilled people that know what the right questions are, what are the follow-on questions. You need to be able to test the credibility and credulity of the issuers that are putting them into the market. And that's just human capital, passion, training, and experience."

Investors must ask the difficult or uncomfortable questions and demand accountability as well as performance. What problems is the company or product addressing, and who benefits? Sharon Vosmek cited MIT research that confirmed that simply having a more diverse and inclusive team with the ability to innovate can empower a company to outperform. How far through the organizational hierarchy or along the value chain does that diversity philosophy—or any stated SRI objective—continue? Does it extend end-to-end, or is it just on the surface?

These are critical due diligence questions that deserve clear answers. I note that this applies not only to what's being invested in, but also to financial companies and advisory teams marketing their investment products to you, if you are an individual investor.

INSIDERS, NOT OUTSIDERS

Contemplating addressing societal ills in investment analysis used to be a frustrating and seemingly futile exercise. But SRI investors are innovating actionable steps to be part of the solution. As Amy Novogratz mentioned, "The world's not in great shape, and we need to figure out how to move into a future that can support us. We all need to really step up a bit and do what it takes to get real solutions to help them take off."

"We can't just be an investment shop," Jenn Pryce declares. "We also have to think about how policy helps resolve the systemic issues." That's the role of every business, government, and policy and decision maker. Investment managers can do their part by identifying areas of outcome that they want to target, as Simon Bond explained. "We established an oversight committee, which replicates what you would see from a risk committee on the financial side. So, if you've got a risk committee holding your feet to the fire on the financial side, you should have something equivalent on the social impact side."

Jenn Pryce, for instance, works very closely with the people and communities her investments strive to support and serve, because, as she emphasizes, it's not just about data. "Every investment has an impact scorecard. It has a section on community impact . . . and is evaluated on the five dimensions of impact of the Impact Measurement Project." There are multiple stakeholders and it's about fixing a market that is broken, in order to efficiently and effectively allocate monies to the right kinds of projects while measuring the social intensity of the outcome.

Similarly, Tammy Newmark collaborates with local institutions and organizations to come up with creative ways to deploy natural resources and capital investment. "Natural resources are critical globally," she explains, "because we're all now recognizing the tie between climate and biodiversity and planetary health. And they are very much tied to local and rural communities and populations. So that's why, when we look at deals and when we invest in companies, we want to see that the companies are in collaboration or have working partnerships with the local communities, that there is a vested interest among all stakeholders for long-term sustainability."

Radha Kuppalli concurs, "The engagement that we have with communities is incredibly important. You need to have that social license to operate."

ACRONYMS, LABEL-MANIA AND GREEN/IMPACT WASHING

It wasn't possible to avoid the subject of "green washing," or even "impact washing" in a single interview. Whenever there's a gold rush somewhere, less-than-honest actors are soon to follow, in an attempt to grab a piece of the pie from unwitting investors. Arguably, there are asset managers and companies looking to game the SRI trend. So, exposing greenwashing should be one side of everybody's equation, while rewarding those who act responsibly is the other side.

Several interviewees complained that a proliferation of acronyms, labels, and a lack of common language risks confusion in the marketplace and provides cover for bad actors. Bram Bos considers what he calls "label-mania" in the Green Bond space as the single biggest challenge for the sustainable fixed income sector. "It's a self-labeled market and there's no formal law at the moment," he observes. "The European Union has tried to implement regulation to address that, but it's not there yet." He further adds that, "you need to allocate additional resources to filter those less-green bonds out of your portfolio . . . not only at the moment you're buying them but once they're in the portfolio, you have to really monitor how the proceeds are being used."

Eric Rice confirms that "impact washing" is clearly the biggest issue in the impact investing space today. Why? "Because," he says, "it's a big fat opportunity for people if they can relabel their strategies or tilt their strategies towards something that resembles impact . . . and there's a lot of bad product out there."

Because there are financial incentives these days in the market to slap a "green" or SRI-related label on an offering, one must look past the acronyms and adjectives to the underlying investment and ask, "Would this investment be taking place anyway, whether or not it was labeled as 'responsible?'" If so, Mark Dowding maintains that we're "dumbing things down in a disappointing way, and it's not clear that the green bond issuance in and of itself is actually driving the delivery of a policy that wouldn't otherwise have occurred."

Investors can and should vote with their wallets and use whatever influence they have to push for more compelling incentives, greater standardization, and more thorough and transparent reporting. And, as Daniel Klier acknowledged, investor commitment needs to be combined with good policy. Policymakers in both the public and private sector play a critical role and we should collectively push them in the right direction.

BIODIVERSITY: THE NEXT SHOE TO DROP

Nearly all of the interviewees demonstrated that Net Zero 2050 was forefront in everyone's mind. But it also became apparent that with the recent UN recognition that more than 50 percent of global GDP is dependent on the world's natural capital, addressing carbon footprints is only just a start. Addressing biodiversity is going to be the next conversation we will all have, and the next big shoe to drop for investment managers.

The world's economy is reliant on natural resources, or natural capital, and our interdependent economies have been utilizing and extracting these resources quicker than they can replenish themselves. Alina Donets observed that over the last decade there's been improved understanding of climate change, but natural capital is a broader subject and equally important. However, there's no consensus on what needs to be done or how to do it. Therefore, we're still at the point where a lot of this remains unaddressed.

Jed Emerson elaborates further, "We have done a very poor job of accurately pricing ecosystem services. We have allowed companies to offload their environmental costs to the commons and not actually carry that cost as part of their price of doing business. And many of the companies that today are thought to be very profitable would not be profitable if they had to actually carry that ecosystem rent."

Eric Rice compared the world economy to an enormous ship that's now being moved in the right direction, but only gradually. As he notes, "The economy is not going to stop using oil tomorrow—so we need to be pushing on every lever that we have. On the companies. On governments. On our joint trade associations, to find ways collectively. And what I see in 2021 is that our path towards 2030 is encouraging."

A VISION OF THE FUTURE

As these interesting and engaging interviews came together to form the arc of this book, patterns emerged—of hope for a better, more sustainable future supported by track records of success and competitive financial returns. Multiplier effects were identified, that ensure that those returns don't only flow in one direction, but also enrich the lives of those among us who have been historically and systemically disadvantaged, marginalized, excluded, and forgotten.

In some cases that means a sustained flow of capital into spaces where it effectively facilitates solutions at both macro and micro levels. The risk to vulnerable borrowers may be lessened, while investors who are comfortable with a degree of risk reap reliable rewards while exerting life-changing positive influence in communities facing daunting socio-economic problems.

I was told about groundbreaking technologies that have been designed to ease the suffering of humankind and help restore and preserve our planet's precious and vital natural resources. Bold experiments were described, that ultimately met with more success than failure. Innovations were discussed, with explanations of how they are deployed to disrupt traditional obstacles, disprove long-standing and problematic myths, and pave a broader and healthier path forward.

All in all, the interviewees provided fresh, informed, and rather surprisingly encouraging perspectives. Matt Patsky, for example, cited the fact that only 30 short years ago "there was liability sitting on the books of the tobacco companies that was unrecognized." But since then, investors helped to lead the charge that convinced both tobacco companies and policy makers to make substantial changes that have literally saved millions of lives. While exclusionary investment philosophies have been useful change agents, today positive inclusion is coming to the forefront, as Simon Bond described when he said, "we don't just exclude a few things and then just carry on as normal."

The new normal of SRI investing is not just a pipe dream; it's already in the pipeline. Tammy Newmark highlighted this optimistic point of view, describing how she's been recently encouraged by a push she's observed, "across all of those different leverage points to better address those types of issues." While acknowledging the challenges ahead, she believes that investors are increasingly focused on commitments to social equality, justice, and inclusion. "I feel like that's important to raise awareness," she says, "to be aligned with our investor interests, and to help change how the whole sustainable investing industry will evolve."

Mark Dowding also describes seeing "a real demand on the part of investors to be able to invest in strategies which are making a measurable difference and change." The momentum is building from people acting. It is a welcome respite from the doom and gloom splashed across today's headlines suggesting that time is running out to rescue humanity and the planet from a catastrophic end. To the contrary, these interviews provide evidence that time is still on our side, thanks to a concerted effort and urgent awareness of the need to act.

"The world has evolved in the last three or four years," notes Dave Chen. "Many of the institutional investors have evolved with sustainability or climate or climate adaptation overlays across their entire portfolios. And that's accelerated over the last two years."

START WHERE YOU ARE

So, what are some of the ways SRI investors can participate in that regard, while avoiding the pitfalls and maximizing success for themselves and those they want to help? There is consensus among the experts we interviewed that it begins by identifying one's own personal priorities, values, and commitments and defining your desired outcomes. As the ancient Chinese philosopher, Lao Tzu famously wrote, the journey of 1,000 miles begins with a single step.

"Start where you are," advises Jed Emerson. "Don't get too wrapped up in the language and the terms and the labels." Dig deep to find answers that make sense, on your own terms, regardless of the jargon.

Picture the kind of impact you want to make. Then do as these and other experts have done. Initiate conversations and begin nurturing relationships with those who share your same goals and values. As much as possible, educate yourself (and others) on the issues, practices, and the processes needed to achieve the financial and sustainability outcomes you want.

Along the way, also keep in mind what Sharon Vosmek said: "We should never underestimate the power of that body of research that shows that when we are presented with facts that challenge our assumptions, we don't learn from those facts. We become further entrenched in our assumptions. And that's just human nature." Challenge the assumptions and biases of other people who offer you financial products and guidance and develop the habit of also continuing to audit your own assumptions with open-minded objectivity.

FIND JOY IN YOUR INVESTMENT JOURNEY

Amy Novogratz has experienced how she and other forward-thinking colleagues are intentionally "investing in a vision that we will have a future that doesn't put our environment at harm." But beyond the pledge to do no harm, she says, is pivotal momentum that actually yields the priceless dividend of joy. "We're really on this road together . . . and it's a fun experience. This is a moment in history and we're all doing different stuff together, like we're making change, we're building, we're using creativity. It's bonding, it gives you meaning. I think if you ask our investors, most would really just enjoy being a part of what we're building."

Ben Rick likewise summed it up in very personal terms by saying "I just never cease to be amazed at how impressed I am with people who have pursued a life based on the desire to do the right thing and give something back." You are among the people he's talking about, and today, as Jed Emerson points out, "All capital has impact and all companies have impact. The issue isn't whether you're an impact investor or not."

You are an impact investor, whether the impact exerts good in the world or has an adverse impact. The choice is yours, and the products available to the conscientious investor are, fortunately, more varied, focused, accessible, and attractive than ever. Opportunities are available, whether your inclination is to invest in stocks and bonds, innovative technology, community building, charity and philanthropy, human rights and equality, healthcare, affordable housing, commercial real estate, agriculture/aquaculture, private finance, clean water, or consumer products and retail trade. You name it . . . there's an SRI entryway with your name on it.

With that in mind, it is my hope that you will feel the words and insights of these world-class investors and know that you are not alone in this journey as you pursue your own goals of investing with purpose and intent. And remember what Ralph Waldo Emerson said—the joy will always be in the journey, never the destination!

Chapter Eleven

Short Lessons Learned—My Closing Questions

At the end of each interview, I grabbed a final few minutes to ask each interviewee a series of five quick questions—telling them to give me whatever came to mind. The intent wasn't to hear a long explanation, although at times I got one, and not every question was always answered. But for the most part, all interviewees, who were all so gracious with their time, indulged me as I asked:

1. What is the single most important challenge in SRI right now?
2. What do you know now that you wish you knew when you started in SRI?
3. What's a lesson learned from an investment that "ticked all of the boxes" but didn't work out?
4. What's a lesson learned from an investment you were skeptical of that did work out?
5. If someone wants to get into SRI, where should they start?

I've summarized many of their responses in the following chapters.

Chapter Twelve

What Is the Single Most Important Challenge in SRI Right Now?

Peter Arensman: "I think in sustainable investments in Ag Tech and Food Tech, scaling up is the challenge, because everything goes much slower than for example, in information technology."

Bram Bos: "It's 'labelmania' as I call it, the over-innovation in the labeled bond market."

Basil Demeroutis: "It's the absence of clear regulation and confusing financial incentives. For example, you get charged a lower rate of VAT on building a new building than you do on refurbishment. The incentives are in the wrong place."

Jean-Philippe de Schrevel: "Impact washing. There is a lack of transparency with many players and you have the danger of throwing the baby out with the bath water. Because those guys cast a shadow on what we're doing. And this is very damaging."

Alina Donets: "It's transparency because transparency of information allows for effective capital allocation. It allows for better communication. It gets better outcomes."

Mark Dowding: "Trying to navigate that every client seems to have a different set of requirements. It's very difficult to standardize different people in different jurisdictions. I think there may be more standardization over time. But from a regional point of view, it is going to be difficult delivering strategies that meet the needs of all of your clients."

Marisa Drew: "It would be access to reliable, high quality, defensible and comparable data. Because that is a big hurdle for the industry to accomplish the things we want to accomplish. And the consistency of data, the accuracy of it, isn't really there yet in so many spaces. That's what holds the industry back both from confidence in the financial markets but also the ability to know that you are actually on the right track."

Jed Emerson: "How to scale with authenticity, how to keep the integrity of the practice as we go about the task of changing the face of systemic capitalism."

Daniel Klier: "I think the biggest challenge is that everybody talks about it, but not everybody means the same thing. We need common language and clearer definitions. We need to move from a marketing narrative to something that's a lot more tangible."

Radha Kuppalli: "The central challenge is driving more capital into emerging markets."

Matt Patsky: "It is getting harmonization and standardization of what we're asking companies to report, so that we have the ability to compare across industry and then across the entire system of how companies are doing. So, we need the data, we need it standardized, and we need a timeline. Then we can really have the ability to make sense of it all."

Jenn Pryce: "I think it's a lack of knowledge of how to structure products that meet investor demand and community need. There are not many entities that sit between private capital and community and can understand both, and therefore structure a product that can speak to both audiences."

Mitch Reznick: "Greenwashing. I fear that is rising because sustainability is 'hot' right now. There are some in every corner of the capital markets that take a superficial approach to sustainability to exploit the opportunity. If these shift from the few to the many, it could undermine the credibility of those with substance in their approach to sustainability and ESG.

Data is also a major challenge. The reality is that for smaller companies and private companies there is a dearth of data to quickly and efficiently build a sustainability profile for a company. The data is dated and a little bit stale, whereas investing is forward-looking. The variation in ESG assessments for any given issue can vary widely, which is why overreliance on these services could lead to suboptimal outcomes.

Also, most sustainability data is mapped to equity tickers. This probably sounds a little bit esoteric, but it is sometimes tough to map that data to the actual bond-issuing entity. For example, sometimes climate data of a private, high-yield company is mapped to the private equity fund that owns the company. That is the wrong connection to make but the PE firm is not the issuer of the data. This is why it is really important to have a proprietary, credible approach. Human capital is required."

Eric Rice: "It's clear: impact washing. Why? Because it's a big fat opportunity for people if they can relabel their strategies or tilt their strategies towards something that resembles impact. But you have to do it right, and there's a lot of bad product out there. A lack of authenticity in impact investing could easily undermine this nascent industry."

Micah Schulz: "It's tackling embodied carbon in materials. That's the most important challenge for real estate."

Sharon Vosmek: "I think venture capital's greatest challenge, if it wants to be relevant to this next set of problems that we have to address—climate crisis, pandemics, health, feeding the planet, a growing population—is that it needs to professionalize itself and grow up."

Chapter Thirteen

What Do You Know Now That You Wish You Knew When You Started in SRI?

Peter Arensman: "The Triple P business model canvas, which all of the students now are being taught. I was taught the single layer normal model canvas—just go for profit."

Basil Demeroutis: "I think it's the integration of the 'E' and the 'S.' That these aren't separate activities. I think it took us a lot of time [to realize this]. We've obviously came to that conclusion, but I wish we had known that a bit earlier. I think it would have short-circuited a lot of stuff."

Jean-Philippe de Schrevel: "The role of technology. I didn't see it coming. I should have, but if we had identified how technology would be the driving force for the accessibility and affordability of our work sooner, we would have specialized in that very early."

Jed Emerson: "I wish I had understood that at the end of the day, this is all the same parade—and the amount of energy that people put into defending this practice against that practice, or this mindset or this label. It makes no sense to me because it's all one thing. It's all about blended value. I wish I had become aware of that earlier, because I think that would have saved a lot of hassle."

Daniel Klier: "Mostly I think how long it takes to take a senior level commitment through an organization. What we're really talking about is system change. You can only change the system if you change every moving part of the system, the way you measure, the way you incentivize, the way you report. And the complexity of integrating ESG properly in the system is something that I think we all underestimate. In most organizations, that started as a side department that was doing ethical investing and sustainable investing. Now everybody is moving that side department into the core. But to get into the core, it's a fundamental change where you need to change every part of the system."

Stewart Langdon: "One thing would be to invest harder in technology because it makes such a difference in generating financial returns but also to delivering socially impactful products."

Philipp Mueller: "It's a very structured process involving multiple teams, from a risk team to a legal team, to an investment team, to the impact team, to the portfolio management team, to credit monitoring. It's very complex to do it right in the markets we are in, and it requires a significant platform and is personnel and resource intensive. I thought it would be relatively straightforward."

Matt Patsky: "The acknowledgement that no company is perfect. If you start by looking for only perfect companies, you'll end up frustrated and with very little. I can remember in the earliest days thinking there just aren't enough companies to invest in, and that's the wrong frame of reference. You've got to acknowledge that companies are on trajectories, and you've got to dig deeper and make sure you're seeing the progress they're making. Also, sometimes it's information that's not even disclosed. I mean, you've got to dig."

Jenn Pryce: "It's a complex problem that we're trying to solve—and finance is only one piece of the solution. So, you need to work with government; you need to work with business. It needs to be a multi-stakeholder solution at the end of the day. We can't just be an investment shop."

Mitch Reznick: "How to create more precision in the risk assessment process and to assess what the most material factors are in each sector. To not be spoon-fed but to know these factors from my own experience.

Understanding the materiality of factors, knowing the right questions to ask and how to weigh those in an investment framework. Having a much better feel for what are the most important, the most material factors, by sector, and knowing how to convert that into investment thinking."

Ben Rick: "That success would come from more listening rather than more talking."

Micah Schulz: "The importance of fighting as hard as you can on a new project, to get in there early when a building is being designed and developed and push those boundaries as high as you can. It's so easy to value engineer initiatives out for a whole host of reasons and retrofitting is just so much more expensive than getting it right up front. The market's moving so quickly that you're amazed to look back and say, "'I thought we were being so ahead of the market, but now it just feels like it was almost essential that we did that.' I think that's an important lesson that I've learned through experience over time."

Chapter Fourteen

What's a Lesson Learned from an Investment That "Ticked All of the Boxes" but Didn't Work Out?

Bram Bos: "A bank in India issued a green bond which we bought for our portfolio. Last year, we learned that they were financing the biggest open-pit coal mine in the world in Australia. The one thing we learned from this is that emerging markets are a different world than developed markets in terms of transparency and credibility for sustainable finance. They're way behind."

Basil Demeroutis: "It was a big box retail deal that was ripe for transformation, and it was not very sustainable. We thought we could turn it around to make it sustainable and socially impactful. In the end, we weren't really able to achieve much. What we learned there was that you need to have a willing tenant. Unfortunately, our tenant was a big, huge multinational and all they cared about was the bottom line. You've got to have people around you who are willing to come on this journey. If it's not the right people, you need to fish elsewhere."

Jean-Philippe de Schrevel: "An investment that I was really believing in was one we made in India in a chain of primary care hospitals. I really admired the CEO and the founder, a really charismatic leader. He started launching new units, new hospitals across different states, too quickly, eagerly, and ambitiously. The lesson learned is that you can have a charismatic leader and founder. But if this guy is not followed by a very solid, bigger management team—whoever he is, and whatever his ideas and however fantastic they are—it's not going to be put into practice. The execution and the solid middle management of a social company is essential."

Mark Dowding: "Early in my career I had invested in a bond called Yosemite Finance, linked to Enron which blew off in 2001. It was short-dated, AAA rated. I trusted in the credit rating, and I thought it was going to be fine, and it ended up being worth nothing. It obviously was an example of corporate fraud. Having a robust ESG framework is something that helps you identify something like corporate fraud. By having that framework, it meant that when we looked at an issuance by Wirecard a couple of years ago, it sent up all sorts of red flags. We gave it a really shocking ESG score and before we looked any further, we'd already eliminated it as an issuer that we'd invest in."

Marisa Drew: "I'm an angel investor, and I think where I've got it wrong is when I didn't fully appreciate the cost side of a given business model. As an angel investor I'm thinking about 'is there a big enough market?' because if you start with a big market, that sets you in a good place for any kind of a new business model or plan. And sometimes the companies check all the boxes and then you're just blind to something. I think the big takeaway is that with high revenue growth models, if you can't manage the growth, it will take you down. There are many things that can break down because of too much demand for the product and lack of operational expertise, or the ability to respond to growth."

Patrick Drum: "I had invested in an India-based health care company that I did a 60-page credit work up on. I even engaged with them. They had almost a 3-decade exposure, high credibility recognition in the Middle East, and at least two women on the board. And with all the governance and all the work that I had done, they had fraud. With issuers in the emerging markets, it's all about governance and it's a hard nut to crack, particularly in that region subject to the culture and context. Those are my three C's: credit, context, and culture. That's it."

Daniel Klier: "Two different points here. One is the bigger thematic decisions. Many people made bad investments in hydrogen, not because they invested in the wrong companies but they invested too early. And secondly, ESG is not ESG. You can have the same company looked at by five different vendors and you will look at it through very different sustainability lenses. Companies may be issuing green bonds while having a business model where some investors would say, 'actually, that's not green.' I think these are conflicts that will be with the industry for a long time, because I always say 95 percent of the economies are neither brown or green, but somewhere on the spectrum."

Radha Kuppalli: "We had an investment called the Malua Biobank in Sabah, Malaysia. Essentially, we were trying to monetize the biodiversity value of this incredible rainforest in Sabah through the sale of biodiversity conservation certificates. It was a voluntary biobank and we wanted to sell the biodiversity value into the palm oil supply chain. It was very well structured as an investment, but the demand was completely untested. We spent years and a lot of social capital with the government of Sabah, but ultimately it wasn't successful as an investment.

"We learned so much about taking a risk, the challenge of voluntary demand for biodiversity products, and how to structure an innovative investment. Frankly, in some ways we were just 10 years ahead of our time, because now there are plenty of people who are trying to do that, looking at new ways of financing these biodiversity conservation projects. The structure was fundamentally sound. If we were doing that now, with the FinTech technology that we were just talking about and recognizing what people are valuing now in terms of nature, maybe it would have been a successful investment. I guess the lesson learned is that timing is everything."

Stewart Langdon: "I think the most obvious example was one where we made a bet on a company that had really good technology, but unfortunately the execution wasn't quite there. I think the learning was that you can have the best idea in the world, but unless you can execute on it, it's just hopeless. And so, ever since then, execution has really been at the top of my list—rather than having a good idea or a good technology."

Tammy Newmark: "I think what we have learned is that, first, we need very strong working relationships and partnerships. That's why we have a very high-touch involvement. Second is that we have to really know that there's going to be listening, learning, pivoting, and adapting. And at times there isn't. And when that's the case, then there's nothing you can do to rescue the business."

Amy Novogratz: "We invested in a company that was promoting sustainable agriculture while selling a consumer-facing product that was really transparent and sustainable, from different farms. And we knew it was early, but we wanted to believe that if we pushed the right levers, we could tip the space into caring more about purchasing it and increasing the value of sustainability. We learned a huge amount about the retail space from that. About what is possible. It did push the conversation forward. Did it help us get to where we are? Absolutely. Was it a good investment? Not at all."

Matt Patsky: "In the end, we're dependent on people to execute and humans have flaws. If the execution is flawed, that doesn't mean they were bad people. It just means they didn't have the right skill set to get the job done. So, we've learned that if something didn't work, to encourage them to go ahead and feel comfortable that they can pivot. Experiment with changing the model, because it's not working. It's not going to work. We've demonstrated that it doesn't work. So, let's rethink it."

Jenn Pryce: "We invested in a fund that provided small business loans across the African continent, but they didn't have people in those communities. They were relying on technology to get economies of scale, the right economics and capital into the hands of people. And it didn't work. It is relationship lending. The economic model never penciled out. They needed to put people in places, and that cost more than they ever thought. I now have great skepticism about the idea that small business lending can be digitized. There's a certain part of the market where it's not effective. We were losing money and the impact is not what we had hoped."

Mitch Reznick: "Not everything is under management control, despite their intention. Even if there's a willingness and desire to have control and convey that, they do not. That's just a fact of life."

Ben Rick: "There's been a problem in the UK with deals where financial success was expected to come from pure growth by aggressively scaling operations. Where you have socially motivated businesses competing directly with organizations that aren't socially motivated, and the root of success is just expanding capital in the pursuit of scale, that hasn't turned out that well in the UK."

Sharon Vosmek: "I don't mind investing in husband-and-wife teams, but my failure was in a company that happened to be a husband-and-wife team. It was a phenomenal business. The product was definitely needed in the market, it was right timed, and I actually think it's superior to anything that's out there. The ultimate failure was governance. The husband and wife were both on the board and they were both in the executive suite. The consequences to the rest of the organization were profound when their marriage became the relationship of note for the business. Their marriage ultimately determined the future of the business and that wasn't successful. Anyone they hired couldn't get into their inner circle. My learning there was, you need to make sure that you have a clear business role, so that you don't have to rely on marital roles and others can come into spheres of influence."

Chapter Fifteen

What's a Lesson Learned from an Investment You Were Skeptical of That Did Work Out?

Peter Arensman: "Because we thought the valuation was too high, we passed on one investment which, in the end, we regretted. My lesson is, when there's less than 10 percent valuation difference, don't walk away. You should reconsider."

Basil Demeroutis: "The Windmill Green was a good example, that we were able to get rents that were 30 to 35 percent above our underwrite. Even though we had a pretty well articulated ESG strategy, it was a bold decision and nerve wracking. And maybe we thought it wasn't the right decision. You've got to go all in. There are no small metrics. Authenticity and being empathetic is so important. It's everything when you walk in that building. It's how it makes you feel."

Jean-Philippe de Schrevel: "There was a financial inclusion company in Mongolia that was going to do microfinance banking in Ulaanbaatar, but also provide financial services to herders in the steppes of Mongolia. I was thinking, wow, that's just mind boggling. I could not understand how they were going to do that. But they really did it, through strong execution capabilities, a very disciplined approach, and very inventive and innovative ways of serving those populations.

"And that's why I'm not turning down any deals anymore just because of the environment or the country. I learned to not be scared by any country situation, as long as the team knows how to behave, adapt, innovate, and work hard to deliver. They can succeed. Here they succeeded dramatically."

Mark Dowding: "I wish I'd bought some stock in Tesla a couple of years ago. I bought a Tesla car as a bit of an experiment to see how it works. A month after having the car, I was raving about it—best car I've ever owned, and I still love it today. I went from being a real skeptic to a real believer in Tesla. If I was only able to put my money where my mouth was, I probably would have paid for that car a couple of times over by now."

Marisa Drew: "I regret not investing in companies where I was the user of the product and thought, wow, this is really solving a problem or a need; it's making my life easier. I just didn't translate my usage pattern to how big those businesses could become. Why wouldn't I invest in the company if I think it's so fabulous?"

Jed Emerson: "Jacqueline Novogratz came to me before she launched the Acumen Fund and she said, 'I've got this great idea. We're going to raise philanthropic capital. We're going to make investments in micro enterprises in emerging markets. What do you think?' And I just said, 'It's not going to work as a foundation. People don't think that way. People think in terms of charity. I've spent my whole life trying to bridge that divide, blah, blah, blah.' Of course, she and her team have done an excellent job over the 20 years since, proving me wrong, doing phenomenal work and making a real contribution to the space. I think we all get our blinders."

Radha Kuppalli: "Our saw milling business. There's a joke in the forestry sector: 'How do you make a small fortune? And the joke is, you take a big fortune and invest in a sawmill.' We actually bought two sawmills, which were the primary customers for two forests owned by one of our funds, from a company going into bankruptcy. We never operated a sawmill before, we were very nervous about it, but we thought this is the right thing to do to protect the value of the forest. We bought those mills for $40 million, and now they're worth hundreds of millions of dollars. Good investment."

Stewart Langdon: "I passed on an insurance investment in India which I really regret. I met the company in 2012 when the entrepreneur was raising money. I think the valuation was $50 million and it had kind of just got off the ground. I remember he had a big lead over any of his competitors, but the company was still very small. I just couldn't quite see how technology would change the way insurance was bought and sold in India. Anyway, he will IPO his business in the near term. People are talking about, I think, a valuation of $3 billion or $5 billion.

"It was before the smartphone thing happened and I just couldn't see how that would change everything, so, unfortunately, I passed on that one. The lesson learned on that was again, technology—underestimating the ability of technology to change things quickly."

Tammy Newmark: "I'm more conservative in businesses than others on my team, and there are new, next generation ideas that I can't connect with the product. There have been a few companies within our portfolio that have gotten a lot of buzz and been very successful that I would not have opted to invest in at first."

Matt Patsky: "We were looking at an investment opportunity that was bringing back rice production to Ghana, reducing rice costs to the end purchaser to one third of what imported rice was. And I was skeptical of the model and skeptical that they had the right people. At the end of the day, it worked. The business model was good and it's thriving. That's one that was missed. It would have been great to be able to tell the story of having participated in it."

Mitch Reznick: "I've been really surprised most recently by companies in the most carbon intensive industries. How quickly they have shifted from superficial interest in mitigating climate change to accelerated interest in mitigating climate change. I mean, we're talking about energy companies, steel makers, cement makers, building materials, the largest contributors. How quickly they've seen the light. I think it was wait, wait, wait, go, go, go. Because they see that the economy is in structural change and they want to be on the right side of that for lots of reasons."

Eric Rice: "About eight years ago, there was this 'impact' company that was making electric vehicles that were very expensive. I thought, it's a fancy car for rich people. Why is that impactful? And my analyst said, 'No, you don't get it. This is a company that is going to move all of the luxury car market into the EV space. Because of that, it's going to impel all of the internal combustion market into this world of EV. You don't understand how big this is going to be.' I didn't, but we did invest. And, of course, it made an enormous difference in multiple ways. It's an impact company."

Ben Rick: "Small businesses that are really niche-y that don't really have scale, but they have ambition. They can either continue in a business-as-usual way or maybe by replicating their services in a really small way. Businesses that seem unambitious can be successful for very long periods of time."

Sharon Vosmek: "When I met my husband, he had just joined a startup of 12 people called Netscape. I knew the people and what they were doing. I knew how qualified they were. I knew all the things an investor should have known to invest, and I still didn't invest. Because I couldn't see what people were going to do with the internet. Here's why: I wasn't a believer in the vision, and that was so good for me to learn back in 1995. I'm not an innovator. I may not know where this market's going to go. I rely on entrepreneurs to take me to markets. I individually struggle to see where things are going but I found that experts help me see into the future."

Chapter Sixteen

If Someone Wants to Get into SRI, Where Should They Start?

Bram Bos: "What is most important is personal enthusiasm and belief in ESG and green. If you don't have that, then working as a green bonds or sustainable finance professional is probably not the right place to be. And where to cut your teeth . . . I think the Netherlands and France are great places to start your career. Europe is still quite far ahead compared to the rest of the world."

Jean-Philippe de Schrevel: "First of all, know yourself and know your strengths and your capabilities. Number two, be genuinely focused on what you like doing. There's a broad range of entry points into the field of impact investing and you should do what corresponds to your heart, and then your brain, and then your skills. And then, just do it. Don't wait. There's no downside."

Mark Dowding: "Be curious, look to the future and inform yourself from different viewpoints. A number of analysts at BlueBay have taken the ESG CFA charter and found that to be useful. This is an area within our industry which is seeing a material amount of growth that should be creating opportunities for talent. The message would be, 'go for it.'"

Marisa Drew: "I would say for someone early in their career, don't necessarily sweat the sustainability bit. If you really want to be in the investment world, first get a good solid grounding in either investment structuring, product creation, capital markets or sales—or any other area that's broadly in and around that investment space—being a relationship manager, etc.

"The sustainability piece, because this is such a high, high, organic growth area that now touches all aspects of finance and it will be so for decades to come, almost by definition, you'll get exposure to sustainability as an overlay because you can't be a good relationship manager if you can't talk to your clients about sustainability. You can't be a good product creator these days, creating investment products, if you don't understand the ESG overlay. That's almost a necessity that'll come as part of getting that good, grounded finance foundation. If you want to specialize later in sustainability, there will be plenty of opportunities that will be available as sustainable finance truly does become the 'new norm.'"

Jed Emerson: "Start where you are. I mean, don't get too wrapped up in the language and the terms and the labels. Anything can be viewed through an impact lens and can be managed on that basis. So, if you're in a firm that is doing whatever type of investing, all you have to do is start asking uncomfortable questions about the practice and the process and you can become an impact investor.

"The other part is to read. I am genuinely shocked at the number of people who have come into this space in the last 20 years who lead with their ignorance. It's not that they're stupid, it's that they don't know what they don't know because they think this is a new idea. They think that because they were successful in finance, all they've got to do is learn some of this terminology and they can be successful in impact."

Daniel Klier: "First of all, it's everywhere now; it's no longer a little side activity. You have it in your sustainable supply chain teams, in your bond teams, in your asset management teams. The first important recognition is it's not something where you need to join a certain team, but it's increasingly part of every line of business.

"The second is, it's bringing together financial know-how and sustainability know-how, which not many people have. You can approach it from either end, but you need to build the other capability. You can be the best sustainability expert, but if you don't understand financial markets there's no chance that you can be a better investor. But if you don't understand sustainability, you will also fall short. The key is bringing in that combination and building your skillset through academic experience and real-life experience.

"Third, frankly, this is still such an evolving field. One just needs to get started."

Stewart Langdon: "Get into investment banking or management consulting and get the training at a top organization, and then bring that tough training and great skillset into the sustainable investing space. If you can get a job straight off the bat in sustainable investing with that type of experience, that's even better. But it's not easy to do. Doing a tough stint early in your career at a top bank or consulting firm is a great thing to do."

Philipp Mueller: "What is most important is to have the intrinsic motivation and the sense of purpose. I think it helps if you've been an investment professional elsewhere so you enter as someone who's already been in the financial industry. This obviously helps you to grasp the concepts and to have some educational background."

Tammy Newmark: "What I tell people is to get your foot in the door anywhere. Within the impact investing space, there are a lot of players beyond impact investing. You could work for an environmental conservation organization or a social entrepreneurship group or an accelerator. But if you want to go into impact investing on the investment side, you've got to work at a financial institution. To become a finance person, you need that finance training."

Amy Novogratz: "There are so many great pitching events and conferences focused on this space right now, and a number of dedicated funds. I would either invest in a fund or create a network and connection to it. There are also a number of accelerators now, which is a great opportunity. We have an aquaculture accelerator in our portfolio, Hatch Blue, helping early-stage companies become investable. They're usually looking for mentorship and other ways of helping beyond just capital. It's a great way to get into the space and be a part of it."

Matt Patsky: "You could get into Sustainable/Impact Investing now with almost every asset management firm and almost every asset owner because everybody's looking at getting into this field. It's kind of exploded to where really you could go into the State of New York's retirement plan and work on sustainable investing. You could go into almost every European pension plan. They've all got to be working on how to do more of this. It's an exciting time to be entering the field as it has now truly gone mainstream."

Jenn Pryce: "The best way I think is an apprenticeship. You've just got to get in there and do it. I have found that they don't teach this stuff in business school yet. There's no course you can take. Find an organization that's doing the work where you feel like you can be empowered and mentored."

Ben Rick: "It's counter-intuitive, but I still think at this point, some kind of mainstream financial world experience. You can almost consider it as part of your formal education, to get exposure to the stuff that will be helpful for you later. Just because of the immaturity of the [SRI] business, I still think it's helpful for young people to have cut their teeth for a number of years in a more conventional finance setting. Ultimately, social investment isn't at the stage where it can offer graduates the training that they might get elsewhere in the way that a larger organization might be able to. Those basics will come in really handy in your career.

"Then you need to find an organization where you are really aligned with the topic and the area of work. If green bonds is your thing, go work for an organization that is buying green bonds. If working with domestic violence is your thing, you need to find an organization that's doing that. A big part of being in this space is aligning with the social mission."

Micah Schulz: "My perspective is you don't need to be an expert to have a big impact. You can have a big impact without being schooled in sustainability, but by having an open mind and a curiosity and willingness to learn about things like environmental impacts, technological changes, and shifting social trends.

"The other thing is being open to and hungry to find really high-quality expert advice. I think if you do this, you can bring insightful knowledge into day-to-day investment business and customer decision-making and really make a massive difference.

"I would suggest focusing on a way to package sustainability expertise with very practical building operation or investment expertise. Then you can commit your skills to what I call the pointy end of the investment decision-making process. So, you're not sitting on the side as somebody who just understands everything about sustainability but doesn't actually get the real-world process where change will be effected."

Sharon Vosmek: "I do think they need to be approaching it inquisitively and talking to lots of different people, including organizations like Astia. Not just venture firms, but nonprofits that are sitting at the edges of venture firms. There are many like us. There are accelerators or incubators. There's Stanford. Ask lots of entrepreneurs, ask lots of types of organizations, ask policy people, even elected politicians. I'm a real believer in an inclusive approach to asking."

Chapter Seventeen

Extended Conversations

For some readers, the interviews in this book may leave them wanting to know more, so I've conveniently posted extended interviews in a podcast format for your listening pleasure.

These are focused, lively, wide-ranging, long-format discussions that eschew the "sound byte" format that is all too common in today's financial media universe. They cover everything from the early personal journeys of each interviewee—and what motivated and attracted them to commit their life energy to SRI—to insights on how they developed and executed their investment strategies and what challenges they face today. The original conversations lasted between one to two hours—and some were even longer but I have edited them down into a more manageable size in a podcast format.

In most cases, the parts of interviews I excerpted for this book represent a relatively small portion of the time we spent together, so there is minimal overlap with what's in this book and a lot more in-depth elaboration on the topics. So, it's a chance to go way below the surface with these impressive people and gain additional insights and useful lessons from world-class investors.

All these discussions are available to you for free at the companion website SRI360.com. I developed SRI360.com to be the leading source for the latest trends and insights from industry professionals who collectively have overseen trillions in sustainable responsible investments. It presents exclusive articles, podcasts, webinars and more lessons from world class investors who are driving positive change with market returns that go beyond the niceties of SRI; Find out what they're doing and how they're doing it.

I hope you enjoy listening to these interviews as much as I enjoyed conducting them.

Here's the list, alphabetized by first name:

Alina Donets—SRI360.com/Alina
Amy Novogratz—SRI360.com/Amy
Basil Demeroutis—SRI360.com/Basil
Ben Rick—SRI360.com/Ben
Bram Bos—SRI360.com/Bram
Daniel Klier—SRI360.com/Daniel
Dave Chen—SRI360.com/Dave
Eric Rice—SRI360.com/Eric
Jean-Philippe de Schrevel—SRI360.com/Jean-Philippe
Jed Emerson—SRI360.com/Jed
Jennifer Pryce—SRI360.com/Jenn
Marisa Drew—SRI360.com/Marisa
Mark Dowding—SRI360.com/Mark
Matt Patsky—SRI360.com/Matt
Micah Shulz—SRI360.com/Micah
Mitch Reznick—SRI360.com/Mitch
Patrick Drum—SRI360.com/Patrick
Peter Arensman—SRI360.com/Peter
Philipp Mueller—SRI360.com/Philipp
Radha Kuppalli—SRI360.com/Radha
Ron Gonen—SRI360.com/Ron
Sharon Vosmek—SRI360.com/Sharon
Simon Bond—SRI360.com/Simon
Stefano Bacci—SRI360.com/Stefano
Stewart Langdon—SRI360.com/Stewart
Tammy Newmark—SRI360.com/Tammy

Notes

CHAPTER ONE

1. Douglas Broom, "This Is Why Food Security Matters Now More Than Ever," *World Economic Forum*, November 23, 2020, https://www.weforum.org/agenda/2020/11/food-security-why-it-matters/.

2. Andrea Bohmholdt, "Evaluating the Triple Bottom Line Using Sustainable Return on Investment," *Remediation Journal* 24, no. 4 (2014): 53–64. doi:10.1002/rem.21404.

3. Bert Scholtens, "Indicators of Responsible Investing," *Ecological Indicators* 36 (2014): 382–85. doi: 10.1016/j.ecolind.2013.08.012.

4. James Chen, "Environmental, Social, and Governance (ESG) Criteria," *Investopedia*, March 5, 2021, https://www.investopedia.com/terms/e/environmental-social-and-governance-esg-criteria.asp.

5. Judith Rodin and Margot Brandenburg, *The Power of Impact Investing* (Philadelphia: Wharton Digital Press, 2014).

6. "Overview Of Sustainable Finance," *European Commission,* 2021, https://ec.europa.eu/info/business-economy-euro/banking-and-finance/sustainable-finance/overview-sustainable-finance_en.

7. Richard Hudson, "Ethical Investing: Ethical Investors and Managers," *Business Ethics Quarterly* 15, no. 4 (2005): 641–57. doi:10.5840/beq200515445.

8. Sidney Lumet, *Network*. Metro-Goldwyn-Mayer (1976).

9. Susan Lund et al., "The Near-Term Impact of Coronavirus on Workers," *McKinsey & Company*, April 2, 2020, https://www.mckinsey.com/industries/public-and-social-sector/our-insights/lives-and-livelihoods-assessing-the-near-term-impact-of-covid-19-on-us-workers.

10. Tiana N. Rogers et al., "Racial Disparities in COVID–19 Mortality Among Essential Workers in the United States," *World Medical & Health Policy* 12, no. 3 (2020): 311–27. doi:10.1002/wmh3.358.

11. Mia Rozenbaum, "The Increase in Zoonotic Diseases: The WHO, the Why and the When?," *Understanding Animal Research*, July 6, 2020, https://www.understandinganimalresearch.org.uk/news/research-medical-benefits/the-increase-in-zoonotic-diseases-the-who-the-why-and-the-when/.

12. I. Khan, D. Shah, and S. S. Shah, "COVID-19 Pandemic and Its Positive Impacts on Environment: An Updated Review," *International Journal of Environmental Science and Technology* 18, no.2 (2020): 521–30. doi:10.1007/s13762-020-03021-3.

13. Khan et al., "COVID-19 Pandemic and Its Positive Impacts on Environment," 521–30.

14. Rebecca Lindsey "Climate Change: Atmospheric Carbon Dioxide | NOAA Climate.Gov," *Climate.Gov*, August 14, 2020, https://www.climate.gov/news-features/understanding-climate/climate-change-atmospheric-carbon-dioxide.

15. Lindsey, "Climate Change: Atmospheric Carbon Dioxide | NOAA Climate.Gov."

16. Francesco Bassetti, "Water Scarcity: Glaciers Sound the Alarm—Foresight," *Foresight*, March 18, 2021, https://www.climateforesight.eu/water-food/glaciers-melt-water-security-is-under-threat/.

17. Susie Neilson, "The Arctic Is on Track to Lose More Ice This Century Than at Any Point Since the End of the Ice Age. Photos Show the Dramatic Melting," *Insider*, October 18, 2020, https://www.businessinsider.com/photos-reveal-extent-of-arctic-ice-loss-2020-9.

18. "Transforming Our World: The 2030 Agenda for Sustainable Development | Department of Economic and Social Affairs," *United Nations*, 2015, https://sdgs.un.org/publications/transforming-our-world-2030-agenda-sustainable-development-17981.

19. "The UN Secretary-General's Strategy for Financing the 2030 Agenda," *United Nations*, September 24, 2018, https://www.un.org/sustainabledevelopment/sg-finance-strategy/.

20. "Unparalleled Worldwide For 500 Years," *Fugger.de*, 2021, https://www.fugger.de/en/fuggerei/unparalleled-worldwide-for-500-years.

21. Rachel Wimpee, "Supporting Economic Justice? Ford's 1968 PRI Experiment," *Rockefeller Archive Center*, November 1, 2019, https://resource.rockarch.org/story/supporting-economic-justice-fords-1968-pri-experiment/.

22. Giving USA, "Giving USA 2020: Charitable Giving Showed Solid Growth, Climbing To $449.64 Billion in 2019, One of the Highest Years for Giving on Record | Giving USA," *Giving USA | A Public Service Initiative of The Giving Institute*, June 16, 2020, https://givingusa.org/giving-usa

-2020-charitable-giving-showed-solid-growth-climbing-to-449-64-billion-in-2019-one-of-the-highest-years-for-giving-on-record/.

23. S. Celik, G. Demirtaş, and M. Isaksson, "Corporate Bond Market Trends, Emerging Risks and Monetary Policy—OECD," *OECD.org*, February 18, 2020, https://www.oecd.org/corporate/Corporate-Bond-Market-Trends-Emerging-Risks-and-Monetary-Policy.htm.

24. Michael J. Moore, "Goldman Sachs Agrees to Acquire Asset Manager Imprint Capital," *Bloomberg*, July 13, 2015, https://www.bloomberg.com/news/articles/2015-07-13/goldman-sachs-agrees-to-acquire-asset-manager-imprint-capital.

25. Staff Writer, "Impact 20: Ranking the Largest Private Markets Impact Managers | New Private Markets," *New Private Markets*, June 29, 2021, https://www.newprivatemarkets.com/impact-20-ranking-the-largest-private-markets-impact-managers/.

26. "Schroders Acquires Majority Stake in Leading Impact Investor Blue Orchard," *Schroders*, July 26, 2019, https://www.schroders.com/en/media-relations/newsroom/all_news_releases/schroders-acquires-majority-stake-in-leading-impact-investor-blueorchard/.

27. "Trends Report 2020 Executive Summary," *Ussif.org*, 2020, https://www.ussif.org/files/Trends%20Report%202020%20Executive%20Summary.pdf.

28. Dee Gill, "Is the $1 Trillion Coastal Housing Market a Future Financial Crisis?," *UCLA Anderson Review*, March 31, 2021, https://anderson-review.ucla.edu/is-the-1-trillion-coastal-housing-market-a-future-financial-crisis/.

29. "Rising Seas Erode $15.8 Billion in Home Value from Maine to Mississippi," *First Street Foundation*, 2019, https://assets.firststreet.org/uploads/2019/03/Rising-Seas-Erode-15.8-Billion-in-Home-Value-from-Maine-to-Mississippi.pdf.

30. "Fault Lines: How Diverging Oil and Gas Company Strategies Link to Stranded Asset Risk—Carbon Tracker Initiative," *Carbon Tracker Initiative*, October 29, 2020, https://carbontracker.org/reports/fault-lines-stranded-asset/.

31. Jonathan Watts, "BP's Statement on Reaching Net Zero By 2050—What It Says and What It Means," *The Guardian*, February 12, 2020, https://www.theguardian.com/environment/ng-interactive/2020/feb/12/bp-statement-on-reaching-net-zero-carbon-emissions-by-2050-what-it-says-and-what-it-means.

32. Jurriaan M. De Vos et al., "Estimating the Normal Background Rate of Species Extinction," *Conservation Biology* 29, no.2 (2014): 452–62. doi:10.1111/cobi.12380.

33. Ashley Bittner and Brigette Lau, "Women-Led Startups Received Just 2.3% of VC Funding in 2020," *Harvard Business Review*, February 25, 2021, https://hbr.org/2021/02/women-led-startups-received-just-2-3-of-vc-funding-in-2020.

34. Tom Eckett, "Tesla and the ESG Conundrum," *ETF Stream*, January 12, 2021, https://www.etfstream.com/features/tesla-and-the-esg-conundrum/.

35. SSE Initiative, "Model Guidance on Climate Disclosure: A Template for Stock Exchanges to Guide Issuers on TCFD Implementation | Sustainable Stock Exchanges," *Sustainable Stock Exchanges Initiative*, 2021, https://sseinitiative.org/publication/model-guidance-on-climate-disclosure-a-template-for-stock-exchanges-to-guide-issuers-on-tcfd-implementation/.

36. Initiative, "Model Guidance on Climate Disclosure: A Template for Stock Exchanges to Guide Issuers on TCFD Implementation | Sustainable Stock Exchanges."

37. Anastasia Petraki, "UK Unveils Its Post-Brexit Sustainability Strategy," *Schroders*, November 18, 2020, https://www.schroders.com/en/uk/adviser/insights/markets/uk-unveils-its-post-brexit-sustainability-strategy/.

38. Available in free digital format from the author's website at www.blendedvalue.net.

39. REDF (the Roberts Enterprise Development Fund) is the 2nd venture philanthropy fund created in the United. States which has invested in various strategies to create and expand social enterprises that they defined as market-based businesses operated by nonprofit organizations to create transitional employment for formerly homeless people.

40. Blended Value refers to a conceptual framework in which nonprofit organizations, businesses, and investments are evaluated based on their ability to generate a blend of financial, social, and environmental value. Blended Value suggests the true measure of any organization is in its ability to holistically perform in all three areas. For more, please see www.blendedvalue.org.

41. Walter Brueggemann is an American Protestant Old Testament scholar and theologian widely considered as one of the most influential Old Testament scholars of the last several decades. He has argued that the Church must provide a counter-narrative to the dominant forces of consumerism, militarism, and nationalism.

CHAPTER TWO

1. Max Roser, "Future Population Growth," *Our World in Data,* last modified in November 2019, https://ourworldindata.org/future-population-growth.

2. Monique Grooten and Rosamunde Almond (Eds.), "Living Planet Report—2018: Aiming Higher," *World Wildlife Fund*, 2018, https://www.worldwildlife.org/pages/living-planet-report-2018.

3. Rosamunde Almond, Monique Grooten, and Tanya Petersen (eds.), "Living Planet Report—2020: Bending the Curve of Biodiversity Loss," *World*

Wildlife Fund, 2020, https://www.zsl.org/sites/default/files/LPR%202020%20Full%20report.pdf.

4. Earth Overshoot Day, "How Many Earths? How Many Countries?" *Earth Overshoot Day*, last accessed August 26, 2021, https://www.overshootday.org/how-many-earths-or-countries-do-we-need/.

5. J. Poore and T. Nemecek, "Reducing Food's environmental impacts through producers and consumers," *Science* 360, no. 6392 (2019): 987–92, doi: 10.1126/science.aaq0216.

6. Deena Shanker et al., "Beyond Meat Just Had the Best IPO of 2019 as Value Soars to $3.8 Billion," *Fortune*, May 2, 2019, https://fortune.com/2019/05/02/beyond-meat-ipo-stock-price/.

7. Uday Sampath and Shounak Dasgupta, "Beyond Meat Surges on PepsiCo Plant-Based Snack Deal," *Reuters*, January 26, 2021, https://www.reuters.com/business/pepsico-beyond-meat-partner-develop-new-plant-based-snacks-2021-01-26/.

8. "PepsiCo Goes Beyond," *PepsiCo*, January, 2021, https://www.pepsico.com/news/story/pepsico-goes-beyond

9. Gene B. Sperling, Rebecca Winthrop, and Christina Kwauk, *What Works in Girls' Education: Evidence for the World's Best Investment* (Washington, DC: Brookings Institution Press, 2016), https://www.brookings.edu/wp-content/uploads/2016/07/What-Works-in-Girls-Educationlowres.pdf.

10. Ibid.

11. Q. Wodon et al., *Missed Opportunities: The High Cost of Not Educating Girls* (Washington, DC: The World Bank, July 2018), https://openknowledge.worldbank.org/bitstream/handle/10986/29956/HighCostOfNotEducatingGirls.pdf?sequence=6&isAllowed=y.

12. "Transforming Our World: The 2030 Agenda for Sustainable Development | Department of Economic and Social Affairs," *United Nations*, 2015, https://sdgs.un.org/publications/transforming-our-world-2030-agenda-sustainable-development-17981.

13. Mark Hall, "The Greatest Wealth Transfer in History: What's Happening and What Are the Implications," *Forbes*, November 11, 2019, https://www.forbes.com/sites/markhall/2019/11/11/the-greatest-wealth-transfer-in-history-whats-happening-and-what-are-the-implications/?sh=3e4d047f4090.

14. Matt Egan, "Crisis Hangover: Millennials Are Scared to Invest," *CNN Business*, March 11, 2015, https://money.cnn.com/2015/03/11/investing/investing-millennials-stocks-markets/.

15. Kaya Yurieff and Donie O'Sullivan, "Facebook Employees Stage a Virtual Walkout Over Zuckerberg's Inaction on Trump's Posts," *CNN Business*, June 1, 2020, https://edition.cnn.com/2020/06/01/tech/facebook-employees-twitter/index.html.

16. Edward Helmore, "Hundreds of Google Employees Urge Company to Resist Support for Ice," *The Guardian*, August 16, 2019, https://www.theguardian.com/technology/2019/aug/16/hundreds-of-google-employees-urge-company-to-resist-support-for-ice.

17. "Redefining the C-Suite: Business the Millennial Way," *American Express*, last accessed August 26, 2021, https://www.americanexpress.com/content/dam/amex/uk/staticassets/pdf/AmexBusinesstheMillennialWay.pdf.

18. Imogen Tew, "Advisers Risk Becoming 'Out of Touch' with Next Generation,"*FT Adviser*, September 26, 2019, https://www.ftadviser.com/investments/2019/09/26/advisers-risk-becoming-out-of-touch-with-next-generation/.

19. "Sustainable Signals: New Data from the Individual Investor," *Morgan Stanley*, last accessed August 26, 2021, https://www.morganstanley.com/pub/content/dam/msdotcom/ideas/sustainable-signals/pdf/Sustainable_Signals_Whitepaper.pdf.

20. ESG Clarity, "ESG a priority for Around 80% of Millennial Investors," *ESG Clarity*, January 3, 2020, https://esgclarity.com/esg-a-priority-for-around-80-of-millennial-investors/.

CHAPTER THREE

1. The web page was taken down in 2008. For access to a working version, visit archive.org and look for a website version of www.dilbert.com from 2007 or before or try clicking on this link: https://web.archive.org/web/20071012014302/http://www.dilbert.com/comics/dilbert/games/career/bin/ms.cgi.

2. Total Portfolio Activation, A Framework for Creating Social and Environmental Impact across Asset Classes, Joshua Humphreys, Ann Solomon, and Christi Electris, Tellus Institute, August 2012.

CHAPTER FOUR

1. The Greenhouse Gas (GHG) Protocol Corporate Standard, a joint initiative of World Resources Institute and WBCSD with the aim of keeping the global temperature rise below 1.5 degrees Celsius, classifies a company's GHG emissions into three "scopes": Scope 1 emissions are direct emissions from owned or controlled sources. Scope 2 emissions are indirect emissions from the generation of purchased energy. Scope 3 emissions are all indirect emissions (not included in scope 2) that occur in the value chain of the reporting company, including fifteen categories of both upstream and downstream emissions

including purchased goods, waste generated, fuel-related activities, use of sold products, investments, franchises, and employee commuting.

2. CLIC is used by Lombard Odier to describe an economic model geared toward sustainability, social justice, and responsible stewardship of the environment and is discussed later in this interview.

CHAPTER FIVE

1. Andrew Calder, Matthew Kolodzie, and Vivek Selot, "Green Bonds, Green Iis the New Black," RBC Dominion Securities Inc., April 4, 2017.

2. "Global green bond issuance hit new record high last year," Nina Chestney, *Reuters,* January 24, 2021.

3. Refers to Article 8 of the EU Sustainable Finance Disclosure Regulation (SFDR) which is a set of EU rules designed to make the sustainability profile of investment funds more comparable and better understood by end-investors. Article 8 is applied "where a financial product promotes, among other characteristics, environmental or social characteristics, or a combination of those characteristics, provided that the companies in which the investments are made follow good governance practices."

4. Refers to Article 9 of the EU SFDR Article 9, also known as "products targeting sustainable investments," covers products targeting bespoke sustainable investments and applies "where a financial product has sustainable investment as its objective and an index has been designated as a reference benchmark."

CHAPTER SIX

1. Kiki Yang et al., Bain & Co., Private Equity Investors Embrace Impact Investing, 2019.

2. Ibid.

3. Ron Gonen, *The Waste-Free World: How the Circular Economy Will Take Less, Make More, and Save the Planet Power of Impact Investing* (New York: Penguin Publishing Group, 2021).

CHAPTER SEVEN

1. Dean Hand et al., 2020 Annual Impact Investor Survey (Global Impact Investing Network, 2020), 16.

CHAPTER EIGHT

1. Sarah McBride, "With WhatsApp Deal, Sequoia Capital Burnishes Reputation," *Reuters,* February 21, 2014.

2. Benjamin Mullin et al., Quibi Is Shutting Down Barely Six Months After Going Live, *Wall Street Journal,* October 22, 2020.

3. Deborah Gage, "The Venture Capital Secret: 3 Out of 4 Start-Ups Fail," *Wall Street Journal,* September 20, 2012.

4. A. Woolley et al., "Why Some Teams Are Smarter Than Others," *New York Times,* January 18, 2015, SR5.

5. More recently, the potential impact to global GDP growth has been estimated substantially higher by McKinsey Global Institute, "The Power of Parity: How Advancing Women's Equality Can Add $12 Trillion to Global Growth," September 1, 2015.

6. I. Elaine Allen et al., "2007 Report on Women and Entrepreneurship," Global Entrepreneurship Monitor 2008, https://www.babson.edu/media/babson/site-assets/content-assets/about/academics/centres-and-institutes/blank-institute/global-research/global-entrepreneurship-monitor/reports/gem-2007-women-entrepreneurship-report.pdf.

7. S. Colt, "John Doerr: The Greatest Tech Entrepreneurs Are 'White, Male, nerds,'" March 4, 2015, https://www.businessinsider.com/john-doerr-the-greatest-tech-entrepreneurs-are-white-male-nerds-2015-3.

8. BAP (Best Aquaculture Practices) is a comprehensive and well-known certification system for ensuring the sustainability of aquaculture products. BAP certification is intended to assure consumers that the seafood they are buying has been produced in a manner that is considerate of the animal's welfare, the environment, workforce and community, food safety, and traceability.

9. GLOBAL G.A.P. (G.A.P. is an acronym for Good Agricultural Practices) is a widely implemented farm certification scheme translating consumer requirements into Good Agricultural Practice. Certification by GLOBAL G.A.P. is often a prerequisite for doing business with large businesses.

10. B Corp certification is a certification of "social and environmental performance" conferred by B Lab, a global nonprofit organization with offices in the United States, Europe, Canada, Australia, and New Zealand, and a partnership in Latin America with Sistema B.

11. The "2X Challenge" calls for the G7 and other DFIs to collectively mobilize *$3 billion* in commitments that provide women in developing country markets with improved access to leadership opportunities, quality employment, finance, enterprise support and products and services that enhance economic participation and access.

12. *Roundup* is the brand name of a systemic, broad-spectrum glyphosate-based herbicide originally produced by Monsanto and is a widely used herbicide in the United States.

CHAPTER NINE

1. Marty Swant, "The World's Most Valuable Brands," *Forbes,* July 27, 2020.
2. "Nature Risk Rising: Why the Crisis Engulfing Nature Matters for Business and the Economy," *World Economic Forum*, January 2020.
3. The acronym REDD refers to "reducing emissions from deforestation and forest degradation in developing countries," the title of the original document published by the United Nations Framework Convention on Climate Change (UNFCCC) in 2005 with the objective of mitigating climate change through reducing net emissions of greenhouse gases through enhanced forest management in developing countries.
4. NABERS (National Australian Built Environment Rating System) is an initiative by the government of Australia to measure and compare the environmental performance of Australian buildings and tenancies. A NABERS energy rating is required for all new buildings over 2000 square meters and buildings that are up for sale or lease.

Index

About the Author

R. Scott Arnell is the founding partner of Geneva Capital S.A., an alternative investment advisory firm based in Geneva, Switzerland specializing in sustainable and responsible investment opportunities. Since founding Geneva Capital, he has focused on mobilizing private equity investment into companies and investment funds primarily in Europe, Asia, and emerging/frontier markets. Prior to founding Geneva Capital, Arnell had over 20 years of international financial & business management experience serving in senior executive international financial and business operations management roles at multiple Fortune 500 companies in the consumer products, high-tech, and internet telecoms sectors. He has extensive business experience in Europe, Asia, and Latin America and lives in Switzerland, the Netherlands, and Mexico.